Learning from L.A.

Learning from L.A.

Institutional Change
in
American Public Education

CHARLES TAYLOR KERCHNER
DAVID J. MENEFEE-LIBEY
LAURA STEEN MULFINGER
STEPHANIE E. CLAYTON

HARVARD EDUCATION PRESS
CAMBRIDGE, MASSACHUSETTS

Library of Congress Control Number 2008928881

Paperback ISBN 978-1-934742-02-0
Library Edition ISBN 978-1-934742-03-7

Published by Harvard Education Press,
an imprint of the Harvard Education Publishing Group

Harvard Education Press
8 Story Street
Cambridge, MA 02138

Cover Design: Perry Lubin

The typeface used in this book is Adobe Chaparral Pro.

Contents

Acknowledgments

"I'd like to thank the Academy . . . ." Not *that* Academy. For more than three decades, I have been part of an academic community at the Claremont Graduate University and a member of a profession that encouraged my colleagues and me to write this book. Only an institution that allows sustained effort and the opportunity for thinking through one's subject—and rethinking, and thinking again—could create the particular rendition of the institutional change story we tell here. To CGU, my colleagues and friends, students past and present, I offer heartfelt thanks.

Also, this book was made possible by the financial support of the Annenberg Foundation and the encouragement of its executive director, Gail Levin. She championed support for an investigation of reform projects in the Los Angeles Unified School District knowing that such efforts, including those financed by the Foundation, had not been viewed as productive in many quarters. The grant did not place any conditions on our work, and Levin encouraged us to follow the data regardless of where it might take us.

The research that led to this book drew on many sources and methods. My colleague and co-author, David Menefee-Libey had been studying LAUSD since the early 1990s, and his research files and interviews proved most valuable, as did interviews conducted by his students at Pomona College. In the late 1990s, he and I collaborated on an evaluation of LAAMP, and those interviews and records formed a valuable backdrop to the interviews we undertook after we began this project. In addition, we made extensive use of LAAMP and LEARN archives, which are housed at Loyola Marymount University, and many of those we interviewed provided us access to their files. Jefferson Crain, executive officer of the board for LAUSD, provided helpful access to board minutes and recordings.

The research was informed by scores of open-ended interviews. These became part of a massive searchable database, kept with MaxQDA software, that linked our documentary sources and allowed analysis across individuals and reform programs. Phillip Glau and the able transcribers at Production Transcripts provided timely and accurate rendering of many of our interviews. We also used Endnote software to keep track of the reports, newspaper stories, and academic literature, well in excess of 8,000 documents.

During the process of research, we captured the efforts of two of the most re-markable graduate student scholars I have known in my long academic career. Stephanie Clayton came to the project as she was completing her master's de-gree in history at Claremont Graduate University. She brought both a critical eye and an insatiable appetite for archives. Her briefings and summaries served as the basis for much of the event narrative. Laura Mulfinger brought amaz-ing breadth of talent and energy to the research. She interviewed, found facts, critiqued, drafted, and edited, all while organizing the somewhat undisciplined work patterns of the senior authors. Both have become full coauthors, and it is a pleasure to recognize them as such.

Jeanne Fryer interviewed LEARN administrators and principals. Anthony Ortiz and Marco Villegas investigated the reward and incentive system for prin-cipals. The book also benefited from the research contributions of DeLacy Gan-ley, Jason Abbott, Weijiang Zhang, Susana Santos, and Jennifer Stokely.

A number of academic colleagues read earlier drafts or portions of the book and provided helpful comments. Mark Blyth, whose own research provided an in-tellectual touchstone for our ideas about institutional change, graciously read our first attempt at conceptualization. The phrase "permanent crisis" originates with him. Bill Boyd saw some glimmer of possibility in our early work and organized a presentation at Stanford University and at the American Educational Research Association around the notion, and the group of authors that participated there grew to write *The Transformation of Great American School Districts,* which preced-ed this book in publication. David Tyack, Larry Cuban, Guilbert Hentschke, Pris-cilla Wohlstetter, Tammi Chun, and Judith Raftery commented on the book's ar-gument and provided helpful suggestions about data and sources.

Caroline Chauncey at Harvard Education Press is a jewel of an editor. She ad-vocated its publication and helped us reshape its contents to better draw out the stories of those who helped us learn from L.A. Joanna Craig wielded a skilled editorial pen, improving the readability of the manuscript, and Dody Riggs saw it through publication with dispatch and good humor. Jeffrey Perkins helped it gain public attention.

Our most profound debt is to the men and women who allowed us to tell their story. Some are mentioned by name in the chapters of this book. Others, by choice, remain anonymous. Without sources from within the reform programs and from the ranks of teachers and administrators of LAUSD, we could not have attempted this effort. We can only hope that we treated that which they shared with us with fidelity and care.

Charles T. Kerchner

INTRODUCTION

Discovering a Changing Institution

This book, or the research behind it, started as a chronicle of the large reform projects in Los Angeles undertaken in the 1990s. Between them, the Los Angeles Educational Alliance for Restructuring Now (LEARN), and the Los Angeles Annenberg Metropolitan Project (LAAMP) spent upward of $100 million and involved thousands of educators and civic leaders. The conventional wisdom was that LEARN and LAAMP failed, and the Los Angeles Unified School District (LAUSD) and public education in Los Angeles County looked much the same structurally at the decade's end as they had at the beginning.

Very rapidly, however, we began to see an underlying story that went beyond a simple project narrative: The whole institution of public education was changing, and Los Angeles provided a vivid case study of the dismemberment of old institutional assumptions and the audition of new ones. In order to understand the reform projects of the 1990s, it was necessary to understand the system shocks that LAUSD had endured during the previous decades. When we looked back over half a century, we found a school district that had been delegitimated and whose powers and functions had been hollowed out. When we looked back to the founding of the modern school district in 1903 with its separation from city government, we realized that virtually every assumption of the Progressive Era founders had been violated.

So, instead of a short-term project rise-and-fall story, we found ourselves preparing to tell the story of long-term institutional change. The research task became overwhelming. We had to get the sweep of history essentially

1

right without becoming mired in details as the manuscript changed from a chronicle to a case study of institutional change. Some historical detail was necessarily truncated to bring the book to manageable size. For readers interested in the event histories, we have posted many of our notes and background papers at www.mindworkers.com. In addition to concern about detail, we found ourselves writing about the dynamics of a transformation still under way. Most of the research on institutional change is historically retrospective, written well after change took place. Here, the change is only partly complete, stuck in what appears to be a permanent crisis with no easy resolution in sight. Thus, how can one say with confidence that we are witnessing institutional change?

We found confidence (and comfort) in a set of ideas. The dreamers who planned how LAUSD might be transformed thought in remarkably similar ways. From the 1960s on, they wanted a way of breaking down the bureaucracy and moving decisions and resources to the schools. They wanted a usable standards and accountability system and an end to bell-curve education. They wanted greater variety in schooling and the ability for families to choose among educational offerings. And they wanted somehow to reconnect schooling and the grassroots, giving communities and families both greater involvement and more say in how schools worked.

In addition, we discovered a relentless march toward new institutional forms using a change process that intensified over time. If what we were witnessing was simply a disturbance with an eventual return to normalcy, then we would not have seen repeated auditions of the same ideas with each trial becoming more operationally sophisticated and politically forceful. Finally, we saw that Los Angeles was not alone, and in *The Transformation of Great American School Districts: How Big Cities Are Reshaping Public Education* (Harvard Education Press, 2008), the institutional change process is seen in other large cities as well.

WHAT DOES IT MATTER?

What does it matter that we are witnessing institutional change rather than project failure? It matters because public policy would have us do different things in each case. Project failure leads to increased external oversight of the failing school district, increased regulation and organizational rigidity. It leads to increasing blame and scapegoating and to a frenzied search for new programs offering a quick fix. The task is to set things right within the existing institutional shell.

Conversely, if we are witnessing institutional transformation, the task is to restructure politics and policy in ways that propel replacement of old institutional forms with new ones. As we suggest at the conclusion of the book, policy would be less directed toward shoring up the existing hierarchy and more toward creating a working network of schools, less toward protecting remaining islands of power and privilege and more toward making the existing system of shared power work, less about trying to fix blame and more about trying to change incentives.

HOW WE TELL THE STORY

Prologue. The story begins with a celebration. For a brief moment in 1993 it appeared that a grand civic coalition would be capable of fostering bottom-to-top change in LAUSD. But in some ways, LEARN and LAAMP were "the dogs that caught the car." The chase was exciting, but they found that their small organizations could audition ideas but not transform the District.

Chapter 1: The Progressives. Underneath the rise and fall of these projects, one finds a set of ideas forming a new institution of public education. We draw parallels between the Progressive Era of the early twentieth century and the current reform climate. Former mayor Richard Riordan and teacher union president Helen Bernstein—an unlikely pair in a largely antiunion town—were in many ways the prime movers. (The current mayor, Antonio Villaraigosa, follows in Riordan's footsteps and has his political support; although one is a Republican and the other a Democrat, they share an antipathy toward the existing school district and a determination to overtake it politically.) They had some historical kin among the Progressives of the early twentieth century: fiery and shrewd advocates such as John Randolph Haynes, a physician turned social entrepreneur, and Caroline Severance, a suffragette who became California's first female voter and promoter of the new German idea of kindergarten.

The keystone of Progressive Era school governance was to take schooling out of politics and turn it over to professional educators, whose work was watched over by apolitical trustees. But by the time LEARN began, the District was governed by a series of interest groups. United Teachers Los Angeles

(UTLA) was the most powerful of them, but there were scores of others that lobbied, participated in school board campaigns, protested, testified, and organized. The school board itself became home to aspiring politicians who used their visibility and experience to run for other elected offices. The superintendency fell into such disrepute that the last two holders of that office were noneducators, something as unthinkable as amateur brain surgery just forty years before. The underlying bureaucracy provided stability but became an object of near-universal derision.

In the Progressive ideal, and in reality for decades, a professionally dominated, apolitical school district was possible because it could control its own functions. Nothing was more crucial than the district's control over its own finances, personnel decisions, curriculum, and standards for achievement. Such local control in Los Angeles, as elsewhere, has been replaced by a federated governance system with massive power lodged at state and national levels, in interest groups, and among book and testing organizations.

Apolitical governance and local control allowed a logic of confidence to surround the District. The District had a positive organizational saga in which it spoke well of itself and people spoke well of it. It had little external scrutiny, and internally the linkages between resource allocation and results were not heavily monitored. Today, this has been replaced by a low-trust logic of consequences in which both management operations and school achievement outcomes are closely watched from outside the District.

In the second and third sections of the book, we turn to the process of institutional change. The steps we lay out are not entirely sequential—one does not stop before another begins—but they are roughly chronological:

1. The old institution is discredited and delegitimated.
2. Significant portions of its most vocal clients exit the system.
3. The functions of the system are removed, "hollowed out," and given to other levels of government.
4. There are frantic efforts at reform and the auditioning of new ideas.
5. There is a defining crisis, or a recognized end to a long term boil of crisis and uncertainty.
6. The new institution is operationally recognized. Someone writes a text about how it should operate.

Each chapter addresses one of these steps.

Chapter 2: Withdrawing Legitimacy. By 1920, Los Angeles public schools became the epitome of the reform-minded Progressive Era. The school district created a complex, integrated hierarchy that provided a wide array of social services as well as elementary and secondary education. High school enrollment and graduation soared during the pre–World War II years, and the school board of community elites mirrored the ethos of the local business elite. It was considered the "best in the West," a school district that others could and should emulate. But beginning in the 1960s, the institution's legitimacy began to be discredited. A desegregation lawsuit made public the extent to which the District did not create success for African American or Latino children, and an aura of distrust descended. Desegregation lawsuits and racial politics were followed by student activism and collective bargaining. Meanwhile, the federal and state governments increased the use of targeted funding, and public education became the primary vehicle for the War on Poverty. All of these developments challenged the Progressive Era norms of unquestioned professional dominance and local control. Within L.A. Unified, these specially funded programs created organizational fiefdoms, each with walls of suspicion protecting it from its neighbors. Relatively few new resources went into regular classrooms.

Chapter 3: Exit and Entrada. Institutional decline becomes more likely—and politically acceptable—when the most vocal of those who use the system exit it. Like many big city school systems, LAUSD experienced wrenching demographic changes in the years following 1950. In the space of fifty years, a student body that had been 85 percent white and mostly middle class became nearly 85 percent students of color, mostly poor. During the same period, the city underwent equally dramatic social and economic changes. Its manufacturing economy collapsed, and many of the largest corporations were bought or merged. The business elite lost its iron grip on the city's politics. Once again, Los Angeles became a port of immigration, and the city's schools were filled with immigrant children, just as they had been a century earlier.

Chapter 4: Hollowing Out. The same actions that delegitimated the ethos of the early-twentieth-century Progressive idea of a locally controlled school district also diminished its capacity to function. Proposition 13, California's property tax reduction measure, along with successful tax equity lawsuits, effectively stripped the ability to make revenue decisions at the local level

and made the school district the fiscal ward of the state. Teacher unionization, legalized by a 1975 collective bargaining law, severely limited the District's ability to assign and discipline its employees and to set its budget
priorities according to managerial priorities. A shift from at-large to subdis-
trict-based school board seats effectively ended the tradition of elite governance and created a system dominated by interest groups. And an activist
state government tied the financial purse strings with an instinct to control
education curriculum and standards.

Chapter 5: New Ideas. By the mid-1980s, some District policymakers came
to believe substantive change was necessary and began to draw up large-scale
plans. The tone of their reports, and the urgency of their message, was in
marked contrast to the District's reaction to the beginning of large-scale federal funding in the 1960s. Then, reaching out to disadvantaged children was
considered a manageable problem. By the 1980s, the District's failure to educate them created a crisis. Reformers inside the District acknowledged that it
could not meet society's expectations for educating children without making
substantial changes.

A series of four plans emerged over the course of the next decade. They
are remarkable because of their continuity. Four key ideas—decentralization,
standards, choice, and grassroots participation—are present in all of them.
Clearly, there was a common theory of action about how to move forward.
Only the will and capacity for action were lacking.

The school board approved the District's most definitive plan, *The Children Can No Longer Wait*, just as the recession of the early 1990s hit and just
after the District had settled a bitter teacher strike with a 24 percent salary increase over three years.[1] The District could not afford its own reform
plan, and as it happened it could not afford its labor settlement either. Amid
mutual recrimination, the salary increase was rolled back and programs were
severely cut.

In the face of this inability to act, the momentum for school reform shifted
to civic reformers outside the District. As with the District plans, LEARN
engaged in a long planning process, one intended as much to build a political constituency as to develop a finely honed plan of action. As we read in the
Prologue, the reform coalition pressed the school board to agree, and LEARN
as a reform program was born.

Chapter 6: LEARN. Schools began signing up to join the LEARN program in the summer of 1993. More than half the schools in LAUSD joined an effort that, in effect, auditioned a new institution of public education. LEARN's decentralized school implementation depended on continuing cooperation between the school administration and reformers, the capacity of the school district to deliver the support and training schools needed, and the ability of the schools to think and plan outside the institutional box. The assumption that the school district was willing and able to implement the reforms it had agreed to proved to be wishful thinking.

It was not that people did not try. Everyone tried. It would be hard to over-state how hard people worked on LEARN. An intricate political deal involving at least four levels of government was pulled off, allowing LAUSD to avert financial disaster and turn its attention to the reform project. A LEARN office was established in the District. Cohorts of schools applied, stepping forward with a positive vote of 75 percent of the teachers. But in the end it was not enough. LEARN was considered a threat to the administration, the school district never could deliver the budgetary flexibility to the schools that it had promised, and as the program rolled along it ran out of friends and gathered enemies.

Chapter 7: LAAMP. By the second year of its operation, LEARN was joined by another reform player: philanthropist Walter Annenberg's 1993 challenge grant to public education. As originally written, the Los Angeles Annenberg Metropolitan Project would have been a straightforward extension of the LEARN idea, with the addition of combining reforming schools together into "families." But LAAMP itself changed the course of reform. The Annenberg Foundation wanted to spread beyond LAUSD and into the surrounding metropolitan area. By funding the reform—the Annenberg money and matching funds raised locally topped $103 million—it nudged the agenda toward more parental involvement and an even more externally driven reform than LEARN had created. LEARN's coalition was big institutional players—business, teacher union, school district. LAAMP's board was more politically and culturally diverse. Its board "looked like Los Angeles," and in some ways it was in greater opposition to the school district. It was also more explicitly focused on increasing grassroots, parental participation. Yet, at the same time, it excluded the teachers' union and the central administration from its board. The reform movement had become almost entirely external.

LEARN and LAAMP invested heavily in technical assistance and professional development for the participating schools. It did so partly because the school district lacked the funds for staff training. LEARN schools were supposed to be the pilots that charted the course for the rest of the District, but one of the effects of externally driven change was to separate the LEARN schools from the rest of the school district. LEARN schools reported to a separate school reform office, not their local administrators, and the office became estranged from the rest of the administration. By the end of the 1990s, the school board had appointed a superintendent who was not friendly to the LEARN program, and the program was starved for resources.

Chapter 8: Implementation. At the beginning of the LEARN program, it was thought that once the impediments of a rule-bound bureaucracy were pushed aside, then teachers and principals would be freed to solve achievement problems, which they were willing and capable of solving. This assumption proved wrong. The notion of learning communities was abstract and ambiguous, and they required drastic shifts in the work roles of both teachers and administrators. Despite training and technical assistance, it was very difficult for teachers and principals to work through issues involving devolution of control. Principals, in particular, found themselves surrounded by incentives to follow the District's existing command and control model of administration, and frequently there was little attention to how teaching and learning was supposed to change.

Forcing a focus on teaching was made more difficult because there was no common accountability mechanism and nothing in the system that connected a teacher's daily activity to the results obtained. California even abandoned its testing program during the time of the LEARN program so that the schools, which were reluctant to measure their efforts against hard targets, had an easy excuse not to. By the end of the program, the state had begun to focus hard on testable outcomes. But these measurements were not present as schools designed their plans, and external test score accountability ran counter to the home-grown and grounded notions of accountability that were being developed in the schools.

Still, more than half the schools in the District, most of them elementary schools, signed up for LEARN. Evaluations of these schools showed that breaking the old institutional boundaries was difficult on all sides. Teachers in LEARN schools who took on new roles often found themselves at odds with the remaining staff. Some of the site action plans were more romantic than actionable, and the schools faced the usual problems of transience in personnel.

Chapter 9: Permanent Crisis. As LEARN and LAAMP came to an end, LAUSD was declared to be in crisis and the reform programs were declared dead. Civic attention switched to an attempt to take over the school board, and a noneducator superintendent, former Colorado governor Roy Romer, was installed as superintendent. The word "crisis" implies a tipping point, a road taken or not, a slippery slope. But in Los Angeles, something close to *permanent crisis* descended on the District. When asked whether the District was nearing a crisis, a veteran administrator responded, "We've been in one for ten years." Their crisis is not so much one of decay or corruption as it is of systemic uncertainty about what to do next. The reality is that a school staff cannot simply go to a shelf and find a set of classroom practices that will meet the achievement expectations of the public in Los Angeles or the requirements of the No Child Left Behind Act.

It may well be that the new institution of public education will be born less of design than of continued experimentation tied with the ribbon of history: the trying, adopting, and discarding of reform elements. If a single crisis point exists, it will be one ascribed by history.

As LEARN and LAAMP closed their operations in 2000, some of their leaders feared that the civic coalition that brought about LEARN would collapse when the leaders left the field. The economy of Los Angeles had changed radically, depriving the city of Fortune 500–level corporate leadership. Many of the younger leaders had not attended public schools in Los Angeles and had no emotional or civic ties to the system. This fear proved unfounded as the current decade is witnessing a fountain of emerging leadership, mostly from Latinos in political offices and community-based organizations.

Chapter 10: Charter Schools. At the same time that LEARN was starting, the California legislature enacted a charter school law. The charter school movement maintained a mostly separate existence from the large civic reform initiative. But as LEARN came to an end in 2000, much of the energy, and many of the people who were active in LEARN, found themselves organizing or running charter schools. The successor organization to both LEARN and LAAMP turned into a charter school management organization with the announced goal of establishing 100 schools in the city.

While LEARN sputtered, the charter school movement expanded rapidly. There are now more than 100 charter schools in Los Angeles. In addition, the school district operates more than 160 magnet schools or centers, thus creating a critical mass of schools in the city that are not subject to the traditional line authority. By 2005, these elements were starting to converge. Charter operators had developed independent political reach and influence, and one organization has taken over management of a District high school. Public education in Los Angeles has begun to look more like a network than a hierarchy.

Chapter 11: Beyond Crisis. To move beyond permanent crisis and toward a network form of organization, the politics of education needs to be restructured in ways that recognize four new realities. Governance has become inherently pluralistic and multi-interest rather than being controlled by a tight elite. Power is spread across governmental levels instead of being localized. Operating control is spread throughout the network rather than at the top of the hierarchy. And a low-trust logic of consequences has replaced the old institution's logic of confidence. Each of these new realities has an idealized and hopeful face, but also an all-too-obvious ugly face with conspicuous flaws: narrow self-interest, gridlock, lack of competence, and lack of system capacity. Politics will not be restructured quickly or through a single project or piece of legislation. Rather, it needs a sustained process that uses both evolutionary trial and error and systemic intelligent design.

Chapter 12: Five Policy Levers. The history of reform efforts in Los Angeles provides important lessons about the institution of public education, and these are recounted in the final chapter. There is little doubt that the old institution has been delegitimated and hollowed out and that there have been repeated auditions of new institutional ideas. There is also little doubt that the District is in a state of permanent crisis, unable to enact new institutional forms and make them work.

While the notion of devising a single grand design for the new institution is appealing, it is unrealistic. Instead, we advocate five public policy measures to build around networks of schools, which, if combined with some long-range and continued systemic thinking, would end the crisis and institutionalize new forms of education and operations:

Legislate authority for LAUSD to devolve into networks of autonomous schools,
with finance and operational authority centered on the schools. These
need not be formed all at once, thus allowing a workable transition
from existing operations to the new system, but the autonomous
networks would benefit from existing charter school policies, including simplification of state controls, and from the operating lessons
generated by LEARN and LAAMP.

Legislate weighted-student formula finances. Moving money directly to the
schools provides the necessary force for forming networks rather
than little hierarchies. Without legislation, fiscal decentralization
will always be tentative and temporary.

Create positive incentives. The current assessment and accountability system is built almost entirely around negative incentives. Creating positive incentives, particularly for students and their families and also
for teachers and administrators, opens the possibility for engagement and growth rather than increasingly unproductive regimes of
fear and compliance.

Finance a student learning infrastructure that would allow students and
their parents much greater access to information, self monitoring, and
resources for learning. It would open-source the curriculum, thus ele-
vating the teachers to creators and developers of pedagogy rather
than being the subjects of its operations.

Deliberately build in choice and variety. LAUSD already operates a sophisticated and widespread choice system of more than 100 charters and
160 magnet schools, most of which are in high demand. Yet, legislation and support are needed to link the autonomous network idea
to incentives to design novel and interesting schools, to deliberately
experiment at the edges of the system.

In drawing together the lessons of the past for the design of the future,
there is plenty to learn from Los Angeles. The public policy problem is not simply to put forward ideas, such as the five above, but to keep them active for a
sustained period—in the same way that charter school advocates have done.

3/15/93

Euphoria

On March 15, 1993, the boardroom at 450 N. Grand Ave. was packed, the crowd awaiting political theater. And a good show it was. Balloons and placards gave the austere boardroom in the old, now-demolished Los Angeles Unified School District (LAUSD) headquarters a festive air. The crowd had marched to "450" clogging Grand Ave., filling the board chambers, and overflowing into adjacent rooms. The audience of reform supporters brought forth the fruits of a two-year effort to form a new organization called LEARN and to build support for it. LEARN was an acronym for Los Angeles Educational Alliance for Restructuring Now, but it was very seldom referred to by its full name. The slim document that had been set before the school board contained a blueprint for fundamental change in the nation's second-largest school district: 639,781 students in 637 schools.[1] The organization was to be radically decentralized. Teachers and principals in participating schools were to become operators of something akin to a producer's cooperative; individual schools would gain control over their own funds, and in return they were to be accountable for results. Hundreds of hands had touched the LEARN plan on its way to finalization, the result of the planning process that was as much political campaign as it was deliberation.

Speakers addressed the pros and cons of the plan, and finally Robert Wycoff, the president of ARCO and LEARN's chair, walked to the microphone.

It's been a long and unifying journey since the morning of August in 1991 when we stood in the courtyard of Ivanhoe Elementary School and issued a call for every member of this community to join us. Along that journey our

ranks grew to include the 600 members, these 600 trustees from every cor-
ner of the community—a coalition of unprecedented diversity and inclusive-
ness. The consensus that we reached as a result of this coming together is
quite extraordinary. It represents thousands of volunteer hours of passionate
debate, thoughtful listening and creative exchange.

But this is a plan that is not simply a final blueprint, which provides the
details of how we're going to go about operating our schools on a day-to-
day basis, how our children should be taught. Instead it is the beginning
of a new system, a new process that will free our local schools to make the
changes necessary to improve themselves. It will recreate our neighborhood
schools changing from a centralized command and control system to an output driven system.

We must begin now with your vote. A vote that I very much hope is
unanimous.[2]

A unanimous vote would "demonstrate that Los Angeles has finally put
aside its internal disputes in an effort to work together to provide a decent
education for our children." For Wycoff, consensus and unity were extremely
important, and he believed that "if we all work together . . . we will be an
unbeatable political force." Through this unity, "Sacramento will listen to us.
The federal government will listen to us and provide the financial and other
support we need." In closing he promised that "LEARN will not go away."

Wycoff finished, and there was one more demonstration of support. The
seven-person board had already seen two marches on its headquarters, and
LEARN supporters twice overloaded the District phone system, but members
were astonished by what happened next: To sustained applause, some seven-
ty-five children entered the chambers carrying baskets containing thousands
of petitions. The process took several minutes, and the applause turned into
a cadenced clap. Wycoff abashedly apologized to board chair Leticia Quezada,
saying, "I didn't understand how many 85,000 was." School board members
later said they had never seen anything like it.

Supporters—the vast majority of those gathered—sensed that they were
at a historic turning point for the schools. Superintendent Sidney Thompson said the vote would "determine the future for generations to come for
all our young people." He and his staff were "fully and totally committed to
this," and he assured the school board, the LEARN leadership (which was
called the Working Group), and the public that they would meet this challenge, which would be "work of joy because we know that we're going in the
right direction."

Board member Mark Slavkin, who was to be one of LEARN's most loyal advocates, called the program "a gift" to the community and a cause for celebration. He lauded the clear goals and achievement standards that the program promised. Achievement standards would allow the schools to spend energy on what matters. "We spend too much time on the process and the paper work and the rules—and too little time on student outcomes. LEARN understands that." He also understood that shifting authority was important: "There are no kids . . . here at 450 N. Grand, and somehow we've put the power as far away from the kids as possible. We have to turn that around."

When the vote was taken, all seven board members supported LEARN, and loud applause followed.[3] After adjournment, board members, the superintendent, and community leaders literally held hands. For at least one shining moment the stars aligned.

UNDERCURRENTS

Although they were hardly recognized during the collective celebration, dissent rippled through the meeting in portentous undercurrents.

Mexican Americans felt left out, at least many from existing interest groups. Whether any particular group had been slighted or discouraged from participating is debatable, but it was clear that the big civic coalition that formed LEARN did not speak for everyone. Parent organizer Sigifredo Lopez, speaking in Spanish, questioned the legitimacy of employee unions and the business elite speaking for the welfare of parents, particularly Latinos: "They're here to think for us. Do they think that we don't have our own thoughts or know how to do what needs to be done?"

Lopez's question raised a broader point of "who were these people, and what right do they have to reform our schools." It was clear that the LEARN coalition was broad and contained many of the city's influential names. Yet, as events would later show, the LEARN coalition may have prevailed because the school district was weak, not because the reformers were particularly strong.

There were issues about moving power away from the existing hierarchy. The reform plan would allow faculties to vote to remove their principal. "Does this mean that principals must go around kissing derrieres, bringing cookies, flowers and such to the teachers so that they won't be moved after two years?" asked community member Bonnie Christensen.

Rosalinda Lugo, a leader with the United Neighborhood Organizing Committee and LEARN board member, warned against politics or bureaucracy creeping in. "And that's something that this school district has been very good at doing, politicizing things and creating bureaucracy."

Then, there were doubts about whether a big, radical reform could be implemented. Union president Helen Bernstein, who represented the District's 35,000 teachers, had been a part of LEARN from the beginning and had brought United Teachers Los Angeles into the reform arena. Yet, she cautioned that a new vision is "pipe dream unless created twice." The mental image of change had to be linked to actualization. Actualization would prove to be actually hard.

Board member Julie Korenstein observed that prior reforms had never been implemented. "I saw *Priorities for Education* sit on a shelf," she said, referring to a 1986 District-developed plan. Other reforms, she said, starved because of a lack of money: *The Children Can No Longer Wait*, a plan developed in the late 1980s that had broad school board support, and School Based Management (SBM), which had become part of the contract with the teacher's union in 1989. Her colleague, Roberta Weintraub, sounded a similar theme: Money was the problem. Yet, she understood that LEARN had been "born of absolute desperation on the part of our whole community to make [the District] work." She was adamant that LEARN continue to advocate for the District in Sacramento and Washington. She inquired about the group's plan for fund-raising.

Indeed, the District was broke. Board member Jeff Horton spoke of "the terrifying budget dilemma" the District faced. Its $7.5 billion budget was endangered by a stubborn recession that continued to deprive the state's coffers of income and sales tax revenue. LAUSD's ability to control its own finances had ended in 1978 with the passage of Proposition 13, which essentially froze property tax rates. Horton argued that involving community and parents in LEARN would create the necessary support to turn to "the powers that be, the electorate, the legislature, whoever it be, and California deserves better than forty-first in the nation. And I see LEARN as the vehicle to move the entire community to demand a fair share of this state's wealth for its children and young people." Korenstein said that she wanted to see the same fervor shown in LEARN applied to busloads of people confronting governments in Sacramento and Washington, "because if we don't do that we'll be right back here a year from now, two years from now and there'll be a new program, a new proposal presented to the board because there wasn't enough money."

LEARN's answer was that they were in it for the long haul. "That's what it's going to take," said board member Weintraub in announcing her intent to vote for LEARN. Theodore Mitchell, the dean of education at UCLA and later the president of Occidental College and CEO of the New Schools Venture Fund, similarly declared, "We're there for the long haul."

Seven years later, LEARN had gone out of business. The Los Angeles Annenberg Metropolitan Project (LAAMP), which had supported and extended LEARN's reforms to create families of schools, was closing shop. Much of the civic infrastructure created around the reform plan was coming apart. As this is written, a few schools still fly LEARN banners, and they have some decisional privileges denied to other schools, but for the most part the reform program is part of the District's archeology.

When asked for his assessment in 2003, Richard Riordan, one of LEARN's founders and later the city's mayor, said, "That's simple; LEARN failed."

Or did it?

AN INSTITUTIONAL VIEW

If one looks at LEARN, LAAMP, and other efforts to reform the Los Angeles Unified School District as *projects,* it's easy to conclude that large-scale reform didn't work. Project failure nearly goes without saying. Projects fall neatly into a rise-and-fall story. Projects start, build up expectations loftier than themselves, and fall apart during their implementation. The LEARN archives even contained a copy of the oft-repeated six phases of a project: enthusiasm, disillusionment, panic, search for the guilty, punishment of the innocent, praise and honor for the nonparticipants.[4]

Many reform participants and supporters came to this conclusion, and it is not surprising that a large number of them are now working on efforts to build new types of schools independent of LAUSD. Charter schools are the favorite vehicle, and even the District itself has embraced the charter idea, at least tentatively.

But what if LEARN and LAAMP were simply part of a much larger institutional change? When reforms are looked at in this way, one comes to a different conclusion about their worth. Instead of seeing them as failed projects, they become *part of a still-incomplete process of institutional change.*

This is a book about institutional change and how it came to the public schools of Los Angeles. It is a book about how a set of widely accepted ideas about how public education should be structured and operated came to be discredited and discarded. It is a book about how civil rights advocates, tax cutters, immigrants, labor unions, and educational reformers all auditioned new ideas in the political marketplace. It is a book about how new ideas were accepted, rejected, modified, and compromised beyond recognition.

The story it tells is contrarian and counterintuitive, because many believe that LAUSD is, as commentator Sandra Tsing Loh has written, "a gelatinous Borg." It absorbs energy meant to change it. But as we show, the school district and its surrounding institution are vastly different from what they were forty years ago. Even so, as Tsing Loh writes, its essence is less discernible through crisp deciding moments "than through endlessly snarled court decisions, civil codes, state laws and charter restrictions."[5] The very complexity of the relationships between the District and its institutional environment masks the profoundness of the changes it has undergone.

The institutional perspective differs in several ways from the usual analysis of reform projects. Most obviously, the scope of expected change is different; it involves looking for changes in the entire institution of public education in which school districts are set. Institutions are the big chunky parts of society, and public education ranks along with law, religion, and the economy as among the most fundamental. Any individual school district is the recipient of rules and resources from parts of the institution external to the district itself, and any school district engages in political and commercial transactions with other parts of the institution. Thus, an examination of LAUSD and how it changes is not complete unless one considers its relationships with several levels of government and interest groups including employee unions and advocacy organizations.

In social science research, the term "institution" has a very specific meaning.[6] The word can be applied to informal and diffuse institutions like a barter economy or patriarchy. But in our analysis here, we mean the term in the more formal sense: an institution as a system of rules and pattern of organization. By the 1920s, Progressive reformers had built the Los Angeles school system into a fairly cohesive institution with internal rules, both formal and informal.[7] It had structures, including offices, communication systems, divisions of labor. It had resources, including money, personnel with skills and expertise, information, and both formal and informal authority. It had internal incentives, and the people within it had general patterns of behavior. By 1941, the Los Angeles city schools had become "truly agencies of social reform completely run by professionals."[8]

The institutional perspective also differs in terms of its time frame. Projects take months or a few years, and critical observers judge their success or failure almost instantly. The efficacy of LEARN was already in doubt just months after the celebratory school board meeting.[9] Institutions change infrequently. The institutional shell of the Los Angeles public schools was created at the turn of the twentieth-century when the Progressive Era coalition of business and radical interests sought to clean up local government and expand its powers in order to counter the rapaciousness of private interests, particularly the private utilities and the railroads. As was the case throughout the country, the schools were taken away from city government and established in the now-conventional form as independent public bodies.[10]

Because institutional change takes place over a long period of time, it is sometimes difficult to see until there is a defining crisis or until someone labels something as definitively new. Our society is labeled "post industrial" precisely because no one has a sufficiently robust label for what it has become instead. While it is generally accepted that public education has mutated from its Progressive Era roots, the institution is still in the midst of change, and the new era does not yet have a descriptor. Part of the problem in describing what public education is becoming arises because on the outside it largely looks the same. School boards meet, administrators report to work every day and manage the programs they have been assigned to lead, teachers pin student work to classroom walls, and hundreds of thousands of sleepy-eyed children are roused from their beds and sent toward classrooms. But inside, in the operations and functioning, we argue that LAUSD has become a different organization and that the sources of criticism and change have hollowed out its capacity. "It's a little like the way the spider eats the beetle," said one education reformer. "The hard parts on the outside remain, but there's nothing left inside." Over the last forty years, schooling in Los Angeles underwent a radical transformation in how it operated and in how people thought about schooling. School board members used to be civic elites, elected citywide. The school board had the independent ability to raise taxes in order to pay for operations. The board did not meddle too much in how the schools operated. The superintendent was a largely unquestioned leader who commanded loyalty from administrators and obedience from the teachers. Fledgling teacher unions spoke meekly and officially did not bargain. Over four decades, LAUSD had changed in ways that challenged virtually every traditional assumption about how to govern and organize public education.

As it does with other institutions, society depends on the stability of public education. A society is thrown into chaos if land titles are uncertain or contracts become unenforceable. Governments and religious organizations lose trust if the civil service or the clergy become corrupted. In Los Angeles, as in other cities, society depends on a public school system capable of educating any child who walks through the door regardless of race, religion, gender, aptitude, prior education, physical or mental challenge, or immigration status. Even if the schools were to fail to teach them anything, civil society depends on the school's custody and care of its children. Indeed, schools open every morning, and students enter for six hours or so. Even the smallest deviation—such as students leaving schools in 2006 to participate in an immigration rally—is cause for great public concern. The stability of the system's operations continues even if the core goals are not being met. It is possible to have schools where people work every day but where the system doesn't work.

Attempts at changing institutions are often resisted vigorously. Social Security became such a politically charged issue that efforts to change it have become dangerous for politicians. (A similar level of controversy accompanied the introduction of the program seven decades ago.) Efforts to change public education have likewise been resisted. This is the case not only because interest groups oppose change, but also because our norms and thought patterns tells us what is right and proper. David Tyack and Larry Cuban explain this as a "grammar of schooling" that "has become taken for granted as just the way things are." They note that "established institutional forms come to be understood by educators, students, and the public as necessary features of a 'real school.'"[11] A project approach to school reform attempts to retain these forms and still "make sense" to those familiar with the existing system. Institutional change, in contrast, requires rejecting the conventions of this "grammar" by breaking down and restructuring the whole system. Reform projects are often disruptive; school boards are voted out of office and superintendents are replaced. And as the recent history of Los Angeles shows, even a project to overthrow a regime is not enough by itself. Real institutional change requires a change in ideas.

Most of our ideas about public schools are rooted in the Progressive Era, when advocates of governmental efficiency joined with anticorruption forces, scientific management advocates, and pedagogical reformers to create the bedrock ideas and practices on which U.S. public schools are built. By forwarding a systemic vision of better schools, they convinced legislatures and the public to elect school board members independent of party labels and to pare down the size of boards so they were run by "the best men" in the community. This accomplished, the way was paved for the professionalization of school administration and teaching. Teachers became licensed, and increasingly longer periods of college study were required of them. The school superintendency became an appointed rather than an elected office, and professional training programs began in school leadership. The "Administrative Progressives," as they were called, took over and dominated public education for more than fifty years and created virtually every feature that we identify with schooling today. Their inventions included schools with levels or grades, high schools where students gained credits toward graduation, teaching pedagogies based on the experimental method, special schools for immigrants, and special modes of teaching for hard-to-teach children.

Administrative progressivism swept the nation, ushering in knowledgeable professionals as superintendents, rather than political appointees. School districts were given control of their own finances, and school boards were separated from city governments, which were looked on as instruments of corruption and patronage. Pedagogy was freed from rote learning, and urban school districts in particular developed courses based on inquiry and problem solving. California, and Los Angeles in particular, became a prime example of progressivism. As historian Judith Raftery wrote, "By the mid-1920s administrative Progressives in Los Angeles had succeeded in remaking their school district on the model of the scientifically managed corporation."[12]

Because institutions resist change in their core ideas, institutional transformation often requires a crisis coming out of the belief that the existing institution is incapable of delivering what is expected of it. In the case of public education, and Los Angeles Unified in particular, the sense of crisis has unfolded over decades. Thus, in order to understand why the big reform efforts of the 1990s and beyond worked or did not work, we need to appreciate how events of the previous forty years had already moved LAUSD away from an ideal begun in the early twentieth century.

CHAPTER 1

The Progressives

Founding an Institution

When the school board meeting adjourned, the party started. LEARN supporters gathered in the courtyard outside the school headquarters, a grassy oasis in the middle of the city. Because there was no room left in the boardroom, many in the crowd had watched the meeting on large television monitors, and the transition from cheering support to victory party was easy to make. Mary Chambers, who was to run LEARN's day-to-day operations, called these supporters "the worker bees." Hundreds stayed. There was a band and dancing. There was food. There was not drinking—or at least any that people talked about, this being school district property. When the last stragglers had left, about 9:30 P.M., Chambers and Jefferson Crain (a field deputy for board member Mark Slavkin who went on to become executive officer of the board of education, and Chambers's husband), were left picking up the litter.

Behind the worker bees stood a community elite of unlikely collaborators who formed LEARN and saw it move forward. Over the course of a decade, they crafted the first systemic reform of public education in Los Angeles in nearly a century. They organized political support for their ideas, pressuring the school district and board to accept them and, by the end of the 1990s, organizing to oust a school board they thought to be recalcitrant. They provided technical assistance and tried to create a new organizational culture to replace the one that LEARN president Mike Roos described as "an internal culture of go along and get along. It absolutely swallows any effort at change . . . nothing permanent will happen till that culture is gone."[1] Or, as one observer put it, "The culture was insecure and whipsawed, bordering on the paranoid."

THE ELITES

LEARN was said to have begun at a breakfast meeting between businessman Richard Riordan, who later became mayor, and United Teachers Los Angeles (UTLA) president Helen Bernstein. They were seemingly an unlikely pair. Riordan was rich. As union president, Bernstein earned a teacher's salary—$47-something, according to her reckoning. A venture capitalist, Riordan symbolized entrepreneurial capital. Bernstein's union was chock full of old lefties who loved to hate capitalism, and the unionists distrusted LEARN because participating meant dealing with business people, the enemy. Yet, Bernstein and Riordan united behind school reform and became fast friends. When Bernstein died in 1997—struck by a car as she was dashing to a meeting crossing Olympic Blvd.—Riordan said, "It hit me like a ton of bricks. I was with her this morning. I've never seen her look better. She was so vibrant. A wonderful leader of teachers and school reform. A warm and wonderful friend. I can't believe it."[2]

Bernstein's interest in school reform grew out of the 1989 collective bargaining negotiations and the bitter strike which led to a contract that increased teacher salaries by 24 percent, part of which was rolled back when the recession of the early 1990s hit. The new contract also spawned School Based Management (SBM), which established shared decisionmaking councils at individual school sites.

Bernstein became an object of great mystery. "In a world where the right wing is mean and the left wing is idiotic, Bernstein's great vision was to carve out a spot in what can only be called the radical center."[3] She was a passionate unionist who would walk into any meeting—invited or not—and say, "I represent Los Angeles' 35,000 teachers." Yet, she believed that her union had to change in order to save the school district. She used her participation in LEARN to advance teacher voice and interest. A reform activist recalled how if anything didn't go Bernstein's way, it was a big yelling and screaming fight. She knew that the school district had publicly committed to support the reform and that she was the only person who could deliver votes from teachers to join up. She used that knowledge as leverage with the District and LEARN. "Without Helen, without the teachers union, we weren't going anywhere," noted Robert Wycoff, chair of the LEARN Working Group, which was functionally the organization's executive committee. "She was the most enthusiastic reformer we had, and at the same time she was a union person."[4] Moreover she led a severely divided union. Within weeks of the school board approval of the LEARN program, the UTLA House of Representatives voted to oppose the plan. Former UTLA president Wayne Johnson led the opposition faction against his former friend and protégé, Bernstein.

Wycoff and the business leaders were amazed that a unionist was capable of understanding that the District had great difficulties. "She had a zeal for reforming the system that was not too different from all the others," said Wycoff. "That was a big change when we in the business community discovered that the teachers union, who we'd always seen as being behind the failure of the schools, saw that real changes were necessary."[5]

She appeared to be a fearless organizer. She could walk into a room of hostile teachers, and in an hour they had agreed with her proposal. "Helen had the ability to convince teachers a new idea was theirs," said Becki Robinson, who was then a vice president of the union. She exuded confidence and toughness. "And, oh my God," said one reformer, "the woman had a mouth on her like a sailor. She could be very verbally aggressive."

But Robinson also noted that while outwardly Bernstein had no fear, "Inwardly she was scared to death." [6] LEARN vice president and Bernstein's confidante Mary Chambers concurred with Robinson.

> [It was] personally disappointing to her that her members would not follow her in LEARN, and I can remember so many late night phone calls when she would just cry. . . . And she was very afraid and every time she had a confrontation it was very scary for her, which just makes her all the more heroic, because she did it anyway . . . she was as terrified as anybody else would've been, but she did it anyway because she believed so passionately in what she was doing. She was a real hero, an incredible hero.[7]

OTHER ELITES

When the Los Angeles Board of Education voted unanimously to support the LEARN plan, board member Jeff Horton was quoted as saying, "We have never seen such broad participation in a school reform movement in the history of this district."[8] And indeed while the representation was broad, it also included a number of prominent reform-minded community and business leaders—kin to the reformers of the Progressive Era—some of whom would continue their efforts well beyond the life spans of LEARN and LAAMP.

Much like the Progressives, these modern reformers were business executives, academics, administrators, and community organizers. The cast of characters included corporate executives and attorneys such as Robert Wycoff and Virgil Roberts; school superintendents and administrators like Sidney Thompson, Don Shalvey, and Maria Casillas; politicians and political organizers including Mike Roos, Gary Hart, Bill Honig, and Steve Barr; college presidents Theodore Mitchell and Steven Sample; and community advocates such as Peggy Funkhouser, founder of the Los Angeles Educational Partnership, and Rosalindo Lugo of the Industrial Areas Foundation affiliated United Neighborhood Organizing Committee. Their stories, and those of many others played (and continue to play) an important role in the story of school reform and institutional change in Los Angeles.

HISTORICAL KIN

These reformers had historical kin. The LEARN coalition they helped construct was remarkably similar to an earlier alliance of reformers that changed Los Angeles during the early years of the twentieth century. At that time, just as now, Angelenos had become restless with government structures that appeared self-serving, inefficient, and at times corrupt. The Progressives changed not just individual school districts but the entire institution of public education. Economists such as John Commons and Thorstein Veblen argued that many of the so-called economic laws were contingent on the institutions of society. They showed how vested interests, informal structures of power and influence, and the cooptation of dissent shaped organizations. Veblen's *Theory of the Leisure Class* was subtitled "an economic study of institutions."[9] While economic and political theorists were first writing about institutions, the Progressives were busy founding one.

By the early 1900s, Los Angeles had been transformed from a frontier town into a city of more than 100,000, nearly ten times its population just thirty years before. Progressivism in Los Angeles was "less than socialism," but it put a brake on Wild West capitalism. Its political organizing changed the distribution of power in California. In Los Angeles, progressivism was most often seen in conservative "good government" terms, as an attempt to root out cronyism and corruption and preserve capitalism against the increasingly popular Socialist ideas. The typical Progressive would be a middle-class male Republican, a lawyer or businessman or journalist. He was a city dweller and perhaps a migrant from the Midwest who could trace his ancestry back past the Civil War to small towns in the East.[10] He was most likely a Protestant and very often an emphatic one. Protestant theologians such as Washington Gladden and Walter Rauschenbusch called for a "social gospel" to help the poor.

> The starting point of Rauschenbusch's theology was the argument, common to his progressive contemporaries in the social sciences and arts, that Americans misunderstood the origin of their outlook of individualism, in this case individual salvation. Americans were mistaken in believing that an emphasis on personal rather than social salvation was a repudiation of medieval tradition in favor of a natural, primitive Christianity. For Rauschenbusch, primitive Christianity embodied the true nature of man, his social nature. It had been during the artificial civilizations of Rome and the Middle Ages that this truth had been obscured and mankind had been inculcated with the error of individual autonomy and the belief that salvation must be otherworldly.[11]

Spiritual zeal combined with the social idealism of Jane Addams's settlement house movement and John Dewey's intent to provide a set of "guidelines for reshaping the nation's social institutions. . . . They persuaded better-off Americans to help the poor, particularly the foreign-born, to become healthy, useful Americans—under the watchful eye of reformers, of course."[12] Although they were sometime allies, Progressives maintained "a sort of *noblesse oblige* attitude" toward Socialists and trade unionists, who were becoming increasingly active. They stood between labor and capital, though they leaned toward the latter.

The reformers of the 1990s understood the need for change in education, just as did two reformers in the booming Los Angeles of the late nineteenth century: John Randolph Haynes and Caroline Severance. Haynes, whose name lives on in the foundation he and his wife formed, practiced medicine and invested shrewdly. Born in rural Pennsylvania in 1853, Haynes graduated from the University of Pennsylvania with both Ph.D. and M.D. degrees, and, together with his wife, Dora Fellows Haynes, he made a substantial fortune in medical practices. Because of his chronic bronchitis, the Haynes family migrated to Southern California in 1887, where he continued to practice medicine and invest wisely. He became part of the Los Angeles boom, investing in real estate projects, mining, a new company called Union Oil, and downtown construction, including the city's first skyscraper (at twelve stories) and the Majestic Theater.[13]

Haynes's wealth made it possible for him to bankroll reform activities and support political change; indeed, the family foundation continues to support research on the underlying causes of social problems and how to address them. Haynes and others, such as his friend real estate developer, the "millionaire Socialist" H. Gaylord Wilshire, supported such reforms as municipal ownership of gas and electric utilities, regulation of streetcars and saloons, and freedom from corporate monopolies.

Haynes felt no contradiction between making money, enjoying the company of the wealthy, and being an ally of organized labor. He was a member of both the Los Angeles Country Club and the bastion of wealth and propriety, the California Club. At the same time, his pro-labor stance made him a constant target of the *Los Angeles Times*. Historically conservative and virulently anti-labor—particularly after unionists from Indiana dynamited the newspaper's building in 1910, killing twenty—the *Times* characterized Haynes as a demagogue and supporter of violent anarchists.[14] In reality, Haynes was a Christian Socialist, a follower of the Reverend D. P. Bliss, who preached that civic reforms would prepare the way for the coming of the Kingdom of Heaven on earth based on cooperation, fraternity, and justice.[15] It was later said that Haynes "best epitomize[d] the internal contradictions of a movement that could seemingly tilt right and left at the same time."[16]

Caroline Severance and her husband, Theodoric, migrated to Los Angeles in 1875, just ahead of the Southern Pacific Railroad. The Severances had long been active reformers in Cleveland and Boston, abolitionists and supporters of Lincoln and the fledgling Republican Party. But by 1906, Caroline was distancing herself from the militarism of Theodore Roosevelt and saw William Jennings Bryan and the Democrats as the best hope for the country. (When the Los Angeles City Council spent $25,000 on a party to welcome the navy fleet, she suggested that the feast would be better served to the unemployed than the city's elite.) Her sixty-year passion was women's suffrage, and when the vote came to California women in 1911, she was the first to register.[17]

Like Helen Bernstein a century later, Severance was an organizer. Her talent was her ability to draw people together from various walks of life, and the family home on West Adams St. became a gathering place. Her appetite for reform was nourished through women's clubs; although the image of such organizations now seems antique and stereotypical, in the nineteenth century these groups were the primary means of socializing women to civic life and promoting agendas.

> Well aware that most women viewed her most cherished reforms, particularly women's rights, as too radical, Severance moved with deliberate gradualism in order not to antagonize potential converts. She gently nudged women into action by educating them through lectures and descriptive literature. To attract the largest number of members, she divided the club into committees of interest. Many committees were purely for self-betterment through such activities as literary discussions and theatrical or musical presentations; others were clearly aimed at reform: temperance, suffrage, education. By appealing to a variety of interests, she brought many women together into a single club where they might be influenced by the more militant members. Her organizational genius enabled her to raise funds, gain publicity for her causes, set her projects into motion, and step aside and move on to another cause.[18]

In Los Angeles, the women's clubs drastically changed the mission and operation of the public schools through the introduction of the kindergarten program. Severance and her friends were able to take the German "children's garden" and make it attractive, first to middle-class Angelenos and then in poor and immigrant communities. It was not an easy sell. Religious conservatives and traditionalists objected to turning over instruction of the very young to people outside the families as well as to the then-radical notion that play could be a means of learning. The Los Angeles Women's Club sponsored a free kindergarten for poor children, while tuition-based ones were started for the middle class.

The stage was set for introducing kindergartens into the public schools. In 1889 the city charter was amended to give the school board the right to start them, but the state legislature held that only private money could be used to operate them. By 1900, kindergartens had become popular. School board minutes show that the middle-class parents at Colgrove and Dayton Heights schools petitioned for one, as did the immigrant parents at Breed St. and those at 51st St. for a "colored children's" kindergarten.[19] By 1913, the legislature required school districts to establish—and pay for—kindergartens whenever twenty-five or more parents petitioned the board.

The kindergartens opened the door for a host of social services, such as school lunch programs, day-care centers, afterschool playgrounds, summer schools, and medical and dental services, all of which "were aimed at mitigating the harsher aspects of urban life for children." At the same time, they helped change the nature of schooling, discarding large-class undifferentiated instruction for more individualized courses of study, the idea of shaping the school to fit the needs of the child rather than the other way around. Along with kindergarten, schools began to offer special classes for "slow learners" and truants and saw the beginning of vocational education.

One vehicle for Progressive control was the Direct Legislative League, established in 1895 by Haynes and other reform-minded businessmen. The League's success gave Californians three powerful means of expressing voter sentiment: initiative, recall, and referendum. (He, doubtless, would be horrified with the contemporary uses of these mechanisms as a way in which interest groups and the rich can purchase a spot on the ballot for their pet ideas.[20]) The League and its allies considered the Los Angeles school board to be corrupt. The board's nine members were elected by geographic subdivisions that followed the lines of city council wards. In 1897, several members were suspected of taking bribes and of "general dishonesty."[21] The superintendent admitted wrongdoing and resigned. One board member was arrested and another resigned.

In 1903, the reformers persuaded Los Angeles voters to pass a new city charter containing provisions for direct legislation and civil service employment instead of political patronage. The new charter law also reduced the number of school board seats to seven, all of which were elected citywide. The charter set in motion a series of events that centralized and streamlined the school district, ushering in a sixty-year era in which superintendents dominated the District and its operations. One educator wrote, "We have a nonpartisan Board of Education, in fact as well as in name; and we are getting toward the next step in the development, that is, toward what is better than non-partisan—a non-personal administration of public school affairs."[22] Teachers began to take tests and get licenses in order to secure employment. School board members no longer visited schools to inspect and comment on their performance. They no longer hired teachers. The superintendent ran the district, and the board made policy. That year, too, the state legislature passed a compulsory attendance law, making schooling the law of the land. Despite protests from some, the idea of universal schooling until age fourteen was rapidly accepted.

Another Progressive vehicle was professionalism. The worldview of "scientific management" advocates such as Frederick Taylor was highly influential in shaping the early twentieth century reforms that created the contemporary institution of education.[23] His views were in line with the emerging political ideas of the likes of Herbert Croly and Walter Lippman, whose *New Republic* magazine was established in 1916. They maintained that irrationality in politics, greed, and corruption could be replaced by scientific and objective bureaucrats, "pure politics guided by selfless experts."[24]

Scientific management, in turn, embraced a belief in economies of scale: Bigger was better. Not only did Los Angeles grow, but the school district annexed small districts in surrounding cities, and it still serves students from fifteen municipalities. It became the second largest in the country, nearly five and a half times that of San Diego Unified, the second largest district in the state, and larger than the entire enrollment of Wyoming, Alaska, Montana, Hawaii, and Rhode Island combined.[25] With 93,000 employees, it is the second largest employer in Los Angeles County (behind the county government), and it has two and a half times as many employees as the City of Los Angeles. In terms of revenue, it would rank 250 in the Fortune 500.

In another practice borrowed from the business elites, LAUSD became vertically and horizontally integrated. It runs 2,668 buses, nearly as many as the Metropolitan Transit Authority, and it has eleven times as many bus routes. It serves nearly twice as many meals each day as the city's McDonald's outlets. Its 2000–2012 building program is valued at $15.2 billion with 160 new schools—a larger public works program than Boston's "Big Dig."[26] And its musical instrument repair shop is thought to be the largest in the country.[27]

These schools created a pedagogy that was fitted to the perceived needs of their students, a practice that was often made routine by intelligence testing. Much of this reorientation came from Progressive reformers dramatically broadening the American vision of what schools should do for children. Instead of thinking of schools as simply teaching students the "three Rs," Progressives viewed the school as "a fundamental lever of social and political regeneration" in a decaying urban landscape.[28] School would be "recalled from isolation to the center of the struggle for a better life."[29] Students could not learn unless their other needs were provided for, and society would benefit from students who were ready to become self-sufficient and productive adult citizens. Progressives, therefore, created health and nutritional programs and curricula that would educate students about family and community values. They also created diverse curricula that could be adapted to the needs and abilities of particular children, including vocational education and college preparation.[30] "Los Angeles schools became a paradigm of Progressive reform," notes Judith Raftery, whose history chronicles the District up until World War II.[31]

CHAPTER 2

Withdrawing Legitimacy

The First Step in Transformation

The Progressives created school districts that were the objects of civic pride. By 1919 the *Los Angeles School Journal* was to report that the schools system "is recognized throughout the U.S. and that visitors come to study it from other countries."[1] Two decades later, in 1937, superintendent Vierling Kersey issued a guarantee to parents, citizens, and taxpayers that "children in our schools today attain a higher degree of ability in reading, arithmetic, spelling, geography, and history than at any former time." These same children would spend more time on the fundamentals and read "from two to six times better than at any time in the history of our city schools."[2] All this was done efficiently; "great waste in the former ways of teaching and learning the Three R's has been eliminated."[3] Kersey had been state superintendent of public instruction in the 1930s, and he used the language of the social reconstructionist Progressives warning against the dangers of selfish individualism. At core, however, he was a moderate Republican, a member of the Sons of the American Revolution.[4]

The Progressives gave Los Angeles a school system run by professionals and anchored by the leadership of local elites who were thought to exist above politics. These leaders provided models of efficiency, efficacy, and propriety to the school system that lasted for more than a half-century. Things that had appeared controversial early in the century—cafeterias, kindergartens, and health services—had become such a part of daily life that they continued even during the economic pressures of the Great Depression.[5]

In 1958, superintendent Ellis A. Jarvis reported that high school graduates scored in the top 27 percent of students nationally.[6] By its own report,
the District was aware that "educators outside of this District hold the Los
Angeles School District in highest esteem."[7] The National Education Association (NEA) ranked California schools among the top four in the country.[8]
Indeed, as a now-retired administrator said of his early days in the District,
"it was *the* place to work, people lined up to teach in L.A.; they would move
across country."

How was it possible, then, that the system the Progressives established to
be responsible, effective, and efficient would become the object of near-universal derision some thirty years later? How was it possible that the movement toward professional domination would be so weakened that by the end
of the twentieth century the district superintendent would be a politician
from another state, and after him a Navy admiral, rather than an educator
steeped in the school system's history? How was it possible that progressive-
minded civic reformers could declare the schools in crisis and organize thousands of citizens to follow them? How is it possible that there was hardly
a public murmur of protest from within the school district when outsiders
staked their claim on its operation?

The short answer is that the legitimacy accorded to public schools in Los
Angeles was withdrawn. Los Angeles Unified School District was no longer
seen as a symbol of the city's success, as evidence that Southern California
offered America an optimistic preview of the nation's future. The city's school
system was no longer the symbol of opportunity and progress, was no longer
emulated by cities across the nation.

"A symbol," notes political scientist Deborah Stone, "is anything that
stands for something else. Its meaning depends on how people interpret it,
use it, or respond to it. . . . Any good symbolic device, one that works to capture the imagination, also shapes our perceptions and suspends skepticism,
at least temporally."[9] The public education the Progressives created depended
on the suspension of skepticism and the ceding of decisions over important
aspects of what had been private and family decisions to professionals. In her
history of the Progressive Era in Los Angeles schools, Judith Raftery relates
the story of the Molokan Russians, a pious but largely illiterate Protestant
sect that had fled persecution and conscription in the Czar's army between
1905 and 1910. "Schools played no part in the Molokan culture," she writes,
and compulsory attendance [in L.A. schools], which was enforced by truant

officers, took older girls away from the household and boys away from paid work. The elders also feared assimilation, and in 1908 they decided to write the board of education requesting the use of a room at Utah Street School in Boyle Heights for instruction of the children in Russian. The request, and a subsequent one for another room, was granted, and three years later the community expressed its thanks to the board. Repeated throughout the city, these small accommodations for Jews, Swedes, French, Croatians, Germans, and others "reflected the skill with which newcomers asserted themselves" and also the capacity of the school district to make marginal accommodations and thus create legitimacy for itself.[10]

No symbols were more important than professionalism and local control. The professional claim to special technical competence was the key to pushing away partisan politics and meddlesome local politicians. Local control assured people that trusted individuals were looking after the welfare of the city's children, that they were being taught according to locally accepted norms, and that the schools were efficiently run. As schooling became more and more institutionalized, it was the legitimacy of the symbols rather than any absolute level of performance that counted. "Thus, the key constraint for educational institutions in this view is the need to maintain the trust and confidence of the public at large—in short, to maintain legitimacy by conforming to institutionalized norms, values, and the technical lore."[11]

But beginning in the 1960s, a series of events brought the District under increasingly hostile scrutiny. Great growth had created fiscal strains and a continual search for funds that ultimately led to fiscal dependency. Desegregation lawsuits filed in 1963 brought into sharp question the assumption that the school district was being run for all its children and that even though inequities existed in society, the public schools lifted everyone. And Great Society legislation broke the logjam of federal aid to public schools, thereby reducing local control and creating active interest groups among the targets of federal assistance. In combination, these events led to an awakening of the community and resulting demands, including dramatic walkouts in 1968. These demands were coupled with increasingly public data about student achievement, which showed that the District was not educating all its children. In 1970, Los Angeles teachers went on strike in the first show of force for what would become United Teachers Los Angeles. By 1975, California passed collective bargaining legislation legitimating a competing voice to that of the dominant school administration. Just as surely as teacher unionism changed the power balance between teachers and administrators, it challenged the administrative regime.

THE SYMBOL OF PROFESSIONALISM

The school superintendent was the embodiment of "neutral professional competence."[12] Along with its Progressive Era counterparts, city managers and administrators, the superintendency was based on the acceptance of the idea that school administrators had special knowledge that separated them from ordinary intelligent people, that they should be respected and left alone in the operation of schools. By the end of the 1950s, it was possible to write that "many educators are insistent in urging, in effect, that the schools are the special province of the professionals, the voters being a necessary evil who must be reckoned with because they provide the money."[13] In this view, the school board's primary functions, aside from directing the district's business affairs, are to hire and support a competent professional as superintendent, defend the schools against public criticism, and persuade the people to open their pocketbooks.

Professional control depends on a symbolic "deal" with the public: Citizens will withdraw from close scrutiny in exchange for high levels of perceived competence and control exercised in the best interests of the public, or at least the part of the public that controls things. Nothing demonstrated competence more than the school district's ability to respond to Los Angeles' monumental growth. Its economic vitality and the financial well-being of the city's pro-growth elite depended on a school district that could respond to huge population influx and mobility.

The District responded to the rapid population growth after World War II by building a record number of new schools. "It builds the equivalent of a new 21-room school every seven days, investing approximately $3,000,000 weekly in new construction," the District reported in the summer of 1967.[14] The new, postwar students were called "in-migrants," as many of them came from other parts of the U.S. rather than other countries. But growth came with a price; growth produced pains. Classes sometimes had more than sixty students. Textbooks were old and in short supply; there were complaints about poor equipment, bad lighting, "and many other things that handicap the teacher."[15] Schools were on double session, and the strains on the bureaucracy were beginning to show.

When the school district was scrutinized, it was largely over money. In 1963, the *Los Angeles Times* editorialized in favor of construction bonds: "For if the bonds are not approved these youngsters' education will be shortchanged by the half-day and limited sessions that will result. Don't let them down."[16] Yet themes emerged that would come to prominence following the conservative reordering of political thought thirty years later. In the late 1950s, the paper floated the notion that schools could be partly supported by student tuition.[17] In 1958, it advocated merit pay for teachers instead of scales "rigged like those of Civil Service clerks."[18]

However, professionalization of the schools also had its detractors. By 1950, Robert Harris, who was editor of the *Los Angeles Daily News* and later a journalism professor at UCLA, wrote, "In recent years, for example, the administrative headquarters of the Los Angeles city schools on N. Hill St. has grown into a sort of junior Pentagon. From this scholastic acropolis on Ft. Moore Hill the orders, the syllabi, the courses of study, the outlines covering methods of instruction are ground out by the ream and disseminated through the administrative chain of command to the teaching rank and file."[19] The schools, Harris said, were democracy's ark, and periodically steps must be taken to get rid of what was impeding it, and his plea was to focus on teaching and learning.

Rhetorically, administrators favored teacher professionalism. "We should have faith in the teachers and others in the 'firing line,'" said Jack Crowther when he was named superintendent in 1961.[20] But Crowther's idea of teacher professionalism was different from a growing teacher voice.

Teacher Unionism

By 1963, Arthur Corey, executive secretary of the California Teachers Association (CTA), told delegates to the American Association of School Administrators convention that labor is trying "to cajole or, if necessary, to force teachers into unions."[21] The CTA, like its parent the NEA, had not yet endorsed collective bargaining, but the American Federation of Teachers (AFT), including a chapter in Los Angeles, had recently been successful in organizing. Wisconsin had passed a collective bargaining law, and a firebrand named Albert Shanker had led teachers in New York City on a strike. The CTA, which at that time included administrators, was worried, very worried.

Instead of collective bargaining, Corey said, what was needed was professionalism for teachers, "for school administrators to let teachers enter the policy-making process of their school systems. . . . Participation of teachers in the development of policy must be achieved if teaching is to have professional status."[22]

However, in Los Angeles collective bargaining gave teachers voice even before the state passed a teacher collective bargaining law. In 1968, United Teachers Los Angeles (UTLA) was formed through a merger of the American Federation of Teachers Local 1021 and the District's NEA affiliate. In 1970, UTLA went on strike, crippling the school district for five weeks.

The strike demands went well beyond salary. UTLA presented a sixty-seven-page school improvement plan. "The main thrust of the proposals is to give teachers a major voice in operating the school programs, even including such matters as textbook selections. UTLA argues that teachers are professionals, and should have some decision-making authority, and should not simply take orders from top administrators."[23] The teachers rejected a 5 percent salary increase on the grounds it was not accompanied by educational improvements. UTLA president Robert Ransom stated, "We must get the public and the Legislature to realize that we cannot continue to cut the school budget year after year and still maintain a school system."[24]

Interim superintendent Robert Kelly did not disagree that the District was in financial crisis. He had headed a delegation to Sacramento to plead for bringing the state portion of the general funds revenue back up to one-half, where it had been a few years earlier. But they got nowhere, and the histories reported that Governor Ronald Reagan "said firmly he is opposed to acting in response to the strike threat and that 'taxes are already too high.'" Kelly said that "unless there is considerable help from Sacramento, I'm afraid our direction must be to cut the school budget rather than increase. We simply have no bargaining room."[25] (In 1996 the school district tried a voter referendum to raise tax rates, but it had been defeated by a large margin.)

Where Kelly—following the superintendent's craft of making as few waves as possible—looked for reasonable agreements among reasonable people, UTLA sought to broaden the political conflict, and did so successfully. Central to UTLA's strike strategy was its public criticism of the District's and state's failure to provide adequate schooling for all children. The union appealed directly to the public, civic groups and state legislators, describing deplorable conditions in schools. They drew endorsements from a wide range of organizations, including the Black Educators of Los Angeles, the East Los Angeles chapter of the Association of Mexican-American Educators, the Special

Education Teachers Council, the AFL-CIO Los Angeles County Labor Federation, and the Southern California Joint Council of Teamsters. The *Los Angeles Times*, no friend of organized labor, editorialized in favor of the teachers.

> The school crisis has in fact been growing for years, and has been visible for all who cared to see. It is a crisis that has been fed by sublime neglect on the part of Governor Reagan and a majority of the Legislature. That neglect continues even now. The governor's tax reform program provides no new state money for local schools, though the need clearly is desperate. Four years ago Reagan pledged to increase the percentage of state aid to schools. Now he says financing is essentially a local problem. This, in our view, is a deplorable abdication of leadership.[26]

Even Los Angeles mayor Sam Yorty endorsed the strike, accusing Governor Reagan and the state legislature of being irresponsible in not providing the funds necessary to avoid it.[27]

Having lost control over the agenda, Kelly was then undercut by two of his own board members who sided publicly with the striking teachers. School board member Robert Docter told a rally of thousands of teachers, "I am proud of you. You know what your responsibility is and you are exercising it."[28] Another school board member, Julian Nava, produced charts showing the "huge educational bureaucracy" that overpaid administrators and ignored teachers. He also took a swipe at state superintendent Max Rafferty, whose job Nava was seeking, saying the financial situation was "living proof of the failure of the educational bureaucracy throughout the state."[29]

After five weeks, the District agreed to a contract that gave teacher representatives "the power to consult with principals on issues affecting the local school, including assignments, promotions, curriculum, textbook selection, grievances, pupil discipline and 'any other matters that may affect the conditions of teachers or the welfare of students.' These provisions give the teachers the first meaningful voice in the operations of the District."[30] The agreement was later nullified in the courts, but the strike established the union as both muscular and antagonistic. Even though the union would gain substantial influence with the school board as a result of its electoral support, it was not accepted as a working partner in educational reform; and on the few occasions that opportunities for genuine partnerships came about, the union was internally conflicted over whether working on the educational issues that were central to the 1970 strike was "real unionism." As one nationally known union leader said, "UTLA's really good at one thing. Fighting." However, the teachers did not strike again for nearly twenty years.

In 1975, California passed collective bargaining legislation, replacing its experiment with wide ranging "meet and confer" discussions with employees with a statute modeled on the tradition of the 1936 National Labor Relations Act. The statute attempted to preserve what were called "managerial prerogatives" by limiting the scope of bargaining to wages, hours, and other terms and conditions of employment. The California law endorsed a legal fiction that educational policy could remain in the hands of the school board even after it had allocated most of its budget in the teacher contract and in the contracts of other workers. The collective bargaining law was named the Rodda Act, after its author, Senator Albert Rodda, who had been president of the California Federation of Teachers, Local 31, in Sacramento before his election to the state senate. He recalled how, as a young teacher, he had been badgered by the school board when he spoke to them on behalf of the union: "In other words they were questioning my right as a representative of the teachers to appear before the board. . . . I can still remember going home on the old streetcar."[31] The indignity was remembered years later when Rodda carried the collective bargaining bill in the legislature.

Desegregation: "Knocking on Doors"
In 1963, schoolteacher and civil rights activist Elnora Crowder journeyed to Watts to find a plaintiff to challenge LAUSD in a desegregation lawsuit. The task was surprisingly difficult. "She went house to house like 'an Avon lady' ringing doorbells." She recounted how, after convincing African American high school student Mary Ellen Crawford and her family to sign the complaint, she "put Mary Ellen in my car and raced downtown to the law office where we signed the complaint"—the beginning of a twenty-six-year-long struggle.[32]

The District never became integrated in the way that the plaintiffs envisioned. Demographic change, middle-class flight (particularly among whites), and massive immigration were the forces that changed the face of LAUSD over the next forty-five years, but the lawsuit cast light on the District and subjected the Progressive Era symbol of a school district advancing the interests of all to critical external scrutiny. The court rulings and racial politics that preoccupied the school board for the next quarter-century began the process of hollowing out the authority of the District and, in particular, the superintendent.

The lawsuit also raised powerful symbols about the District's fairness in dealing with what appeared to be common sense accommodation. At the turn of the twentieth century, immigrant groups granted the school district legitimacy because the District made accommodations to their language and cultural beliefs.[33] These grants of legitimacy were essential to establishing an institution of public education, because the system depended on these immigrants sending their children to school. Even among African Americans, whose leaders took seemingly modest steps to chip away at obvious discrimination—asking for more "colored teachers" at Jefferson High School in 1934, for example—the system was still viewed as legitimate. Efforts toward political organization first found success not in a city council district but in a citywide election for school board in 1939, in which Fay Allen, an accomplished musician who had been decorated by Woodrow Wilson for her work in World War I, became the first African American to serve on the board.[34]

African Americans who were part of the Great Migration to Los Angeles during and immediately after World War II tolerated the city's discrimination because it was a less harsh than what they had faced in the South.[35] Their children were not so patient.[36] Particularly galling was the assertion by some school board members that segregation did not exist. In 1963, in the face of a protest at a school board meeting—something that was unheard of a decade before—board member Charles Smoot "stoutly denied that segregation, de facto or otherwise, existed in the Los Angeles schools. 'I resent pressures put on this board,' he said, 'we represent majorities too.'"[37] At the same meeting, board member J. C. Chambers asserted that if black history was not taught in the schools, it was because there was so little of it. (In fact, a Negro History course had been approved by the District in 1939 and had been offered at Jefferson High School.)[38]

The lawsuit did not begin with a great popular uprising against segregation, which was enforced by restrictive real estate covenants and perpetuated by the way the school district drew its attendance boundaries. Even though the American Civil Liberties Union (ACLU) filed *Crawford v. Board of Education of the City of Los Angeles* in 1963, they originally preferred to work with the school board through nonjudicial means. And even in the initial lawsuit they sought only to integrate Jordan and South Gate high schools, which were less than two miles from each other; one was entirely black the other almost all white.[39] But "the mayor, council, and citizens deluged the Board with protests against any tampering with the existing school boundary, otherwise known as the 'Alameda Wall.' Alameda Street, which Jordan borders at 103rd St., was considered too wide and hazardous for high school students to cross, though a few blocks away elementary pupils were making the crossing."[40] By 1966, the plaintiffs came to believe a citywide solution was necessary and filed an amended suit.

The District's pattern of disingenuousness continued to destroy its legitimacy. In 1962, the ACLU sought a school-by-school racial census, but the board balked, saying that it did not want to "do anything that would put into any individual's record a designation of his race."[41] In 1963, the California Fair Employment Practices Commission demanded racial data, and the District had to comply but conditioned its response on the confidentiality of data.[42] (Interestingly, the District conducted and published what they called *Nationality and Racial Background Surveys* in the 1930s.[43])

For school administrators, integration became a no-win issue. Either support or opposition invited backlash, and the controversy moved the issue from inside the organization, where a professional hierarchy was dominant, to either the courts or electoral politics.

The Crawford case also focused the more general problem of race relations on the schools, making them the center of social discontent rather than other societal institutions. Reasoning that as long as housing was segregated the schools would be segregated too, the National Association for the Advancement of Colored People (NAACP) and the ACLU first turned their attention to passing fair housing legislation in 1963, but it was overturned by a backlash referendum.[44] Educational civil rights advocates had no choice but to go after school segregation directly. Even though the housing referendum itself was overturned by the U.S. Supreme Court, too much time had passed for a cordial resolution between the school board and the ACLU.[45]

In 1965, the Watts riots lasted for almost a week and killed thirty-four people.[46] Nearly a year after the riots, the McCone Commission, which was appointed by Governor Edmund G. "Pat" Brown to investigate the riots, documented and lamented the inferiority of LAUSD's black and Latino schools. As a remedy, the commission recommended an extensive program of "compensatory" education with remedial courses and small student/teacher ratios. The commission did not even mention the possibility of desegregating the District's schools.[47]

In February 1970, Superior Court judge Alfred Gitelson ruled that the segregation of the District's schools violated state law and required immediate remedy. The ruling was termed one of the most "significant court decisions on racial segregation outside of the South."[48] While for many pro-integrationists Judge Gitelson's order looked like a victory, the school board and antibusing groups refused to concede defeat. Labeling Gitelson as the "busing judge," antibusing groups successfully defeated his reelection campaign later that fall, thus sending a clear warning to all elected officials. Meanwhile, the school appealed the case to the California Court of Appeals, another elected body, who then held the case for five years, giving anti-integrationists much-needed breathing room to further entrench their antibusing agenda in the school board through subsequent elections.[49]

In the meantime, the school board started to reorganize the District along decentralized lines. Although suspect because the resulting neighborhood boundaries were still largely segregated, the board's action was not in conflict with the desires of minority parents but was in accordance with the changing demands of these groups.[50] The centralization of the school district in the early 1960s created an "impersonal, massive, administrative bureaucracy" that was unresponsive to individuals and local communities. When the mainstream minority advocacy groups, such as the ACLU and the NAACP, were unable to bring LAUSD into compliance with state desegregation laws, many saw this failure as a sign that the board was not the means by which they would attain their goal of equal education.

There were several different responses to this failure. Organizations such as the United Parents Council began to advocate for local control. Legislators in Sacramento built a coalition in support of breaking up the district.[51] Community organizations in Latino and Asian American communities expressed open concern about possible negative effects that busing might have on bilingual and bicultural programs already established in their local schools. By the end of the 1970s, even members of the African American community were openly expressing doubts. For example, Aaron Wade, superintendent of Compton School District, questioned the effectiveness and necessity of integration in a 1979 interview with the *Los Angeles Times*.[52]

The state supreme court eventually weighed in, but, confusing matters even further, in 1976 it ruled that the appellate court was correct in labeling segregation in Los Angeles as de facto, but it did not agree that the District was not obliged to alleviate it. Citing state law, the court sided with integrationists and ordered the school board to create and implement desegregation plans under supervision of the trial court. The court also changed the terms of desegregation from a set formula derived by the state to a vague condition that the District would undertake "reasonable and feasible steps to alleviate harms of segregation." This ruling was therefore both a reaffirmation of the board's duty to integrate and a substantial shift in the ground rules for carrying out this task.[53]

Responses also emerged from within LAUSD, including two programs that would bring lasting change. While both were ostensibly implemented as integration programs, their effects on the District were decidedly different. The first program was, in reality, an odd one in light of the community's and the board's adamant opposition to busing. Titled Permits With Transfers (PWT), this voluntary busing program shipped minority students out of their increasingly overcrowded and run-down schools to outlying white schools in order to bolster the dwindling enrollment in those areas. The other program also involved busing and was also voluntary. Magnet schools were created primarily in white neighborhoods to draw students of different ethnicities and races to the same campus by offering special educational opportunities. The District hoped that PWT would alleviate the need to build new schools in minority areas, which they were barred from doing by Gitelson's 1970 order, and they hoped that magnet schools would help slow white flight.[54]

The lawsuits did not bring integration to Los Angeles schools. By 1981 it was realized that no remedy available to the courts, other than massive metropolitan busing, would create racially balanced schools. But the lawsuits did aid and abet the institutional delegitimation of the District, and, along with teacher unionization, they changed the politics of the District from good government conservatism to a highly polarized and racialized distrustfulness of the administration. Plaintiffs in the lawsuit raised the ideals of fairness and justice, which effectively countered the older metaphor of an American melting pot, which advanced diversity but was complicit in policies that kept the city segregated and people of color in their place.

Student Achievement

Beginning in 1966, the publication of achievement data began to puncture the story that the school district told about itself. The education committee of the California Assembly released district-to-district test score comparisons, something that the state Department of Education was legally prohibited from doing, and something that was "professionally frowned upon." Los Angeles scored worse than the state average. "A spokesman for the Los Angeles schools said the results were not unusual because of the wide range of low and high ability children in the metropolitan area." Publishing comparative scores undercut the dominant belief that a district could interpret its own results rather than being held to account by a higher level of government. As Dick Turpin, education writer for the *Los Angeles Times* said, "Educators have argued that publication of district-by-district scores would unjustly criticize schools in low-performing areas. Performance results relate to ethnic and wealth factors and must be evaluated and explained at the local level, they have contended."[55] In essence, it was officially acceptable to have lower expectations for lower income and minority students.

The following year, a front-page headline announced, "L.A. Students Among Poorest Readers in the U.S., Tests Show." First graders were reading at the seventh percentile against national norms on the Stanford Reading Test, and LAUSD ranked last among the ten largest school districts in the state. Scores had declined from two years earlier. Superintendent Jack Crowther said the problem was money. "We have tightened our belts, we have lopped here and cut there. And, frankly, I think we must tell people that our educational program has been harmed." However, the *Times* report also noted that "some [school] board members said the test scores might have been pulled down by low performance in Negro and Mexican-American areas." [56] Indeed, the disparity problem had been recognized earlier in the relatively high dropout rates.[57]

Eventually, this story of underachievement in Los Angeles was joined with national criticism of the public schools. In the early 1980s, the National Commission on Educational Excellence report, *A Nation at Risk,* changed the focus of educational politics from discussions about achieving equity to discussions about achieving excellence. The quality debate destabilized the system because it asserted that education as an institution had failed. The report started the debate by proclaiming, "Each generation of Americans has outstripped its parents in education, in literacy, and in economic attainment. For the first time in the history of the country, the educational skills of one generation will not surpass, will not equal, will not even approach, those of their parents."[58]

As it turned out, the statement, and much of *A Nation at Risk,* exaggerated the academic performance problems of public education. The longer one looked, the more difficult it became to find the great decline in American education. Although the widely watched SAT scores had fallen in the early 1970s, much of their decline has been attributed to changes in the pool of test takers. Moreover, the reading and mathematics achievement of virtually all of the groups monitored by the National Center for Education Statistics had not shown net declines over the 1980s and 1990s. Scores for African American and Latino students have actually improved, though they still remain substantially below those of white students.[59]

In fact, in 1993 the National Assessment of Educational Progress (NAEP) announced that three-fourths of twelfth graders had reached a basic level at which they could "develop interpretations from a variety of texts," "understand overall arguments," "recognize explicit aspects of plot and characters," "support global generalizations," "respond personally to texts," and "use major documents to solve real-world problems."[60] Thus, the vast majority of American students had met the lofty standards set out in the early part of the century. But this was of little comfort. The broad consensus of public confidence in the academic performance of American schools had been lost.

THE SYMBOL OF LOCAL CONTROL

The Progressives understood that the city's schools derived their ability to govern from the state, but even in California, where the state Department of Education is an active agency, important policy and operating decisions remained with the school district. "The desirability of local control of the public schools is an article of faith among most trained educators and many other Americans, including President Eisenhower," political scientist Thomas Eliot wrote in 1959 in one of the first scholarly articles about public education to be published in a political science journal.[61]

The *Times* considered federal money to be a "sell out" and further stated that "our great progress in the post-war era should silence those who demand that school districts must accept handouts from Washington."[62] When there were issues of the efficient use of school taxes, the way forward was not federal aid but "district by district and school by school. [The] challenge is for us to take greater interest in our local districts, elect better board members, get more facts, not rule out good ideas originating with parents, but depend more on experience of school teachers and administrators."[63]

Local control aided professional domination. For years they could "argue politely and persuasively that regardless of the possible merit of any legislative proposal to require the teaching of particular subjects, discretion must be left to each school district. Compulsory uniformity would be a departure from the American way."[64] However, local control worked only so long as the state and national governments had confidence in the schools and local districts could successfully raise sufficient funds. In Los Angeles voters had approved nearly $1 billion in construction bonds in seven elections since World War II.[65]

But by the early 1960s, resistance to taxation was growing. Voters defeated a bond issue and tax override in 1962, and Superintendent Crowther publicly linked the election failure to a slowing of the building program and the short-day sessions, particularly in the San Fernando Valley. In 1965, 27,799 students went to schools that offered either double sessions—one group of students in the morning and another in the afternoon—or a shortened school day in order to accommodate enrollment pressures.[66] "Our best evidence of the need for these facilities is that the children who will occupy them are already here. We aren't guessing—we're counting."[67]

The financial burden of growth created taxpayer stress. The state had reduced the percentage of the total education bill it was paying, and the District turned repeatedly to voters for tax overrides for operations as well as for construction bonds. Even though the legislature began to allow districts to raise taxes without an election, LAUSD continued to lobby for expanded state resources, and it began to look wistfully at the federal treasury.[68] "I'm not against it so long as we can maintain local control but there is that danger," Crowther said in 1961.[69]

At one point it had been suggested that the federal government simply use its taxing power to deliver funds directly to local school districts, but President Lyndon Johnson and Congress had something different in mind when they passed the Elementary and Secondary Education Act (ESEA) in 1965. Social critic Barbara Ehrenreich wrote, "The unique and reassuring thing about American poverty, however, was that it was so imminently curable. American affluence seemed to guarantee that no matter how numerous the poor, or how needy, there would be enough to go around. . . . Poverty seemed marginal, aberrant—as if it only had to be seen to be corrected. 'Suddenly,' enthused Herman Miller of the U.S. Census Bureau, 'we seem to have it within our means to eliminate it completely.'"[70] In LAUSD, federal and state programs targeted particular categories of students and grew rapidly from $4.5 million in 1964–65 to $47.1 million in 1966–67, and from less than 1 percent of the budget to nearly 8 percent.

ESEA changed expectations about school outcomes. Before, it was assumed that the goal was to provide equal and universal opportunity. "If students had access to classrooms, that was deemed to be a sufficient fulfillment of public responsibility. If they failed to thrive in school or dropped out, that was deemed to be their fault, and not our failure."[71] After ESEA, and particularly after sociologist James Coleman's historic study the following year,[72] the equity goal was to provide near-equal outcomes for students regardless of race, gender, or economic condition. In many cases, these state mandates expanded the responsibilities of school districts toward children. Since the earliest days of the public education movement in the United States, schools had always done more than simply teach children reading, writing, and arithmetic. The Progressive education movement of the late nineteenth and early twentieth centuries had established a strong tradition of providing for children's other needs as well.

The school district immediately saw the mixed blessing. In a 1967 report, the District planning team said, "Now, during the 1960s the District has been provided with substantial outside resources to launch a concerted major assault upon problems of disadvantaged young people."[73] It noted that educators had long been aware of the "crippling handicaps faced by environmentally and economically disadvantaged young people in acquiring an education" and that the District was doing everything possible within its regular programs, but that there were not enough resources for a "major attack." Of the 800,000 students in the District (including the community college district), 300,000 were from what were called "disadvantaged areas." About 60,000 students were receiving compensatory education services.

Meanwhile, the state was taking a renewed interest in the schools. In 1962, conservative Max Rafferty was elected as state superintendent of public instruction, with a basic education message critical of alleged "fads and frills" captured in his billboard slogan: "Reading, Riting, Rafferty."[74] Rafferty had gotten his start in 1960 when he became superintendent of the newly formed La Canada–Flintridge school district, a formerly unincorporated and predominantly white and affluent area that had split off from the Pasadena district in the face of growing black and Mexican American enrollments and rising poverty. Rafferty "gained considerable support from conservatives due to his strident criticism of 'progressive' education and related 'problems.'"[75] He defeated liberal Democrat Ralph Richardson for school superintendent in 1962, heralding the rise of activist Republican conservatives in advance of Ronald Reagan's election as governor in 1966.

The California legislature also took renewed interest in local schools. Policy scholar Michael Kirst argues that the California legislature was among national leaders in the early 1960s in asserting state prerogatives over education and challenging local control. In particular, the states worked to "establish minimums of curriculum, teacher qualifications, and facilities below which local school operations cannot fall."[76]

MANUFACTURING AN INDICTMENT

The 85,000 petitions that LEARN chairman Robert Wycoff submitted on behalf of LEARN to the LAUSD board on March 15, 1993, were the products of a months-long community campaign (detailed in chapter 5). Since the previous October, the organization had handed out the petitions at public meetings and mailed them to local residents in an envelope bearing a picture of actor Edward James Olmos accompanied by a multiracial group of seven children, and quoting Olmos as saying, "Our Los Angeles school system is in crisis. Please act now to help reform our schools."[77] The full text of the petition read as follows:

Whereas, the School System in Los Angeles is in crisis; and
Whereas, the failure of the school system is hurting all levels of our society and especially our children; and
Whereas, schools currently exist in major urban areas which work well; and
Whereas, the ingredients for a good school system exist, that is good teachers and principals, concerned parents, and bright students; and
Whereas, LEARN, a non-profit organization of teachers, parents, administrators, business, labor and community leaders drawn from every area and group has developed a comprehensive school reform plan for L.A. schools; and
Whereas, LEARN's school reform plan is currently under consideration by the Los Angeles Board of Education;
We, the undersigned concerned citizens, hereby urge the Los Angeles Board of Education to immediately adopt and implement the entire package of LEARN school reforms throughout the L.A. Unified School District.[78]

The petition was an indictment of Los Angeles Unified on three counts: the District harmed and endangered children, failed to educate its students, and it lagged behind more successful urban school districts facing and solving similar problems.

Taking on the Mantle of Society's Failure

LEARN's leaders and supporters had consistently presented similarly sweeping but vague indictments of the District for years. In 1990, Helen Bernstein and Richard Riordan put it this way: "The bottom line is saving a whole generation of our youth. The litany of social ills—illiteracy, crime, drug use, gang affiliation, homelessness—all have at their root a society that has failed in education. The breakneck speed at which technology is advancing has put demands on education that it currently cannot meet."[79] Thus LEARN, like public education generally, accepted the notion that public education possessed sufficient power to address the ills of society and that it should be blamed if social ills continued.

LEARN's leaders made three points consistently, and each point reflected public opinion found in survey after survey. The first point had to do with quality of life issues, particularly poverty, drugs, and violence. Too many children in the schools—like too many families in Los Angeles—were not safe from the social problems and disorder of contemporary America. A growing number of Angelenos no longer believed that the schools of Los Angeles Unified succeeded at this mission. Four in five residents surveyed in an August 1991 poll, for example, agreed that "the District has failed to control crime and drugs in the schools." Nearly as many, 70 percent, agreed that "discipline is not properly enforced" and that "there is too much racial tension among students."[80]

LEARN's leaders and member organizations stressed these quality of life issues at every turn throughout the evolution of the coalition. In October 1990, Kids 1st, a community organization with ties to the Industrial Areas Foundation and Riordan that later joined the LEARN coalition, staged a rally at the Los Angeles Sports Arena where 15,000 people cheered speakers who called for the District to be more effective and interested in educating their children. The event's organizers and participants expressed particular concern about street gangs and the drugs and violence they brought to schools and communities.[81] The sidewalks, streets, and buildings surrounding schools carried the "tags" of gang graffiti artists marking their turf, and children were not safe to walk to and from school.

Racism remained a persistent problem and had deep roots in the District. Los Angeles Urban League president John Mack, a founding member of LEARN's Working Group, noted in early 1992 that the most troubled schools in the District had predominantly African American and Latino student bodies.[82] Racial conflict exploded in the streets of Los Angeles with three days of rioting that began on April 29, 1992, when a predominately white jury acquitted four police officers accused in the videotaped beating of African American motorist Rodney King. In all, fifty-three people died during the riots, and there was an estimated $1 billion in material damage.[83] Mike Roos, LEARN president, recalled that the riots started "literally on the first day of our first task force meetings." Unable to get to his downtown office, Roos remembered seeing the plumes of smoke and realizing at the time that the advent of the riots would add urgency to the work that they were undertaking.[84]

A second point in the indictment of LAUSD argued that children were not well educated by the District's schools, which consistently performed poorly on standardized tests.[85] Dropouts created an even more profound academic performance problem. The District officially reported that 3–4 percent of students dropped out each year, but common sense demonstrated that these official figures were ridiculously low. For example, Roosevelt High School enrolled 2,075 freshmen in the fall of 1989, but only 828 seniors graduated from the predominantly Latino school four years later, in the spring of 1993.[86]

Business and community leaders also framed the academic performance of the District as an economic problem, undermining the competitiveness of the region's high school graduates as the cold war receded into memory, and Rockwell and Hughes and the other firms that made the missiles and airplanes began consolidating, laying off workers and moving to more business-friendly climates in Atlanta, Phoenix, and St. Louis.[87]

A third point in the indictment criticized LAUSD as a dysfunctional organization cut off from the public and incapable of reforming itself. LEARN's leaders argued this in both absolute and relative terms. Roos told a local reporter that "the District currently looks 'a lot like the [former] Soviet Union,'" an inflexible and dictatorial organization run blindly from the top down.[88] Part of the problem was the scale of LAUSD, the second largest school district in the United States, with nearly two-thirds of a million students. Parents, children, and community members viewed the District as a monolithic and stagnant bureaucracy unable to adapt to a rapidly changing city and its educational needs, and LEARN echoed their criticisms.[89]

LEARN leaders argued that scale, urban poverty, and language problems were unacceptable explanations offered to excuse LAUSD's poor performance as somehow normal or inevitable. They pointed to urban school districts around the country that faced similar challenges but performed better. Throughout the first half of 1992, LEARN Task Forces heard reports about urban districts from across North America—especially Rochester, New York, and Edmonton, Alberta, Canada—that were doing better in fulfilling their complex missions.

This sweeping LEARN indictment of the District presented a point of view common in Los Angeles at the time. It could be heard in general public conversations and was reflected in public opinion polls. For example, in late 1988 the Los Angeles 2000 committee—a civic planning committee appointed by Mayor Tom Bradley—commissioned the RAND Corporation to survey the region's residents about their quality of life.[90] The "great majority" of respondents rated life in the Los Angeles region as good, but nearly half expressed concern about the region's future. When asked open-ended questions about what worried them, they did not spontaneously bring up education and schools as major issues. But when asked directly what they thought of the city's schools, the respondents expressed an ambivalent mixture of criticism and support. On the one hand, 56 percent rated "handling of the schools" as "bad or very bad." Respondents with children in public schools and respondents in the San Fernando Valley were especially critical. On the other hand, respondents expressed support for spending public money on elementary and secondary education.

An Awkward Silence

One odd feature of the public conversation surrounding LEARN's indictment of the Los Angeles Unified School District was the awkward silence in response. There was hardly anything resembling a debate, because few, if any, people stepped forward to defend the District or argue that it was in fact performing well or serving the public effectively. The closest thing one could hear to a defense was offered by Superintendent Bill Anton, who was himself one of LEARN's fifteen-member steering committee, the Working Group. Anton objected when others on the Working Group sent a letter to Mayor Bradley and California governor Pete Wilson in the aftermath of the April 1992 riots arguing that "there is no doubt that the failure of our current public education system is at the heart of the hopelessness which prompted the recent riots in our city." Anton responded, saying, "To blame the school system for all of society's ills is unfair. . . . You don't have to damn the school district. We need help. We need correction. We're not denying that we need to do more and that we need to do a heck of a better job. But to say we are so horrible just feeds into this distrust for public education."[91]

Anton's remarks illustrated the fine line that LEARN leaders were trying to walk. On the one hand, they argued that the District was failing to do its job and that it needed to move in a dramatically new direction. This would require a reorientation of everyone in the organization, from classroom teachers all the way up to the superintendent, and it would require additional resources from taxpayers. On the other hand, LEARN's leaders joined Anton in arguing that public education and the District were not so far beyond repair that they should be abandoned. The reformers were concerned that if LEARN's indictment was too harsh, voters would support a voucher initiative that some business leaders were threatening to put on the statewide ballot at some point. They were also concerned that proposals to break up the District—which had been around since the early 1970s—would be revived, and there would be no LAUSD left to reform.

CHAPTER 3

Exit and *Entrada*

Demographic Change and Political Uncertainty

The school district that the LEARN petition declared to be in crisis had a vastly different student population from the one that had been heralded as "best in the West" a generation earlier. A combination of flight by middle-class families—white, African American, and Latino—deindustrialization, and the largest arrival of immigrants in the United States since the 1910s changed the face of Los Angeles. By the time LEARN started, the students of Los Angeles Unified were nearly two-thirds Latino, almost half non–English speakers, and more than two-thirds poor. These social and demographic transformations did not cause institutional change, but they created the uncertain conditions under which a political sea change could take place.

THE IMPORTANCE OF MIGRATION, GROWTH, AND DECLINE FOR THE POLITICS OF SCHOOLS

The legitimacy challenges that began in the 1960s and led to the LEARN crisis declaration came in a city that appeared in many ways to be a success. Los Angeles began the post–World War II period as the fourth largest American city, and it is the only one of 1950's top-ten cities to grow continuously ever since. Underneath the surface of this growth, however, the Los Angeles economy, its employment opportunities, and its settlement patterns changed shape rapidly during the 1970s and 1980s, both within the city itself and in the wider region.

The particular ways these economic and population dynamics played out had lasting consequences for the politics of educational reform in Los Angeles and other cities. In Rust Belt cities such as Chicago, Philadelphia, Detroit, and Cleveland, decline often brought crisis. First, population decline inevitably meant school enrollment decline, which led to wrenching and destructive changes to school districts. Residents endured the demoralizing experience of watching schools close, schools that had often served as the civic heart of neighborhoods—where parents brought their children to learn and neighbors came together to vote, watch football games, and hear concerts. Superintendents and school boards were forced to lay off teachers and administrators, and recrimination often poisoned these districts' abilities thereafter to carry forward any constructive programs of school maintenance or improvement. Los Angeles, with its stability and even growth, for the most part avoided such wrenching changes driven by population decline.

Second, many Americans view schools as integral to the life and economy of their communities. The decision to move into or remain in a neighborhood or city is often an affirmation of what its schools have to offer. Conversely, people who come to doubt the quality or direction of their city or schools often consider whether they might move so they can find a better life and better schools elsewhere. For schools and school districts, facing such constant judgments by people moving in, staying, or leaving can create tremendous stresses. Los Angeles Unified, in contrast to school districts in the Rust Belt cities, initially encountered fewer stresses because Southern California remained more often a destination than a point of departure throughout the postwar period.

Economist Albert O. Hirschman recognized the importance of such dynamics during the 1960s and explored them in his influential 1970 book *Exit, Voice and Loyalty*. Hirschman often used public schools as exemplars for his analysis, and he began by noting that once people have embraced an institution like a public school or district, they at first tend to be generous when they discover the institution's flaws.[1] That is, many people remain "loyal," or at least tolerant, as long as the flaws are minor. When the people of a city like Los Angeles have elected leaders who establish a school district like LAUSD, or who have moved to that city in part because of the opportunities provided by the education system, the legitimacy of that school district has a certain momentum. People will not turn against the schools lightly, especially at a time when the institution of public schooling commands broad respect locally and nationally, the way LAUSD did in the early 1960s, prior to the legitimacy challenges.

Such loyalty was important to the leaders of LAUSD during those years, and it had become a powerful resource over decades of migration into Los Angeles and dramatic growth of both the city and the school district. Still, tolerance or loyalty has limits when people come to believe that an institution has flaws or makes mistakes. Those limits are reached, Hirschman argued, when people lose their patience with the flaws of the institution and begin to seek change. They usually do this in one of two ways: "exit" or "voice."

Hirschman viewed "exit" as a consumer-style choice made by individuals or families: A dissatisfied person exits by simply abandoning the "product" or institution in favor of a competitor.[2] In the case of a school district, a dissatisfied family can "vote with their feet" by moving away and enrolling their children in the schools of another district. Alternately, they can stay put but enroll their children in private schools or even choose to homeschool them. Hirschman acknowledged the general power of this response: An institution could lose valuable constituents or clients or money. But he also noted that exit is a blunt instrument that may generate confusion or uncertainty: Those in charge of the abandoned institution may not understand what message the exiters are trying to communicate. The exiters' actions do not necessarily give the institution any specific ideas about how to respond and therefore may not lead to improvement or even change. Further, as is often the case when people abandon public schools, exit may bring backlash. Although moving to greener pastures is a quintessentially American action, exiters may find that their neighbors stigmatize and discourage their exit as "desertion, defection, and treason."[3]

Exit is also not the only means by which people signal their dissatisfaction with an institution. They can also express their disapproval through what Hirschman called "voice," by staying put and speaking up, demanding that those in control of the organization change what they're doing. Hirschman continued with the schools example, noting that "one major, if problem-plagued, effort presently underway toward bettering public schools in the large cities is to make them more responsive to their members: decentralization."[4] He explained that voice is easier and more likely under some identifiable conditions, notably a well-functioning democratic political system. He acknowledged the power of this response as well but also noted that it is often messy and confusing and does not necessarily lead to organizational improvement.

Forty years later, Hirschman's analysis offers tremendous insight into the politics of school districts. This should not be surprising, given his frequent use of public education as an example. His exit-voice-loyalty formulation provides tools for exploring what can happen when a school district begins to lose legitimacy, to lose the public's confidence that it is the institution best suited to do the job of educating their children—as the Los Angeles Unified School District began to do in the 1960s.

For decades, the legitimacy of the District had been visible directly in people's behavior: They showed their satisfaction or loyalty by moving into the District or by keeping their kids in the District schools and keeping their complaints to a minimum. As time went on, however, there was evidence of growing dissatisfaction with the District in the growing numbers of people exiting to suburban public schools (although, interestingly, far fewer to private schools than in Rust Belt cities). As noted earlier, there was also evidence of growing dissatisfaction in the messier business of people using voice: complaining about the schools and challenging the legitimacy of the school district's structures and practices.

Hirschman notes, and the story of Los Angeles Unified confirms, that the relationship between voice and exit can be complex. On the one hand, the exit option can act as a "safety valve" for the school district, enabling malcontents to simply walk away, leaving behind those who are less likely to complain. On the other hand, departures can increase the political leverage of those staying behind and demanding change, because it increases the credibility of threats they make to leave if things do not improve.[5] As a consequence, it can increase pressure for innovations like testing-based accountability or charter schools.

On the face of it, the implications of this analysis for LAUSD over the last half-century can be interpreted as positive. There appears, at least, to have been no mass exit from the city, no sweeping vote of no confidence in the city or its schools. The City of Los Angeles grew steadily throughout the twentieth century, and LAUSD's enrollments likewise grew. Figure 3.1 shows that there was a roughly 15 percent decline in total enrollments during the 1970s as the baby boom generation completed its education and some schools closed. But that downturn ended after a decade, and the pattern of growth returned. Although this period was a difficult one for the District, LAUSD has not gone through the wrenching and sustained contractions of urban school districts like Philadelphia or Detroit. It did not have a long legacy of controversial

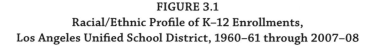

FIGURE 3.1
Racial/Ethnic Profile of K–12 Enrollments,
Los Angeles Unified School District, 1960–61 through 2007–08

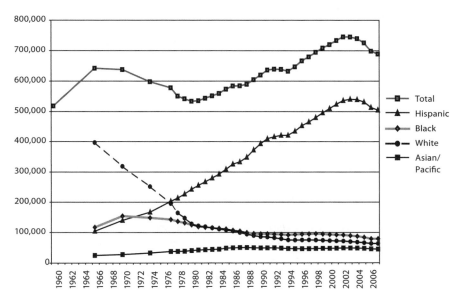

Sources: 1960–66: Sam Hamerman et al., "Report of the Los Angeles City Schools Planning Team" (Los Angeles: Los Angeles Unified School District, 1967); 1967–92: "Annual Ethnic Survey" (Los Angeles: Los Angeles Unified School District, annual); 1993–2007: Educational Demographics Unit, "District Enrollment by Ethnicity," California Basic Educational Data System (CBEDS) (Sacramento: California Department of Education, 2008).

school closings or mass layoffs to poison its reputation in communities or stymie the District's labor relations.

But a closer look at Figure 3.1 reveals that the relative stability and growth of Los Angeles and its school district are in many ways an illusion. While aggregate population and enrollments remained stable or increased, there was tremendous churning underneath the surface; people and groups were simultaneously moving into, out of, and around the city in ways that had dramatic effects on the schools and the District. In particular, there were striking differences along racial and ethnic as well as class lines. As the Anglo population sprawled out into the suburbs, African American migration grew and then subsided, and Latinos from within and outside the United States moved into the District and region in large numbers. During this process, the gradual collapse of large manufacturing in the region led to growing economic inequality and substantial poverty.

Thus, Hirschman's analysis is helpful but requires elaboration. By focusing on the actions of individuals and families, he did not engage the likelihood that certain groups of people might come to disapprove of an institution even as other groups of people are drawn to it. The economy, society, and education system of Los Angeles reflect deep differences along racial, ethnic, and class lines, visible in the simultaneous exit *and* entry of thousands of families each year for diverse reasons. This churning created tremendous uncertainty for the District and, at the same time, created the conditions for deep institutional change.

THE RISE AND DIFFUSION OF "ANGLO" LOS ANGELES

For much of the twentieth century, Los Angeles was a predominantly white, Protestant city. Most of its early population growth came through migration from within the United States. The city's Mexican founders were outnumbered and displaced by waves of white migrants, drawn mostly from the Midwest by economic opportunity and the temperate climate. Political geographer Edward Soja describes the city for the first two-thirds of the twentieth century as "definitively WASPish, for Los Angeles had for decades contained the highest percentage of native-born Protestants of all the largest U.S. cities."[6] This white majority offered a strongly supportive constituency for those establishing the booming Los Angeles school districts as Progressive models for the nation.[7] Whites still comprised more than 80 percent of its residents in the 1960 census.[8]

With brief exceptions, Anglos continued to migrate from elsewhere in the United States into the Los Angeles region for the first two-thirds of the century, but their migration patterns began to shift during the 1950s. First, those already in Los Angeles migrated away from the center city. Initially, this suburban sprawl was contained within the boundaries of L.A.'s school district as home-building moved into the San Fernando Valley north of downtown. Valley communities like Northridge and Van Nuys had distinct identities but were still formally within Los Angeles city limits and school district. Even when sprawl began to stretch beyond the city limits, the founders of many new suburbs sought to remain within the Los Angeles school district, and between the 1890s and the 1940s, the District simply annexed all or part of more than thirty adjacent municipalities.[9] To this day, cities like San Fernando to the north, Maywood and Huntington Park to the east, and Gardena and Carson to the south are all part of the Los Angeles Unified School District, and the precise population of the District itself is difficult to pin down.[10]

Because this Anglo exodus from the central city nevertheless remained within the formal boundaries of LAUSD, it did not have the impact it might have had if these families had simply exited the District. Schools in Los Angeles remained deeply segregated through the 1960s, and most new schools built on the suburban periphery of the District were simply "white schools." In 1960, the population of the San Fernando Valley was 92 percent Anglo, and its school enrollments were overwhelmingly Anglo.[11] Although Anglo families may have exited the core of the city seeking to insulate their children from more "urban" schools, their movements had little impact on the school district's aggregate enrollments or operating budget.

Between 1970 and 1990, while Los Angeles County's aggregate population was growing by nearly two million, its Anglo population decreased by 1.4 million. Not all of this decline was due to migration: During this period, Anglos were relatively older than non-Anglos, and their birthrates were declining. Still, many Anglos moved to the suburbs outside L.A. County and others simply left the region as higher-paying industrial jobs evaporated and competition grew for what jobs remained.[12] This exodus accelerated dramatically during the 1990–95 period as nearly 1.5 million native-born residents left the L.A. region during the post–cold war recession, but it slowed once again as the century drew to a close.[13]

The impact of these Anglo migrations on the demography of LAUSD was striking. On the one hand, enrollment in the District for the most part remained high. In the fifteen years after World War II, District enrollments had more than doubled, driven by the baby boom and continued in-migration from outside the District, climbing to more than a half-million by 1960. (See Figure 3.1.) After nearing 650,000 in the mid-1960s, total enrollments slid back down close to a half-million in the late 1970s and early 1980s before beginning another slow climb that continued into the twenty-first century.

Yet on the other hand, the racial and ethnic composition of those enrollments shifted sharply after 1960, much more sharply than in the general population. The District's leaders carefully avoided keeping enrollment records by race and ethnicity until required to do so by the U.S. government in the mid-1960s, and that refusal makes demographic research on the District difficult.[14] Nevertheless, it appears that "white, non-Hispanic" students comprised a substantial majority until the late 1960s. Anglo enrollments dropped by half between 1967 and 1977, however, and then by half again between 1977 and 1987.

In contrast to Rust Belt cities, where Anglo enrollments declined similarly during this period, Anglo private school enrollments did not increase in Los Angeles. Private schools remain a relatively minor component of K–12 education in the Los Angeles region, with a stable enrollment share just over 10 percent throughout the years since 1960, according to the state's Department of Education. To the extent that Anglo parents were exiting from L.A.'s public schools, most were also exiting from Los Angeles the city.

One striking exception to this pattern can be found among high-income households, both Anglo and non-Anglo. Table 3.1 presents a sampling of nine census tracts around the city with varying income levels. It sorts these tracts—which usually contain between 300 and 1,000 people—by median income for 1990 and 2000 and then shows the proportion of children in the tract who are enrolled in private schools. The relationship is significant: While very few children in the lower income tracts enroll in private schools, a large number of children in the higher income tracts do. While this is by no means a random sample of the entire district, the data are consistent with interviews that suggest some of the most affluent residents of the city have indeed exited the public school system without necessarily leaving the City of Los Angeles. While a small minority, these upper income residents are predominantly Anglos and come from a constituency that formerly offered strong support for the legitimacy of LAUSD.

For Anglos, "exit" may have proven to be far easier than "voice" as a means of expressing frustration with the direction of the city and the school district. Sprawling residential patterns have long made political organizing difficult in Los Angeles, a problem made worse by residents' frequent moves from place to place.[15] Nevertheless, despite Anglos slipping to minority status in the District after 1970, Anglo political leaders and voters continued to control the District's board and superintendency. The school board, which was elected at large until 1979, retained an Anglo majority through the 1980s, in large part because Anglos were more likely to vote in the District's low-turn-

TABLE 3.1
**Median Income and Private School Enrollment for
Selected Census Tracts in LAUSD, 1990 and 2000**

	Median family income, 1999	*Percent private enrollment, 2000*	*Median household income, 1989*	*Percent private enrollment, 1990*
Los Angeles County	$46,452	13.0%	$34,965	14.2%
Los Angeles City	$39,942	14.5%	$30,925	15.8%
Boyle Heights (Census Tract 2043)	$28,496	3.4%	$21,424	10.4%
46th and Normandie (Census Tract 2322)	$28,750	1.4%	$15,221	1.5%
South L.A. (Census Tract 5409.02)	$35,921	10.4%	$23,827	8.8%
Liemert Park (Census Tract 2345)	$39,550	11.1%	$21,485	18.1%
Walnut Park (Census Tract 5347)	$47,008	5.2%	$25,179	8.7%
Westwood (Census Tract 2674.02)	$49,013	26.8%	$34,589	12.6%
Brentwood (Census Tract 2643.02)	$104,430	44.7%	$50,177	41.5%
Beverly Glen (Census Tract 2612)	$144,553	72.4%	$94,412	65.6%
Pacific Palisades (Census Tract 2627.02)	$178,533	61.4%	$89,642	54.0%

Source: American Fact Finder, U.S. Census Bureau, http://factfinder.census.gov

out elections. Many of those Anglo voters proved reluctant to vote for the taxes sufficient to build new schools and finance the expanding responsibilities of the District as enrollments expanded in the 1950s and 1960s, and they elected cautious school board members reluctant to meddle with the segregation of the District.

Anglos were obviously not the only demographic story. By 1960, Los Angeles was home to more than 400,000 African Americans, most of whom had migrated from the South in search of jobs and opportunity. Even larger numbers of Latinos lived in the city and near its eastern boundaries, mostly a blend of multigeneration Mexican Americans and recent immigrants from Mexico.[16] The city still had a relatively small Asian American population in 1960, predominantly Japanese Americans whose families had been in the state for decades, and subsequent immigration from Asia centered on school districts outside of LAUSD. These developments reflect distinct patterns of migration and movement that shaped the District.

THE RISE AND FRAGMENTATION OF BLACK LOS ANGELES

African Americans began to move into the urban core of Los Angeles during the First and Second World Wars. Most migrated from the old South and the trans-Mississippi states of Arkansas, Oklahoma, and Texas, drawn by war industry jobs and the city's reputation for better race relations. That migration continued through the 1950s and into the 1960s as Los Angeles was established as a manufacturing center with strong unions, relatively high wages, and a recession-proof core of military contract–driven industry.[17]

In some ways, Los Angeles earned its reputation as an attractive destination for blacks. African American home ownership rates were much higher in Los Angeles than virtually any city in the United States, exceeding one in three by the 1910 census.[18] W. E. B. Du Bois himself visited in 1913 and reported that "out here in this matchless Southern California there would seem to be no limit to your opportunities, your possibilities."[19] Soon war-driven labor shortages created opportunities for African American men to gain unionized factory and shipyard jobs that were likely to pay well and have benefits comparable to those of Anglos. Los Angeles schools provided better education for blacks than many Southern schools did. Lonnie Bunch argues, "Black Angelenos, while still quite limited by the pervasive influences of racism, were optimistic . . . as they faced the future."[20] Blacks were entering rather than exiting the city, and by 1960 they comprised 13.5 percent of L.A.'s population.

Los Angeles was, of course, no paradise for African Americans. Pervasive racial "covenants" on deeds confined African American home buyers to only certain neighborhoods of the city, and rental housing followed much the same rules.[21] Los Angeles was a deeply segregated city, and the District's "neighborhood" schools were segregated into a three-part system: "white," "Negro," and "Mexican." Although state court lawsuits challenging racially segregated schooling had twice proven successful in Southern California, L.A. Unified continued to build and run segregated schools well into the 1960s. The District's "color blind" refusal to collect or record data on the racial and ethnic composition of school enrollments successfully deflected local desegregation activists to focus instead on neighboring Pasadena, whose school district did collect such data.[22] Segregation in Los Angeles was reinforced not just by the lack of data gathering or the gerrymandering of school boundaries but also by local commercial and political practices. White-owned stores often refused to sell to black shoppers. Police mistreatment of blacks was pervasive and legendary and helped spark the riots that spilled out of Watts in 1965.

African Americans' entry into Los Angeles in large numbers did not immediately give them voice in state and local government. Raphael Sonenshein describes Los Angeles in 1960 as "one of the most backward cities in the nation in African-American political representation. Los Angeles Blacks had yet to elect a city council member or a congressperson. Their only political representative at any level was State Assemblyman Augustus Hawkins."[23] Blacks gained some ground in the 1963 city council elections and in 1965, when the Reverend James Jones won election as the only black member of the LAUSD school board (he was defeated after one four-year term), but the at-large system of electing school board members gave disproportionate power to Anglo voters. Opportunities for African Americans to "voice" through conventional Los Angeles political channels were sharply limited throughout the decade, becoming available really only with the election of Mayor Tom Bradley in 1973, paradoxically around the same time as black enrollments began a decline that continues to this day.

Although African Americans expressed growing dissatisfaction with LAUSD schools, opportunities to exit the city into the suburbs surrounding Los Angeles were constrained by the same discriminatory employment and housing practices that kept them confined to particular neighborhoods in the city itself. Nevertheless, gradually during the 1960s, suburbs like Compton, Englewood, Culver City, and Pomona became destinations, and the African American share of the L.A. County population outside the City of Los Angeles began to climb slowly. Historian Lawrence de Graaf found that by the middle of that decade, the character of black migration into the Los Angeles region had changed: "While between 1965 and 1970 nearly ten blacks moved into Los Angeles for every four that moved out, such a rate of out-migration was unprecedented and reflected a trend of poor, unskilled persons entering the ghetto while more affluent and educated ones left."[24] Although African American enrollments in LAUSD peaked around 1970, the composition of that enrollment was already in flux along economic lines. It continued to reflect the growing poverty of African American neighborhoods thereafter as a result of what de Graaf calls "black flight," thus creating greater challenges for the Los Angeles Unified School District.[25]

The black experience in LAUSD has been complex. After decades of migration to the city from other regions of the United States, blacks stopped coming to Los Angeles in substantial numbers by the mid-1960s, the time of the Crawford desegregation lawsuit, the Watts riots, and the peak of success in the civil rights movement nationally. Like Anglos, many African Americans left the city and county during the economic downturns of the early 1970s and early 1990s, and the departing population was skewed toward those with higher skills and education. A sizable African American population remains in the city, and tens of thousands of black children continue to attend LAUSD schools. Nevertheless, African Americans' ability to influence the District through exit and voice never came close to matching that of Anglos, whose numbers in enrollment they have matched or exceeded since 1980.

LATINO LOS ANGELES: *ENTRADA Y VOZ*

The Spanish founded Los Angeles in 1781, and it remained a small settlement for more than a century. A Mexican American population center developed early in the 1920s, concentrating in the area east of what is now downtown and reaching beyond current city limits into what historians Victor Valle and Rodolfo Torres call "the Greater East Side."[26] These early residents were drawn to the area by the employment opportunities of the emerging city as well as by the more transitory migrant work in citrus and agriculture, and their population grew slowly through the middle decades of the century.

Mexican American families' commitment to the education of their children in Southern California was evident in their early enrollment despite pervasive discrimination and segregated schools.[27] Their earliest political organization and advocacy came in the successful lawsuits challenging such segregation, first in 1931 in the San Diego County town of Lemon Grove and then in 1946 in the Orange County town of Westminster.[28]

The passage of the Immigration Act of 1965 spurred a shift that would see international migration quickly eclipse U.S.-based migration into the city and school district. Prior to 1960, substantial numbers of Mexicans had periodically moved into the region, but many of them had also moved—or been expelled—back to Mexico, leaving a relatively small Latino community centered in East Los Angeles.[29] After the 1965 legislation, immigration into the United States from Mexico and other Latin American countries surged, and Southern California was a major destination because of its vibrant and diverse economy. Los Angeles County drew more than 20 percent of all new migration into the United States for the next two decades, rising rapidly throughout the 1970s and surging again especially after the 1986 Immigration Reform and Control Act. Over the next thirty years, the Latino population in the City of Los Angeles more than tripled, rising from 519,843 in 1970 to 1,728,138 in 2000.[30]

Though the pace of this immigration has since subsided, during the 1970s and 1980s it transformed the city into the culturally heterogeneous metropolis that it remains to this day. Further, almost 70 percent of these new immigrants were younger than thirty-five, which drove a baby boom in the city that brought more children to LAUSD schools.[31] Latino students outnumbered black students in L.A. schools by 1974 and Anglo students by 1978. They comprised a majority of all students by 1984, and LAUSD has become an increasingly Latino district ever since.

Latino in-migration initially centered on the Eastside and neighborhoods around downtown Los Angeles but quickly sprawled into predominantly African American neighborhoods south of downtown. De Graaf notes that this had a double effect, increasing the Latino population but also spurring some blacks to move out of the city.[32] The consequences for Los Angeles schools were dramatic and rapid and complicated by language issues. A substantial proportion of these new migrants spoke only Spanish, and their children presented a challenge to schools and teachers unprepared to teach non–English speakers. Figure 3.2 shows that by 1990, nearly 40 percent of all children enrolled in LAUSD schools were classified as "English Language Learners," and the number grew to 45 percent by the middle of that decade.

This influx of immigrants also fueled a Latino sprawl in the 1970s and 1980s that quickly moved far beyond the boundaries of the Los Angeles Unified School District.[33] The 2000 census reported that Latinos comprised nearly half the population of Los Angeles County, though it also showed that longer-term immigrants had begun to move in and out of the region following employment opportunities in much the same way as Anglos and African Americans had.[34]

One could interpret Latinos' following earlier Anglo dynamics of entry and exit as their communities' affirmation and then critique of LAUSD. However, Latinos only belatedly began to share Anglos' experience of what Hirschman described as the third option: "voice" or political influence over the District. Their opportunities for influence through elected officeholders were long limited by their minimal representation on L.A.'s city council and LAUSD's at-large board elections. Eastside native and Cal State Northridge history professor Julian Nava won election as the school board's first Latino in 1967, and he served until single-member districts were established in 1980. Despite the ongoing surge in Latino population and enrollments, there would not be more than one Latino on the seven-member board until the city council mandated that lines be redrawn in 1993.

Nevertheless, outspoken Latino criticism of the Los Angeles Unified School District began to take a clear focus in the mid-1960s. During the winter of 1967–68, Latino students grew impatient with the lack of improvement in local schools and began to develop plans to make their demands more urgent.[35] Collaborating with members of United Mexican-American Students, a college- and university-based group, as well as teachers, including Garfield High School history teacher Sal Castro, the students launched a boycott on Tuesday, March 6, 1968. The walkout, the first of what came to be called "the blowouts," drew support from 2,700 of Garfield High School's 3,750 students and from the predominantly African American Jefferson High School south of downtown, where 700 of the school's 1,900 students also walked out.[36] Hundreds of students at Lincoln High School and Roosevelt High School, the District's other two East Los Angeles high schools, walked out the following day, and the *Los Angeles Times* began to cover not only the "disorder" of the demonstrations but also the participants' demands for school reform.[37]

In the end, the demonstrators were able to present the outlines of a systematic program of reform at LAUSD. The students called for staffing schools

FIGURE 3.2
Students Classified as "Limited English Proficiency or
"English Language Learners" in LAUSD, 1979–80 through 2006–07

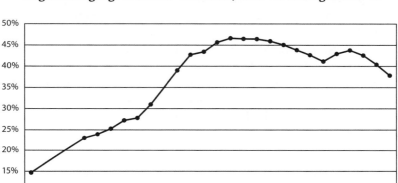

Source: Educational Demographics Office, "Language Census Data Reports" (Sacramento: California Department of Education, 2008).

with administrators and teachers who could speak Spanish and communicate with Latino students and their parents. They demanded that teachers and the District's curriculum show respect for and attention to Mexican American culture and history. They called for reduced class sizes, increased numbers of counselors and other support staff, and the hiring of community members as teachers' aides to assist in instruction. They also demanded an end to tracking and curricula that provoked students to drop out before graduation, or made moving on to college more difficult. Finally, they demanded improved maintenance of campuses and the creation or expansion of libraries at all campuses.[38]

This vocal expression of discontent had wide-ranging consequences. In the broadest sense, it was the first expression of what would become the Chicano movement of the late 1960s and 1970s, a powerful cultural force that lasts to this day.[39] But for the Los Angeles Unified School District, it set the pattern for Latino community activism and reform proposals for decades to come. As LAUSD became a predominantly Latino school district, expressions of "voice" would continue to emerge from neighborhoods and even schools. For example, the Industrial Areas Foundation began organizing at the neighborhood level in the 1980s and later formed Kids 1st, an early participant in what would become the broader LEARN coalition. Community-based leadership and networks would continue to develop with students themselves often playing major roles in advocating for their own education. Many leaders of "the blowouts" would remain in the District as teachers, administrators, and even as one school board member, Vicki Castro, elected in 1993. The issues they raised would thus continue to echo through into the reforms of the 1990s.

THE TRANSFORMED METROPOLIS AND
ITS EDUCATIONAL CHALLENGES

This economic and demographic transition continued throughout the decades after 1970, introducing tremendous uncertainty into policymaking for LAUSD. The District faced many challenges, not least of which was the absence of cohesive and supportive political coalitions in such a racially and ethnically diverse city with such vexing economic problems.

One unprecedented challenge creating uncertainty for the District was that by the end of the 1980s, hundreds of thousands of children were enrolled in LAUSD schools who did not speak English. Figure 3.2 shows that by the end of the immigration surge of the 1970s, more than one in six students enrolled in the school district were classified as having "Limited English Proficiency." This proportion grew rapidly after the 1986 immigration reform, which not only gave amnesty and legal status to many immigrants working in Los Angeles without papers but also enabled them to bring their families to the United States.[40] The children of these newly legalized immigrants—most of whom were Spanish speakers from Mexico—were far more likely to have begun their education in a language other than English.

LAUSD struggled to develop curriculum and effective instructional methods as non–English speakers increased to comprise nearly half of all enrollments. Perhaps more critically, the District struggled to find bilingual teachers who could communicate effectively with these students. The inability of schools to respond to this challenge created widespread public frustration, exemplified by yet another ballot initiative, Proposition 227 in 1998, which mandated a new statewide policy allowing only one year for students to transition into full-time English instruction.

But the greatest unresolved crisis spurred by the economic and demographic transformation of Los Angeles has been, and still is, poverty. Eligibility for the federal free and reduced price meals program is the most widely used indicator of poverty in American schools, and LAUSD's participation in the program is remarkable. Well more than half of all students in the District were enrolled in the program by the early 1980s, and the proportion was steady at approximately three-quarters throughout the 1990s, even as overall enrollment in the District surged.[41] The conclusion is inescapable: The core educational challenge of the Los Angeles Unified School District is educating poor children.

Such pervasive poverty presents obvious educational challenges. It has become commonplace in the United States to view public schools as engines of economic opportunity and development. This is most possible when schools are filled with well-resourced students ready to learn and where schools prepare students for jobs available in a vibrant local economy. By the end of the 1970s, neither of these circumstances was present in Los Angeles. As LAUSD faced a growing crisis of legitimacy, then, it faced a perhaps deeper challenge of how the District should develop educationally. The answers were not obvious.

EXIT, VOICE, LOYALTY, AND CRISIS

This economic and demographic transformation created a political crisis as well, in part because the self-reinforcing dynamics confounded the District's mission. The disappearance of highly skilled, high-paying jobs in the 1970s, 1980s, and 1990s coincided with the immigration of low-skilled workers.[42] When an economy no longer produces the jobs and upward mobility that once paid for the school system, the school system struggles to provide education that can serve as an engine of recovery and growth for the city and region. In Los Angeles, better paid and better educated people continued to exit, which further undermined the capacity of the system to improve itself.

As immigrant student enrollments grew, an additional challenge further complicated any attempts to reestablish legitimacy for the District's policymakers. A substantial number of those immigrant students were children of parents who were not citizens or had come to the United States illegally.

Because they were not citizens, these parents would have no voice in the formal business of governing the District: They could not vote to elect the public officials who would fund the District, hire its teachers and administrators, or set its curriculum or assessments. Nor could they vote when education-related initiatives were put on the ballot. For example, Proposition 187 in 1994 proposed to deny undocumented parents' children the right even to enroll in school. (Proposition 187 won at the polls but was overturned by the courts as a violation of the Fourteenth Amendment's equal protection clause.) Further, the exclusion of these parents from democratic decisionmaking about their own children's education exacerbated a growing misalignment between the voting population of LAUSD and the region, the population at large (which was more Latino than the voting population), and the student population of LAUSD (which was more Latino still). Even if the District were able to reestablish its legitimacy with voters, the interests and values of the electorate did not necessarily coincide with the interests and values of the children served by the school district.

The 1980s and 1990s presented a sharp contrast to the 1950s, when LAUSD was a predominantly middle-class district with financial resources and a supportive and powerful electoral constituency. By the last two decades of the century, LAUSD had few politically powerful advocates or defenders, few people willing or able to develop institutional alternatives to respond to the legitimacy crisis that had emerged and become chronic.

These dynamics demonstrate that in some ways Hirschman's analysis of exit, voice, and loyalty does help us understand the school district's political crisis. Even as hundreds of thousands of individuals and families continued to move into the region and the school district, others did indeed grow dissatisfied with their prospects in Los Angeles, whether because of the declining economy or because of the quality of their schools. Many who were dissatisfied moved away, and many others challenged the District to improve. Together, they ended decades of established legitimacy for the District and created tremendous uncertainty about what would come next.

Yet, the economic and demographic transformations of Los Angeles demonstrate some of the shortcomings of Hirschman's analysis. Hirschman presumed that an organization under challenge would act to regain the confidence of its constituents. Los Angeles confounds this thinking, because the demographic turbulence of the late twentieth century dramatically changed the constituencies of the District. The old constituencies have dwindled, and former leaders have either departed or can claim far fewer followers. The diverse constituencies of the transformed District now contended for leadership and control, and there is no obvious path for the District either educationally or politically.

All this change further undermined and destabilized the institutional foundations of the District, creating uncertainty and inviting new coalitions and ideas. The political setting of LAUSD was difficult to begin with, offering a weak city government, the separation of school governance from city government, and fragmented governance over social services in general. It has never been a responsive political system in which avenues for voice are obvious or transparent, one where exit can have constructive effects. The economic and demographic developments of the years since the 1960s have made the situation even more challenging, as the District has gradually lost its self-sufficient capacity to manage and improve its schools.

CHAPTER 4

Hollowing Out

The Demise of Local Control

Eight months after LEARN was adopted, *Los Angeles Times* columnist George Skelton lamented the political gridlock that had halted educational reform in the state capitol. Governor Pete Wilson, a Republican, had offered up some educational reform ideas, and these had immediately been attacked by the two top Democratic officeholders and would-be gubernatorial candidates. Skelton noted that the state constitution had got it right some 144 years before by taking the leadership of public education out of politics, and then he noted that the "real politicizing of elementary and high school education at the state Capitol can be traced to landmark events in the 1970s and '80s: The granting of collective bargaining rights to teachers, which greatly enhanced union muscle; passage of Proposition 13, which dried up local funding and concentrated power of the purse in Sacramento, and the election of Bill Honig as superintendent."[1]

Capitol gridlock only mattered because the momentum for educational change had moved from the school districts to the state government. LAUSD, like other districts in the state, had waited helplessly as its essential functions of governance and operations were eaten away. The local property tax, once the bedrock of school finance, now provides only about 20 percent of general funds in California. The curriculum—once developed by an army of specialists inside the District—is effectively controlled by the state, which maintains the list of approved textbooks and sets and approves academic standards by grade level. And the actual development of teaching material and methods has largely been contracted out to corporations that not only provide textbooks but also provide detailed instructions about how to teach and at what pace. Judgment of student performance—once a teacher's prerogative—has largely been assumed by testing organizations and the state agencies that contract with them. Finance and pedagogy are further controlled through the use of categorical programs that channel state and federal funds directly to students with specific educational needs or conditions. These programs are even more tightly constrained, and they contain their own monitoring and compliance mechanisms.

In the face of this, LAUSD has had to work very hard to maintain itself. As reform advocate Virgil Roberts noted, "It's kind of like trying to maintain the old mansion, when what you really should do is just tear it down and build a smaller house, or smaller houses on it. There's been this effort to maintain the system, but at less and less of a functional level, just for the sake of maintaining it. And it's been totally hollowed out."[2]

TAX EQUALIZATION AND REVOLT

In Los Angeles and elsewhere in California, the resource tap began to shut off in the late 1960s. Since World War II, public education had enjoyed widespread support in part from the parents of the baby boom generation eager to have schools for their children. "Since 1946, a total of $966,500,000—nearly one billion dollars—has been approved by school district voters in seven separate bond issues to finance construction, necessary equipment of classrooms and related educational facilities," a 1967 District report noted. "In order to accommodate the constantly increasing school population, the citizens of Los Angeles have committed themselves to an unparalleled financial obligation"[3]

Meanwhile, the property tax rate for schools nearly doubled, increasing from $2.40 per thousand dollars assessed to $4.33.[4] When combined with rapidly increasing real estate values, the tax burden on individual homeowners became onerous. "The financial burden, as a result of growth, has created a serious drain on the available resources of the local district property-owner taxpayer. The local property-owner taxpayer has had to assume a greater share of financing the local schools, while the State has steadily reduced its share of financial support."[5] Even in these times, the schools' growth absorbed revenue increases and left programs vulnerable. Jack Crowther, the

District superintendent from 1962 to 1970, is remembered for his opposition to forced busing as a remedy for segregation, but his largest frustration was with the school board and the legislature over finances. "I'm not going to put up with this stupidness any longer. I've been cutting our budgets for five years and I'm tired of it," he said in 1968. "It is heartbreaking to see a great school system start to deteriorate because of lack of funds."[6]

After 1966, voters approved no construction bond measures for thirty-six years, and starting in 1974 declining enrollment further squeezed the District's finances for a decade.

Proposition 13

Things started to worsen fast with the passage of Proposition 13 in 1978. To many, the California property tax limitation measure was life instructing art. Tax limitation crusader Howard Jarvis became the real-life inspiration for Howard Beal, the deranged newscaster in the 1976 film *Network,* leaning out the window yelling, "I'm mad as hell and I'm not going to take it anymore" and encouraging others to follow suit, the prototype for the angry white man.

In fact, there were two proximate causes for the tax limitation measure, which was opposed by virtually every newspaper and interest group in the state. Rising property values and reassessments driven by true market value gave rise to shocking property tax bills. Stories appeared in the newspapers of people who were "house rich" but "cash poor" being taxed out of their property. Widows, who had purchased their homes for a pittance, found themselves living in houses worth more than a quarter-million dollars. At the same time, the state had amassed a huge surplus in its treasury, thanks largely to a progressive income tax signed into law by Governor Ronald Reagan. Inflation had boosted salaries, and ordinary people found themselves in the upper tax brackets. The legislature had failed to agree on a remedy for the surplus or for the tax assessments, and the surplus began to appear "obscene," in the words of state treasurer Jess Unruh.

The combination of the 1971 *Serrano v. Priest* tax equity decision, a revenue limit measure passed in 1972, and the passage of Proposition 13 created the fiscal crisis that forced the state to assume primary responsibility for school finance.[7] The dramatic shift in resources effectively ended LAUSD's control over its own fiscal future. In large measure, financial management became a matter of reacting to state windfalls, in years such as the late 1990s technology sector boom, or, more frequently, shortfalls. The lack of enthusiasm for educational reforms was in part traceable to the omnipresent problem of money.

The education establishment's eventual response to tax limitation was Proposition 98, which guaranteed public schools about 40 percent of the state's general revenue. It passed narrowly in 1988 with heavy assistance from education interest groups including the California School Administrators, the California Teachers Association, and the state Parent Teacher Association.[8] Opponents of the proposition included Governor George Deukmejian, business groups, and some public employee unions.[9] To help ensure its passage, state school superintendent Bill Honig used his remaining campaign treasury—$425,000—to produce and mail a campaign pamphlet to 550,000 California households, urging support of the proposition.[10]

Subsequently, defense of the Proposition 98 allocation has become a central activity of school districts and their advocates. It has taken on a normative quality, something akin to a civil right. When Governor Arnold Schwarzenegger suspended the Prop 98 funding level in the midst of the state's financial crisis in 2004, teacher unions and other education interests placed the governor on the "enemies list" until he repaid the money in 2005.

For Los Angeles, the difficulty with state centralization of finances is not simply the loss of power to tax; it is the lack of information about how to manage the system. The interaction of the revenue limitations has created what Stanford University professor and former state school board president Michael Kirst calls an "incoherent and unfathomable system."[11] In 2005, LAUSD superintendent Roy Romer echoed the comments about the flight of local control that were made by his predecessors some forty years earlier: "But ever since Proposition 13, we can't even debate such priorities and decide on them locally. We have to lobby, like every other interest group, in a state Capitol whose partisan paralysis is on display daily. I have had to ask the District's employees to do more with less."[12]

The dramatic shift in local and state funding can be seen in Figure 4.1. Local revenue declined rapidly in the late 1970s, following Proposition 13, and was replaced by state revenue as the federal share of the total inched up to nearly match that produced from local property tax revenue. The consequences of this shift make the District more vulnerable to shifts in the state and national economy. While property tax revenue was relatively stable, flows from the California income and sales taxes are highly dependent on

FIGURE 4.1
LAUSD Income by Source, 1950–51 through 2004–05

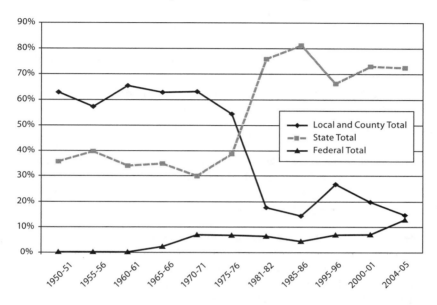

Source: Annual Report of Financial Transactions, California School Districts (Sacramento: California State Controller, 1950–2005).

business cycles, and in a boom or bust economy state, such as California, it means virtually constant budget woes for the schools.

Changes in How Resources Are Spent

The state controls more than just the level of funding for each district in California. Increasingly since the 1960s, the state controls what districts and schools spend their money on. "General purpose" funds, over which school districts have substantial control, have declined from 87 percent of K–12 spending in 1969–70 to less than 70 percent in recent years.[13] Even allocations of these general-purpose funds are often beyond the easy control of school boards and administrators, as a substantial proportion of them is spent on salaries and benefits, most of which are negotiated through collective bargaining mandated by the state. Generally, about 65 percent of a district's operating budget is mediated by its labor contracts. Nongeneral purpose funds that remain must be spent by districts on "categorical" programs earmarked for specific purposes, notably special education, class-size reduction, child care and development, instructional programs targeted at racial and ethnic minority students, and adult education. In addition, virtually all of the 8–10 percent of operating funds that come from the federal government are categorically encumbered.[14]

Although the LAUSD central office is often characterized as bloated, it is comparatively small, and its capacity has been hollowed out, too. A review of spending patterns initiated by an agreement between the District and UTLA showed that LAUSD spent 59 percent of its budget on instruction, more than any district other than Chicago.[15] (By comparison, District of Columbia Public Schools spent about 48 percent of their operating budget on instruction, Baltimore 52 percent, Boston 55 percent, and Chicago 61 percent.) Merle Price, who was a principal and cluster leader during the LEARN era, recalls:

> The other thing that was happening simultaneously with all of the hope for this reform: there was pretty much a dismantling of any central capacity in the District to handle instructional improvement. There were very few people working on such significant areas as literacy, math, science and social studies by the time I became deputy superintendent in 2001, other than a few grant-funded positions. While there was capacity in reading because of Open Court, there wasn't in the other disciplines. So this idea of helping school-by-school with a bottom-up approach absent central capacity was, in hindsight, a mistake.[16]

California's Relative Finance Position

Spending per pupil went from about $400 above the national average in 1969–70 to more than $600 below the national average in 1990–2000. Television journalist John Merrow characterized the decline as "First to Worst," and he was close to right.[17] The state has relatively high per capita income, and in 1970 it spent about 4.25 percent of personal income on public education, about the same as the national average. This percentage declined rapidly beginning in the mid-1970s; and despite its recent rise, it still spends less as a function of personal income than the national average (see Figure 4.2). Given the state's reliance on the income tax, lower spending as a function of income combined with increasing enrollment translates into a large gap between what California spends per student and the national average, as Figure 4.3 shows.

FIGURE 4.2

California Share of Personal Income Spent on K–12 Education Relative to the U.S. as a Whole

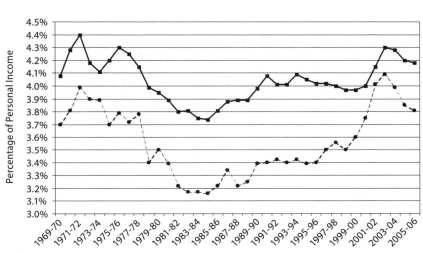

*2003–04 and 2004–05 are estimated.
Note: U.S. includes District of Columbia. Per pupil spending is per unit of Average Daily Attendance (ADA).
Source: California Budget Project, "How Does California Compare?: Funding California's Public Schools," October 2007.

CATEGORICAL PROGRAMS

In 1965, Congress passed the Elementary and Secondary Education Act (ESEA), the federal government's first major intervention into public schooling and the progenitor of No Child Left Behind (NCLB). The categorical funding systems embedded in ESEA and similar state laws broke the hierarchy of LAUSD into budget silos. As was the case elsewhere in the country, earmarked funding created internal divisions both within the schools and the District. Lines of authority and responsibility attached to each specific and accountability procedures.

Both categorical funding and desegregation created substantial goal substitution within the schools. Principals faced more bureaucratic pressure for clean audits and no disturbances with their programs than they faced

FIGURE 4.3

California Spending per Student as Compared to
U.S. Spending per Student

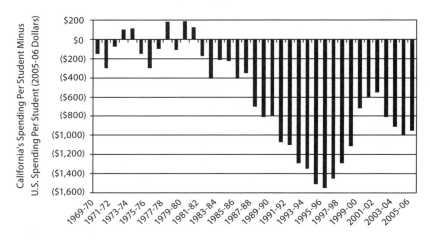

*2003-04 and 2004-05 are estimated.

Note: U.S. includes District of Columbia. Per pupil spending is per unit of Average Daily Attendance (ADA).

Source: California Budget Project, "How Does California Compare? Funding California's Public Schools," October 2007.

pressure for increased student achievement. School politics changed as well. Interest groups formed around each categorical program. Ultimately, categorical programs and desegregation led to what has been called the "the layering and the lawyering" of LAUSD: each program in its own bureaucracy, each with its own rules and compliance mechanisms, and each with its own legal advocates.

Between 1964 and 1966, federal funds increased tenfold for LAUSD, from $4,563,712 in 1964–65 to $47,162,830 in 1966–67.[19] While lauding the external funds that had created "a new vitality" in classrooms and a "new determination that something can be done for the student who had fallen far behind, for the student who is stuck on dead center, for the superior student who needs new challenges," a District report noted, "Compensatory programs observed tended to be 'package deals' and there is not the flexibility built into the projects to allow the principal to adapt the program to the particular school and community."[20] In a preview of the coming critique of categorical funding, the report noted misunderstandings between teachers in the regular programs and specially funded ones, excessive record keeping requirements and unrealistic deadlines, and a disproportionate use of administrative time—30 to 50 percent allocated to specially funded programs—and too little carryover of promising programs into the regular classrooms.[21]

The District began to realize that it could not solve the problems it had been handed.

> To solve the problems facing urban schools and urban societies requires the cooperative effort not only of the Board of Education, but also of the city, county, state and federal governments. These public agencies cannot fully solve the problems without enlisting the help and participation of the business men, churches and others in the private sector of our community. The Committee recommends that initiative be exercised at the highest level of the school district to bring these forces together effectively. No other problem is more important.[22]

Categorical funding also changed the contours of spending. Despite the presence of collective bargaining agreements, long-term spending trends show movement *away from* regular classrooms and toward special education and compensatory education. By one calculation, spending controlled for inflation *decreased* by 18.7 percent in regular LAUSD classrooms over the years 1987–96 while per pupil expenses for special education increased by 50.7 percent.[23]

Even though there were efforts to consolidate categorical programs, by 2007 an external review of how the District allocates its operating funds found more than $2.5 billion in funds "heavily restricted by state, federal, district, and collective bargaining requirements," leading to "proliferation of interventions and programs that can undermine instructional coherence in schools and foster an inefficient use of resources."[24]

Activist State Government

With the taxing authority effectively shifted to the state, operational influence followed in short order. In 1982, Bill Honig, a highly energetic maverick member of the state school board, defeated Wilson Riles, the incumbent state school superintendent who was running for his fourth term in office with substantial support from teachers and school administrators. But Honig's ascent to office symbolized more than an upstart replacing a veteran; it represented a sea change in educational politics.

For the previous quarter-century, public schools had been thrust to the forefront of the fight for equity. Particularly in large urban districts, such as Los Angeles, the issues and conflicts surrounding racial and economic equity drove educational politics and vastly influenced their operations. Honig represented the emergent politics of organizing education around a quest for academic excellence.[25]

The beginning of this was generally marked from a year later, in 1983, when *A Nation at Risk* was published, but in California, as in many things, the future arrived a bit ahead of schedule. When Honig took office, he found that he was not alone in wanting to use the power of the state as a means to shake up the educational system. A legislator and former teacher, Gary K. Hart, had long been associated with educational reforms. He had drafted a bill that contained many of the ideas Honig advocated. State senator Teresa Hughes agreed to introduce what became known as the Hughes-Hart Educational Reform Act, or S.B. 813, in the upper chamber.

S.B. 813 was a 200-page monster that provided new state money for the schools and increased requirements across the board. In Honig's words, it "increased graduation requirements, lengthened the school day and school year, tightened discipline, improved teacher selection, inaugurated an incentive program for top-flight teachers, streamlined dismissal procedures for incompetent teachers, and provided more than $800 million of new money for the schools."[26] None of it created radical reform, but the curriculum frameworks are credited with substantial changes in instruction, probably the state's most effective reform. Comparative test scores—first by district and then by school—were released to the newspapers. There was a groundswell of interest in achievement within Los Angeles and other cities. The emerging politics of excellence created a new constituency that was not directly oppositional to the politics of equity; but it placed reform accountability at the center of public discussions about the schools.[27]

It was in many ways the beginning of what would be known a decade later as "systemic reform." Marshall Smith and Jennifer O'Day popularized the notion in an article published in 1991, and Smith carried it into federal policy when he was deputy secretary in the U.S. Department of Education during the Clinton administration.[28] Honig takes some umbrage that they invented the notion.[29] "I drew it all out over lunch or something on a sheet of yellow paper."[30]

In fact, the state had been active earlier, too. Earlier in the century, the state legislature had been quite aggressive in shaping the organization and administration of school districts, as well as their financing and programs.[31] Kirst argues that the California legislature was among national leaders in the early 1960s in asserting state prerogatives over education and challenging local control. In particular, the states worked to "establish minimums of curriculum, teacher qualifications, and facilities below which local school operations cannot fall."[32]

Collective Bargaining

Even before passage of collective bargaining legislation in 1976, UTLA proved itself a powerful political organization. It first struck in April 1970 when the teachers stayed out for five weeks. The agreement that settled the strike was later nullified in the courts, but the strike established the union as both muscular and antagonistic. Even though the union would gain substantial influence with the school board as a result of its electoral support, it was not accepted as a working partner in educational reform, and on the few occasions that opportunities for genuine partnerships came about, the union was internally conflicted over whether working on the educational issues that were central to the 1970 strike was "real unionism."

Even a decade after the 1970 strike, teachers who had not joined the picket lines were shunned in school staff lounges, and administrators were divided into those who could "work with the union" and the majority who were conditioned to loathe it. Where many union-management relationships passed from antagonism to a close and constructive working relationship, relationships in LAUSD always remained edgy. However, the teachers did not strike again for nearly twenty years.

In 1988, the union began negotiations with a new superintendent, Leonard Britton, who had been hired from Miami with the expectations that he would radically decentralize the schools and create a strong working relationship with the teachers. Things went badly almost from the start. UTLA, having been through a period of budgetary austerity, asked for a 12 percent raise and the adoption of a school-based management model. The District offered 4.1 percent and maintenance of existing medical and health benefits.[33] Relationships deteriorated throughout the school year as the war of words and actions escalated. Teachers began a work-to-rule action, stopping what they considered unpaid activity, including filling out attendance sheets, attending after school meetings, and supervising playgrounds.[34] When the teachers refused to give state-mandated tests in October, Britton said that they were "violating the state Education Code and endangering state funding."[35] Over the next several months, the courts, the Public Employment Relations Board, the mayor, the state school superintendent, and individual school board members sought to intervene. Students demonstrated and boycotted. Paychecks were docked for those teachers who would not turn in grades. A strike was authorized.

The irony in this is that the District and union were headed somewhat in the same direction. Both sides wanted some kind of school site management arrangement. The District proposed "a pilot program to give teachers wider authority. It would create a school leadership council consisting of teachers, parents, clerical workers and students to act as an equal partner with the principal" in decisionmaking.[36] The union also had a plan, and School Based Management was part of the final contract.[37] Its provisions still exist, and the union and school board still process requests for SBM-based waivers from board policy and the union contract.

At the same time as it was seeking more "professional" authority for teachers, UTLA was advancing an hourly wage definition of their work responsibilities. Union president Wayne Johnson defended the work boycott by saying, "Teachers are paid for 120 hours a month and that is essentially for teaching classes. . . . No one can construe [before- and afterschool chores] as paid time."[38] The fundamental definitions of teaching were clashing with the existing work rules in ways that have still not been resolved.

Teachers struck on May 15, 1989. On the first day, more than 90 percent of the teachers stayed out. Student attendance was cut nearly in half.[39] Eight days later the teachers ratified a contract containing an 8 percent increase for *each* of the next three years, a settlement far in excess of any gained in another California district that year.[40] But the teachers' economic joy was to be short lived. By 1991, recession crippled the District, and the teachers accepted pay cuts rather than face mass layoffs.[41]

Yet, in hindsight the 1989 strike was not about money; it was not even about power, although the union clearly drubbed the superintendent. It may well prove to have been the one event that made it apparent that the school district was not capable of reforming or running itself.

Superintendent Britton, who had been brought to Los Angeles to smooth over relations with the union and to forge a cooperative relationship with the union, appeared weak and ineffective. The casualty was not just Britton, who left the District in 1991; it was the *office* of the superintendent and, by extension, the professional management of schools. Although superintendents who followed were liked and disliked to varying degrees, and thought effective or ineffective differently, no superintendent would have been perceived as having control of the district. By 2000, the superintendency would be held by a politician rather than an educator, and there was no public outcry over the demise of professional control.

The strike also hardened relationships between the union and lower-level school administrators, who were ultimately responsible for policy implementation and daily operations. The UTLA attack on them was direct and personal. The union bought bus banners comparing administrators' salaries to those of teachers, declaring them as unnecessary bureaucracy. And the settlement cut deeply into administrative staff and programs.

Just as UTLA became the undisputed political powerhouse in relations with the District, the school board, and to a great extent the state government, it also became the object of efforts to organize reforms around rather than through the District. SBM was seen as a power grab, not an educational reform. By the end of the 1990s, it was possible for a civic leader to say, "There's one thing we agree on. It's impossible to make progress as long as there is the big district, a big school board, and a big union." The political stage was set for radical alternatives.

SCHOOL BOARD

LAUSD is governed by a nonpartisan, seven-member board elected at-large to staggered four-year terms—just as it was in 1960.[42] But the board of today is starkly different in its powers and politics. In 1960, the elected board could raise property tax rates, subject to voter approval, and in doing so it had kept the school district afloat since the early 1900s, through two world wars, the Great Depression, and enormous enrollment growth in the 1920s and again in the post–World War II period. Tax rates grew steadily through the 1950s and 1960s, although the growth came to an abrupt stop in 1969 when the District's taxpayers repudiated board proposals for both a rate increase and a substantial bond issue to build more schools.[43]

The Crawford desegregation case filed in 1963 changed board politics drastically. Before that, "liberal" meant a school board member was for more schools and more school services, which meant higher taxes. To be conservative was to be against foreign interference in public schools and to be for a return to the three Rs. For example in 1957, in the run-off between candidates Edith Stafford and Mary Tinglof, conservatives accused Tinglof of ties to UNESCO, which in the John Birch Society politics of the day would place her loyalties to the United States in question.[44] She was also accused of being a puppet of the teachers union, which was a presence in the District even though collective bargaining was legally decades away. Tinglof also was for more progressive ways of teaching and for spending more money in the schools. Stafford, however, supported the conservative plank of holding taxes steady, teaching the three Rs, and the American way. The *Times* strongly endorsed Stafford and printed several articles outlining the disaster that Tinglof's election would bring. Tinglof won and became a strong liberal voice.

After the desegregation struggle began and throughout the late 1960s and 1970s, school board campaigns and the politics of the board's operation revolved around how a candidate felt about integration, in particular busing. Campaigns became high profile and increasingly expensive and were supported by educational interest groups. Although they continued to run for office without party labels, most candidates were transparently either Democrats or Republicans. And, increasingly, board members sought other elective offices after leaving the board.

In 1965, the Reverend James Jones became the first African American to serve on the school board since 1943. He was highly regarded due to his work with children through the church, but perhaps his biggest draw was that he was a minority who opposed mandatory busing.[45] In 1967, Julian Nava became the century's first Latino board member by defeating the deeply conservative Charles Smoot, the only member who remained opposed to the federal aid that was then flowing into the District. Nava attributed his victory to the teachers who campaigned on his behalf, and he promised to treat them as professionals, not employees.[46]

The late 1960s and early 1970s were particularly turbulent times for the board. In the wake of the 1965 Watts riots, the board was subject to increased picketing, demonstrations, and unrest. African American dissatisfaction with the District was joined by Latino activism in 1968 with walkouts at four predominately Latino high schools on the Eastside and the beginnings of what would become the Chicano movement. The board, and its politics, became increasingly polarized. The dominant liberal wing saw the demonstrations and walkouts as expressing legitimate political aspirations. Indeed, the board voted 5–1 to reinstate first-year Garfield High School history teacher Sal Castro, who had led the walkouts.[47] The conservatives, who were still fighting integration, saw permissiveness and unwarranted disturbance of school operation. In 1969, a conservative slate that called itself "Save Our Schools" won two of the three open seats, marking the beginning of an ascendancy.

One of them, Donald Newman, may well have been the last Progressive Era archetype. Newman was a physician who had served pro bono as the football team doctor for the Wilson High School team. He provided free medical exams for needy young people and was involved in civic and volunteer efforts in the El Sereno neighborhood. He was passionate in his support of better schools for the neighborhood and a new school building, but he did not see any particular reason that the principal of the school needed to be able to speak Spanish, Latino students still being a minority at the school. In a campaign speech, he declared, "Top priority is to solve the turmoil in the schools. I would plan to listen to the students and parent organizations through their elected representatives (not as a mob) and through the professional staff of the Los Angeles city school system."[48]

To William Johnston, who was superintendent from 1970 to 1979, Newman was both a friend and an ideal.[49] In Newman he had found someone who was not particularly doctrinaire and whose goal was to restore confidence in the school district. He was still willing to stick up for it, writing in 1971 after he had been elected board president: "Some of our students are reading poorly: true, but in all of our reading scores where are the variables listed? For example, the mobility of our population, the bilingual problem; our depressed communities where the only bright spot may be the school classroom. The increase in college placement courses in our minority communities give a lie to the statement that because an area is poor all students do badly."[50] In other words, the District was doing as well as could be expected, and support for the administration would allow the schools to become decentralized, something that Superintendent Johnston advocated. The board presidency, he said, was that of a coordinator, to keep the board running smoothly, not a position of prestige.[51] Newman died in office in 1976, and many years later Johnston wrote a biographical tribute titled *The Doc Newman Story*, perhaps the last time a superintendent in Los Angeles would write kindly of a board member. (Johnston memorialized other board members by hanging Paul Conrad's biting political cartoons directed at them in his bathroom above the toilet.)

High-Profile Board Members

Beginning in the 1970s, LAUSD entered a period where school board members became highly visible. Some used the board as a stepping-stone to higher political office. Several are particularly memorable. Kathleen Brown, daughter of one governor and sister of another one, was elected to the board in 1975. She went on to become state treasurer and run unsuccessfully for the governorship. Diane Watson, a former teacher in the District, became the lightning rod for integration and the symbol of a generation of activist black politicians. After serving in the General Assembly and state senate, she is now in the U.S. House of Representatives. Bobbie Fiedler, a San Fernando Valley activist in the anti-integration group Bustop became Watson's sparring partner over integration issues. Fiedler rode the wave of conservatism into the U.S. House for two terms. Rita Walters, an African American woman, was elected in 1979 and went on to serve as a member of the Los Angeles city council from 1991 to 2001. More recent board members who have moved on to higher elective office include Jackie Goldberg, who served two terms each on the L.A. city council (1993–2000) and in the State Assembly; and José Huizar, who, after serving on the board from 2001 to 2005, including two years as board president, was elected to the city council in 2005.

Single-Member Districts

The backlash caused by desegregation and the reality of a school board controlled by whites, but a school district with majority minority enrollment, left many minority groups and other liberals feeling that citywide elections did not give them fair representation on the school board. The board was remarkably white for its school population demographics, with only one Mexican American and one African American. City councilman Zev Yaroslavsky had introduced a bill to repeal the Progressive Era practice of citywide elections for school board members in 1976, but it was defeated at the polls. A similar one passed in 1978.[52] The measure was supported by Mayor Tom Bradley and various labor groups who were concerned with the prospect of an antibusing majority on the board, but the school board members themselves were conflicted on the idea.[53]

Increasing Union Influence

While it may seem as if the creation of districts itself destroyed the Progressive system of professional management, in reality this act stripped away the façade of impartiality and apolitical representation. Throughout the 1970s, school board elections saw the rise of politically polarized elections and a marked decrease in the interest of voters in general, both of which opened the way for interest groups. Various interest groups joined the fray over who controlled the school board, most notably African Americans, antibusers, and unions. Left in its place was an admittedly sullied and perhaps ideologically flawed institution, but it was a truer interpretation of what had been going on for years. By institutionalizing the mechanisms that had already been in existence, school board politics became more transparent and open to more than just one interest group (traditionally middle-class whites).

The teachers' union, UTLA, was the most visible of the interest groups. With the exception of two periods (discussed in Chapter 9), it had supported the campaigns of at least four of the seven board members. In 1987 it successfully targeted for defeat John Greenwood, a member it had previously supported, and was successful in electing the politically liberal Julie Korenstein to represent the conservative San Fernando Valley. Korenstein later said, "To run for the board and not have support of teachers, you don't have a chance in hell of winning. . . . With their support, you have teachers walking precincts, on the telephones. . . . There are 4,000 to 5,000 teachers in the West Valley alone."[54]

UTLA influence and corresponding bragging rights peaked in the late 1990s when President Wayne Johnson asserted that the "political strength of teachers cannot be underestimated" and that "the message is you better listen to us or you are in political trouble."[55] This would be the case for a decade.

Meanwhile, the cost of school board elections escalated. In 1989, Korenstein won her election with less than $75,000.[56] In 1993, the total had reached $130,000.[57] In 1995, a record company executive spent $200,000 of his own money on a losing campaign.[58] In 1999, Caprice Young raised $665,000.[59] When the election was over, former board member Jackie Goldberg reminded the winners that they had just spent $2 million to create "the most negative attitudes toward public education in the history of this city, and now it's their job to change that."[60] In effect, the escalating cost of school board elections was tied to increasingly explicit delegitimation of the LAUSD in its current form.

In what may be one of the most expensive school board races in history, in the spring of 2007 Tamar Galatzan, who was backed by Mayor Antonio Villaraigosa, spent $2,762,540 to defeat John Lauritzen, who was backed by the teachers' union and spent \$1,297,209. All for a job that pays \$25,000 a year.[61]

Regardless of how much money they raised for the elections, the unions found themselves increasingly unable to alter the District's diminished capacity. When LEARN president Mike Roos was asked in 2005 what he knew now that he wished he had known when he started the campaign for the reform effort, he replied after a long pause: "I probably would have wanted to know how absolutely un-empowered, or powerless the school board is in terms of affecting that organization. A faulty assumption, having been a legislator, and having seen time and time again how we could beat the bureaucracy, and absolutely change at least the way they were doing business, either by pure force of law, budget manipulation, or absolute threats."[62]

THE PERFECT STORM

More than forty years after Mary Ellen Crawford's parents were convinced to lend their name to a desegregation lawsuit, Virgil Roberts, one of the plaintiffs' attorneys reflected on the period, saying, "I would think that the decline of school system began with Prop 13. And everything really started to flow from that. There were other things that happened along the way, but what Prop 13 did that affected all of us, because I think it affects all local government, in that it essentially took away locally controlled schools." He continued:

> Up until then a school board had the ability to fix itself because it could raise money. . . . You go from being essentially a suburban city—the whole city was a suburb—with a small minority population that is primarily black, which is what it was when the Crawford case started, to becoming a large city with a huge urban core that is becoming increasingly poor and immigrant. At the same time you have aging facilities, you know, so you have more needs and less money.
>
> It was the perfect storm.[63]

CHAPTER 5

New Ideas

Stability in the Face of Turbulence

The delegitimation of the key ideas of local control and unquestioned professional dominance followed by demographic changes and a hollowing of the District's capacity created an atmosphere that fostered new thoughts about how LAUSD should be run. A consistent set of ideas began to emerge in the 1960s, and these are still in formation. LEARN and LAAMP auditioned and refined them in the 1990s, but they remain largely unconnected to one another. Though, like their predecessors, many of those reformers have left the stage, the persistent and evolving ideas they worked with continue to play a central role in the District's ongoing institutional transformation.

Generally, these ideas are understood in programmatic terms familiar to educators and policymakers: universal high standards, decentralization, greater parental and grassroots engagement, and variety and choice in types of schooling. All these elements have been part of every reform plan proposed for LAUSD since 1967, and they have been part of national policy debates. However, when all four of the ideas are put into action at the same time, they preview a fundamentally different educational system, a new institution.[1]

THE IDEAS

The programmatic concept of having high standards and applying them universally to all students started as an oft-repeated assertion that "all children can learn." The standards movement of the 1990s connected the force of public policy to this assertion, and the current era of tests and accountability connected consequences to it. The expectation of universal achievement moved public education from a period of high confidence in professional educators to one of great suspicion and external inspection. The notion that all children can learn, and that schools should be held accountable to see that they do, represents an enormous institutional change from the bell curve notions that had organized curriculum and instruction at least since the Progressive Era. The "scientific" approach of that era dictated that schools should match their instruction to the supposed attributes of children, which in practice meant that less would be expected of, and offered to, poor children or children of color. Reformers rejected the bigotry of this approach as they embraced the idea of universal standards. "It involves nothing less than a shift from the system of sorting and selecting and tracking to one of inclusion that aims to raise the average achievement of all children and to assure that none fall below an acceptable minimum."[2]

This commitment to universal student learning has transformed the concept of equity and how the school system approaches the overarching issue of racial difference and discrimination. The politics of equity, which began with desegregation lawsuits and around which the first of the reform plans was constructed, initially focused on the issue of access. In essence, the writers of the 1967 Planning Report argued that poor and minority students should have access to the same schooling as more affluent and white students. Within a decade, however, and continuing today, reformers came to recognize that even when all students had equitable access to schools, they might still be offered resources, and instruction and expectations fitted to the old bell curve. Advocates of equity became concerned with the distribution and adequacy of resources for *all* children within the school system, and they demanded that schools engage in practices and produce outcomes that demonstrated the effective use of those resources.

By the late 1980s, these expectations of universal standards and adequate provision began to be felt politically in Los Angeles. A 1989 reform plan illustrated the change in expectations, saying, "It is not incumbent upon the child to prove that he or she is capable of learning, rather it is incumbent upon the District to prove that it can teach every student."[3] These expectations of responsibility would be attached to lawsuits, initiatives, and legislation that challenged the adequacy of the state's education system.

Importantly, this idea that schools and instruction should be restructured for high expectations has persisted even though there is no sure pedagogical technology for reaching that goal and no universal belief that it is even attainable. The idea has also persisted despite resistance by many inside LAUSD. Many, perhaps most, teachers don't believe that all students can "work to standard." Much of the central administration resists providing students a curriculum that would lead to college admission because students seem unprepared for it, and it is easier to provide different levels of substandard curriculum than to devise programs to raise student achievement for all. Yet the idea persists.

Over the course of several plans, reformers elaborated on the core idea of universal high expectations with the addendum of accountability. They have come to argue that schools and districts (and, more recently, students themselves) should be held explicitly accountable for accomplishing goals associated with these expectations. These notions are now commonplace: Accountability requires assessment, which in turn requires tests devised by authorities outside the schools and districts. Further, it requires that the results of these tests be made public and carry consequences.

The second major idea is closely associated with universal standards. Reformers came to believe that because each school operates in a distinct community with a distinct student pool and a distinct set of administrators and teachers, these professionals must be encouraged to find their own ways of meeting universal expectations, at least to some degree. There must be developed some systemwide division of labor in which higher authorities set the expectations, while local authorities are allowed some autonomy or discretion in devising instructional and organizational strategies for success. This division of labor contrasts in many ways with traditional Progressive notions about universal and hierarchical management practices. It has also come to be called "decentralization," although it embraces centralization of some controls and decentralization of others.

As in the case of universal standards, reformers have elaborated on the core idea of decentralization. Based on observation and experience, they have come to believe that even when given this autonomy, many schools, administrators, and teachers lack the capacity to meet the new responsibilities required in a decentralized system. The development of that capacity— and assistance to schools as they develop it—has thus become a part of the decentralization idea.

Decentralization, like the idea of universal standards, persists despite resistance from practitioners. As the event history of LEARN and LAAMP will show, most central office administrators do not believe in decentralization. Even principals, who complain about central office mandates and make a show of "protecting" their teachers from some of them, for the most part are relieved to have the central office taking much of the responsibility. Teachers and their union are likewise nowhere near taking full responsibility for their own practice. Thus, the power of the organizational idea of autonomy and assistance lies in its persistence in the face of this disbelief. At the same time, the event history shows that the District and the charter schools movement has begun to create valuable craft knowledge about how to operate schools in a decentralized environment and how to operate within a network form of organization where power and authority is distributed rather than hierarchical.

The third idea is similarly an elaboration on universal high expectations. Experience and research demonstrated that students and schools performed better when parents were actively involved. Contrary to the Progressive Era idea that educational professionals should seek independence from parent interference, reformers came to believe that parents must become partners in their children's education. In its early incarnations, this idea initially meant that parents should simply be enlisted as volunteers. Some later versions advocated active participation of parents and community members in shared decisionmaking at school sites. Spreading decisional authority to parents challenged both the professionally dominated hierarchy and the Progressive Era assumption about school district governance by community elites. In effect, the reform plans began to recognize a much more participatory politics. Increasing parent and community participation also recognized the increasingly federated nature of school governance, where instead of power concentrated in the hands of the school board (and gently guided by the superintendent), it was widely distributed from the grassroots to state and national capitals.

A fourth idea, less visible in the four plans but increasingly influential in Los Angeles and the United States, can be said to stem from the first three. Some reformers argued that not only should variety among schools be encouraged, but parents should have some choice about which schools their children will attend. Autonomous schools seeking to perform at high levels, especially when adapted to the particular values and visions of local parents and communities, should be expected to develop along different lines. In sharp distinction from the original Progressive Era ideas of scientific management and consistent "best practices," reformers advanced the idea that variety and choice were essential to encourage and enable school quality.

The combination of choice and standards changed the politics of the District, though not by bringing the discipline of the market to bear in ways that closed down bad schools and caused good ones to multiply. Policies to create such a market dynamic were never part of the plans themselves or of any successful political initiative. Instead, the availability of choice turned many of the District's most engaged parents into consumers. In thinking and acting about education, they thought more about finding a good school and placing their child in it and less about automatically acting as boosters for the school in their attendance zone.

The development of these four ideas is clearly visible through the successive reform plans for the District reaching back decades before LEARN.

LEARN'S ANCESTORS

The LEARN plan brought to the school board in March 1993 had two primary ancestors. In 1967, LAUSD responded to the passage of the 1964 Civil Rights Act and the 1965 Elementary and Secondary Education Act. The District had long resisted collecting data that could document the segregation of its schools, and its leaders had long insisted that the District provided quality education for all its students. In response to ESEA mandates, however, the board relented and in 1966 created the eleven-member Planning Team of administrators and teachers who would investigate the District and develop recommendations for reform.

The plan that was produced acknowledged for the first time that LAUSD was becoming a district of Latino and African American students, and it saw the newly authorized federal programs as a means of explicitly focusing on "the crippling handicaps faced by environmentally and economically disadvantaged young people in acquiring an education that will prepare them for full participation in society."[4] On the issue of integration, however, the committee struggled to find some politically acceptable recommendation. None of its ideas were implemented; they included an integrated educational park of 10,000–25,000 preschool to high school students; a national sales tax of 1 percent to support education; and the establishment of a countywide school system.

By the mid-1980s, the politics of planning had moved from a small committee to include hundreds of participants. Superintendent Harry Handler appointed Paul Possemato as associate superintendent of "Policy, Implementation, and Evaluation," a catch-all title that allowed an intellectually inquisitive Possemato to plan reforms but did not give him power to implement them. Over the next five years, committees operating under his leadership created two reform plans.

The first, *Priorities for Education*, was written in 1986, three years after *A Nation at Risk* and in the wake of a series of reforms taken by the state Department of Education and the legislature.[5] The writers of the report sought change, and every aspect of district operations was fair game. By breaking down what they saw as school board micromanagement and an overly rigid central bureaucracy, principals would be able to get their hands on sufficient authority to run their schools. Despite Possemato's efforts to sell the plan, *Priorities for Education* did not gain traction. Nevertheless, shortly after the report's completion, the school board brought Miami superintendent Leonard Britton to L.A. with the expectation that the District would undergo a decentralization and restructuring similar to that Britton and his charismatic deputy, Joseph Fernandez, had fostered in Florida.

The new superintendent ordered another reform report to be written and asked Possemato to lead the group again. The resulting report, *The Children Can No Longer Wait*, was a massive internal reform document that advocated decentralized schools, high standards, integrated professional development, and an intelligent assessment system.[6] The recommendations resulted from carefully gathered opinions and a close reading of the educational reform literature. Although the academic work that would define the systemic reform era was still to be published, and the federal legislation that would make systemic reform the watchword of the Clinton administration was several years away, the report served as a reasonable model for what would have been a very large-scale effort. Subtitled "An Action Plan to End Low Achievement and Establish Educational Excellence," the document stretched to 179 pages and contained thirty-eight recommendations.

Although similar to *Priorities for Education* in its broad strokes, the report was clearly more sophisticated than its predecessor. It was more clear-cut and focused, and it contained an implementation plan spread over several years as well as a specific budget. The annual total cost of the recommendations was estimated at $59 million in the first year (1989–90) accumulating to a total of $431 million by the end of the 1990s. Of the total amount, more

than three-quarters of the expense, $312 million, was to be spent on five rec-
ommendations, three of which later became part of the 1990s reforms: universal access to preschool; reductions in elementary school class sizes; shared
decisionmaking at each site; increases in teachers' hours to allow for professional development; and an expansion of the base budget of schools to
provide for library technicians, nurses, psychologists, music, art, and physical education teachers and counselors, along with funds for substitutes, field
trips, books, and supplies.

When *The Children Can No Longer Wait* was presented to the school board,
it was received as important but impractical. School board president Roberta
Weintraub called approval of the document "probably one of the most important things that we do this year," but she went on to say that she regretted
that the plan's adoption coincided with "horrendous budget cuts," perhaps
$90 million, that the school board was facing in order to pay for increasing
teacher salaries.[7]

The report was adopted by a unanimous vote on March 27, 1989. As would
be the case with future reforms, what was advocated and adopted was implemented only selectively. After a strike- and recession-driven budget crunch
in 1990, the statewide economic boom of the following decade made it possible for the District to eventually adopt all of the high-cost items in the 1989
report. But hardly any of the ideas behind the reforms took root in immediate practice. The District had shown itself capable of recognizing problems
and crafting thoughtful and innovative solutions but incapable of implementing them in a systematic way.

THE LEARN CAMPAIGN

The importance of persistent ideas is visible in the campaign that created
LEARN and that organization's own plan. Ideas from the two 1980s reports
surfaced again in the 1993 LEARN plan, *For All Our Children*.[8] Indeed, there is
evidence that LEARN consciously borrowed from the plans that Possemato's
LAUSD planners created.[9] By this time, however, the momentum for change
had moved outside the District. It was the new ideas that were guiding action
much more than the old institution, which was seen as the problem rather
than the source of the solution.

The pattern of change seen in other institutions presented itself in the
campaign to bring about LEARN.[10] The LEARN planners did not know exactly
what institutional changes it wanted to bring about or what the new con-

figuration of a school organization would look like, but they agreed that the school district was a mess and on a political approach for influencing it. The strategy was that of a political campaign, and the planning exercise became a means to engage business people, community activists, and educators in the formation of an archetypical big civic coalition. Part of LEARN's logic was to create an unbeatable political coalition, such as that found in other urban reforms and recommended by the school reform literature.[11]

In its founding, LEARN was able to combine the forces of three streams of reform activism. The first was comprised of business and foundation activists, led by the Los Angeles Educational Partnership (LAEP). Under the leadership of its president, Peggy Funkhouser, it had introduced several significant teacher-initiated reforms in the 1980s, and the organization had come to the conclusion that a broader agenda was necessary. The second came from the remains of the School Based Management program, which had been negotiated by UTLA to settle a teacher strike in 1989. While some union leaders remained skeptical of LEARN, Helen Bernstein, who had negotiated the SBM provisions and succeeded to the union presidency after the strike, strongly supported the program. The third stream of reform activism emerged from four Alinsky-style community organizations that joined together to launch Kids 1st at-large rallies in 1990.[12]

By the time the LEARN coalition went public, it had an astonishingly broad coalition.[13] Its principal leaders were part of what was called the LEARN Working Group, an informal organization that acted in many ways as a shadow school board. The building of this organization was a deliberate and methodical joining of diffuse discontent to the existing reform ideas. It is widely accepted that Richard Riordan and Helen Bernstein were the original coordinators of the new school reform movement. Riordan became concerned with education in the mid-1980s when he tried to create a program to distribute donated computers in the District. Frustrated by the District's inability (or unwillingness) to cooperate with his efforts, Riordan looked for other ways to help local children. The idea for a pressure group "to force the board to reform" was one he had been kicking around for a couple of years.[14] Through his involvement with Kids 1st, Riordan became acquainted with Bernstein.

While Riordan had substantial personal wealth, he felt that he could not get serious attention from the old guard of Los Angeles. He called on Virgil Roberts, a record company executive and one of the plaintiff's attorneys in the *Crawford* desegregation lawsuit, and Roberts recruited Lockheed chairman Roy Anderson and ARCO president Robert Wycoff, who became LEARN's chair and who was to present the LEARN plan to the school board in 1993. These three prominent businessmen were then able to establish the aptly titled Working Group.[15] The group met twice a month beginning in January 1991 to discuss educational issues and listen to presentations from various consulting groups, including McKinsey & Company and Booz, Allen and Hamilton. The group had decided that they would review all other successful school reforms before they decided on what their plan would consist of. Thus, the ideas that were part of earlier plans, which were reflected in those being tried out in other places, became the ideology around which the reformers organized politically. The *R* in LEARN stood for "restructuring" and the *N* for "now," giving the ideas an urgency.

After a few sessions, the Working Group realized that they needed to find someone who could be a full-time spokesman for their reform. After a careful search, they asked Assembly Speaker Pro Tem Mike Roos to head the organization. His political expertise and stature in the community were two of his best selling points. As a condition of his acceptance, Roos asked that the group also hire his longtime assistant, Mary Chambers.[16] By the end of March 1991, LEARN had a Working Group comprised of twelve members, a president, and a vice president.

The Working Group hired Roos and Chambers for their political skills, not because they had particular knowledge of how to run a school district, and their arrival signaled a shift in the politics of reform from an internal battle pushed by maverick and younger school administrators to an external fight in which the education bureaucracy became the target of a reform effort grounded in a large civic coalition. Roos and Chambers approached their jobs as they had pursued their legislative careers: as a political campaign, the endpoint of which was the adoption of the LEARN plan. From their perspective, the school district would be responsible for implementation. From the spring of 1991 to the early winter of 1993, they worked long hours in an intense campaign schedule pitching the LEARN message at hundreds of meetings as they sought support and funds for the reform.[17]

Part of the campaign was to continue to delegitimize LAUSD even as they worked with its administrators and teachers. They commissioned a Louis Harris and Associates telephone poll to estimate public support for restructuring the school district.[18] Two-thirds of respondents said that the District was not doing a good job preparing high school students for jobs. The majority of parents and nonparents, 80 percent, said that the District had failed to control crime and drugs in the schools. The improper distribution of funds among schools concerned 76 percent, and 70 percent felt that discipline was not properly enforced and that there was too much racial tension on the campuses. A smaller majority of all respondents, 61 percent, agreed that spending and curriculum decisions should be left to the individual schools. In all, the numbers showed that the school district was held in very low esteem by the majority of those polled.[19]

The negative opinions headlined in the Harris poll became part of a two-pronged attack conceived by the Working Group to create a large community coalition to devise a plan and then use this political capital to force the District to act on it. With "best practices" reports provided pro bono by the management consulting firms, the Working Group drafted documents that addressed the seven areas of greatest concern in education: accountability and assessment, governance, parental involvement, school to work transition, professional development, facilities, and social services. The members felt that by focusing on these topics, members of the community could create an all-encompassing reform.[20]

In accordance with their philosophy of community involvement, the Working Group started to recruit business and community leaders to be part of the task forces that would create LEARN reform policies. As the head of this recruitment, Roos began with a mandate to find eighty members of the community to volunteer for the task forces. UTLA members were also given an open invitation to join the effort. The Working Group interviewed the potential trustees and charged them with the responsibility to not only help create the LEARN reform policy but to also be *the* representative of their community organization and to disseminate information to their group. This style of organizing—reaching out to visible or familiar community leaders—left gaps that would create some political challenges for LEARN later, especially in some Latino quarters. But it enabled the creation of a cohesive and dedicated coalition with real political clout.[21]

Despite the prospect of long hours and no pay, more than 600 Angelenos volunteered to join a task force committee. The task forces had the benefit of the significant amount of legwork already conducted for the Working Group. They would each be led by one or more Working Group member and would therefore be governed by someone who was familiar with LEARN's research and goals. Most importantly, the task forces were adding to or correcting a working draft and not starting from scratch. With these resources at their disposal, the task forces were more than approval committees, but they were not, in many cases, originators of LEARN policy.[22]

In December 1991, a month before the Council of Trustees convened for the first time, the impact of the financial hardships of the state on LAUSD was beginning to show. Barely two years after the teachers union had won hard-fought raises, the District's budget cuts began to eat away at the previous three-year contract. Board members claimed that without a 3 percent reduction of all employee salaries, the District would become insolvent. This could mean the intervention of the county and the state, a situation that would threaten the continued existence of the union. Agreeing that the situation was dire, union members accepted a 3 percent pay cut that would be repaid with interest in 1995. The District promised to restore this pay cut in the 1992–93 school year, a commitment they would later regret.[23]

With the new teacher union contract settled, the first meeting of the Council of Trustees was held in January 1992. It was at this time that the trustees were assigned to task forces based on their interests and their previous experiences or abilities. These seven task forces were to meet as often as necessary to create a systemic policy for the Los Angeles school district that would not only be delivered to the board of education but also to the state legislature by June. While the central office was supportive of these efforts (Superintendent Bill Anton was a Working Group member), the leadership was understandably concerned over budget shortfalls precipitated by the recession.[24]

The recession had been particularly difficult in California, and the statistics issued in June of 1992 showed it. While the jobless rate nationwide had hit an eight-year high at 7.5 percent in May, California's jobless rate had risen to 8.7 percent, with L.A.s County's at 9.8 percent. For California governments, this meant large budget cuts and layoffs, which would greatly affect cities, counties, and school districts.[25]

The driving force behind LEARN was the Working Group, but the spirit of it was the task forces. The primary function of each group was to take one aspect of education in Los Angeles, learn as much about related issues as it could, and represent the community while creating a consensus policy. Because representation was the key to being a community organization, Roos and Chambers tried to include as many people as possible. What started out as seven groups composed of approximately twenty members each quickly became seven groups of approximately ninety members each. Some of this is attributable to the eagerness of UTLA members to participate, but it was also a sign that communities in Los Angeles recognized the need for the restructuring of the District.

While never tension free, LEARN leaders were remarkable in their ability to draw together people who were at loggerheads in other arenas. This was particularly the case with the employee unions. Although Bernstein and UTLA participated from the start, two other union leaders joined the Working Group, and their members participated in the task forces: Walter Backstrom of the Service Employees International Union (SEIU), which represented clerical and other service workers, and Eli Brent of the Association of Administrators of Los Angeles (AALA), which represented principals and other front-line administrators. Conflicts about tenure rights, seniority, the power of the school principal, and the role of the administration altogether echoed those that played out during contract negotiations and school board elections. LEARN became another arena for their increasingly vitriolic skirmishes.[26] AALA was apprehensive about the plan's inclusion of teachers and parents in decisionmaking, especially the possibility that these two groups would have the power to fire or transfer a principal. Riordan met their protests with simple honesty: "The bureaucrats are going to be clobbered" by this reform. The teachers were still upset about merit pay, and the SEIU was unhappy about being left out. LEARN was able to calm some of those fears, but the fact remained that LEARN would alter the power structure of not only the central administration but of the school site as well.[27]

Still, the Working Group was a strange organization in that all of the key players in the contract negotiations were members but acted as though they had completely separated their two roles. While they said extremely disparaging things about each other in speeches and to reporters, they were never reported as behaving badly during LEARN meetings. In effect, they were allies when acting under the auspices of LEARN, even though they were known to consider each other bitter adversaries.[28]

Although the unions exerted influence over the policy, the task forces themselves were not considered union run. Reporter Frank Clifford of the *Los Angeles Times* set the scene by describing the meetings of people "dressed in pantsuits and corduroys, blue jeans and running shoes, gather[ed] in downtown skyscrapers to map out political strategies." These strategies were no longer the province of "private elites" but a coalition of people who felt that the city was in crisis and that the whole community was needed to fix a community problem.[29]

Working together was all the more remarkable because of the events of April 29, 1992, when the Los Angeles riots revealed racial tensions that went beyond black versus white and brought national scrutiny to L.A. and its social ills.[30] The potential setback for LEARN was enormous. The possibility of losing money and people was ominous, but the loss of momentum was even more critical. They could not possibly compete with the rebuilding effort of the riot areas, so they decided to link their cause with that of Rebuild L.A. by pointing out the critical need for education in the poverty- and riot-stricken areas. The LEARN publication urged members not to "overlook the urgency of re-invigorating our only real hope for the future [in] the understandable rush to rebuild Los Angeles." Bernstein pointed out that none of the rioters had targeted schools, even though everyone knows that they have valuable computer equipment. Roos kept up his hard-paced speaking schedule, and the LEARN publication, *Action Update*, kept urging task force members to attend meetings. The group that was of greatest concern to core LEARN members was the Council of Trustees, whose members were expected to provide donations and links to other donors or participants. By June 1992, the LEARN Council of Trustees was more than 600 strong, and participation did not substantially decline as the plan, *For All Our Children*, was drafted.[31]

CHAPTER 6

LEARN

Auditions of Large-Scale Change

After the euphoria of spring 1993, when the LEARN plan was approved, the reality of implementation set in. During the summer and fall, the first cohort of schools was selected to participate, and LEARN made the transition from being an organization designed to rally support for change and manufacture consent by the school board to one that had to see the plan through. This implementation narrative illustrates how radical the LEARN reform was, how deeply it cut against the grain of a vertically integrated bureaucracy and, therefore, the extent to which it was resisted. Even though the ideas embodied in LEARN had grown from reform plans developed within the District, the auditioning of those ideas through LEARN demonstrated a lack of will and underscored the fact that the capacity of the District had been hollowed out.

In adopting LEARN, the school board pledged to create a decentralized network as a form of organization in place of its well-established command and control hierarchy. Not everyone applauded this move. The natural reaction was to hold fast to whatever powers remained and to condition reforms on their ability to fulfill the requirements of then-existing policies, labor agreements, and legal restrictions. Upper-level administrators, in particular, saw LEARN as an improper coalition of the teacher's union and the business elite against professional educators and an elected school board. The tendency to delegitimate professional leadership of education, which had first been seen decades earlier, continued even as the business people who dominated the LEARN Working Group advocated take-charge leadership.

107

"SID, I'M GONNA MAKE YOU A STAR"

Perhaps no incident in the seven-year run of the reform programs better illustrates the transition from old institutional form to new than a conversation between Superintendent Sidney Thompson and LEARN president Mike Roos. In separate interviews, each tells essentially the same story. Roos, in one of his many meetings with the superintendent, says, "Sid, do you understand if you do this deal right you could be on the cover of *Time* magazine, then on every poll you would be a leading candidate for mayor?" To Roos, a politician to the core, there could be no greater aphrodisiac than fame or the rush of visibility that comes with leading a movement. Thompson, a career civil servant who rose from the ranks of teacher to become superintendent, was horrified. Roos recalls Thompson responding, "Why would I want to be on the cover of *Time* magazine? It's the last thing . . ."[1]

The difference between the two was more than style, although there was that. Roos is brash and public, always dressed in elegant whiter-than-white shirts, power ties, and tasseled loafers. Thompson, who was the District's first African American superintendent, is quiet and self-effacing, his rumpled demeanor cloaking what an associate called "an organizational street fighter." Each has powers that work in different places. Roos, who was an All American baseball player at Tulane, where he graduated with a degree in political science, excelled at the initiating phase of politics. Thompson, who graduated from the Merchant Marine Academy, understood that the District was beset with external forces and saw his job as moderating their influences enough so that work could continue to get done. "We spent a lot of time reacting," Thompson said. During a period of time when the District was being sued about something virtually every day, he said that one of his operating goals was "to keep the lawyers out of the schools, away from the principals and teachers."[2]

A legislative style and logic permeated LEARN. Roos, who was fifty-three when he stepped down from the LEARN presidency, had been in politics all his adult life. He began as the director of the Coro Foundation, which trains future political leaders, and served as an aide to a city council member before running for the State Assembly in 1977. He rose rapidly through the Democratic ranks, becoming majority leader in 1980 and Speaker pro tempore in 1986, a political ally of the formidable Assembly Speaker Willie Brown.[3]

The logic of control and stability had been part of Thompson's working life since he came to the District in 1956 as a math teacher hired on an emergency credential because there was a teacher shortage.[4] "I had a sense that there was an order, that there was a control, it was predictable. And of course, we all dressed and wore ties and all of that. They didn't relinquish [this attire] until the temperatures went to 100 degrees in the Valley, and then all of a sudden, 'Okay, now you can wear a sport shirt.' But it was ordered. And there was a certain security in that order." The order had disappeared by the 1970s, and he remembered getting a call from the principal at Jefferson High School. "When I picked up the phone, he said, 'Fort Crenshaw, this is Fort Jefferson. How are you doing?'" Thompson repeated the interchange at a public meeting, and it made headlines: "Principal Calls School Fort." "Some of my teachers were very upset," Thompson said, "but others were saying, 'The truth's the truth.'"[5]

Thompson became interim superintendent in 1992 after William Anton, who had negotiated the LEARN agreement, resigned saying that he could no longer abide the school board's micromanagement. Thompson's appointment was subject to intense racially aligned bargaining between black and Latino advocates, the latter favoring the associate superintendent, Ruben Zacarias. A newspaper report at the time of his appointment said, "Thompson's main strength, which is the ability to build consensus among diverse and at times warring groups, is the quality needed most in a superintendent at this time."[6] Thompson vowed to fully implement the LEARN reform plan to bring more decisionmaking to school sites. "And he said he intends to use the recommendations in a recent management audit, which sharply criticized inefficient district operations, to clean house at district headquarters."[7]

Roos and Thompson were to be bound together by LEARN in one of history's more interesting working relationships. Thompson's direct involvement with LEARN, rather than delegating the duty to a deputy, was seen as having a major influence over the internal perception that LEARN was important.[8] Their first task was to make it possible for LEARN to take place at all. In the months before the school board voted to adopt the plan, the District found itself in negotiations with its teacher's union while, at the same time, the recession drained coffers empty. Six months of negotiation ended in the spring of 1993 in what became known as "the Willie Brown deal," which vividly illustrates the demise of local control and the extremely complex nature of LAUSD's governance. Brown, Speaker of the California Assembly, was brought in to forge—and help pay for—a labor contract settlement that would make LEARN possible. The negotiations lasted for months and involved at least four levels of government and more than a dozen influential parties and organizations. The story is told here in some detail because it illustrates how far the District had come from the straightforward local control envisaged by the Progressives.

THE WILLIE BROWN DEAL

In the face of recession, UTLA had accepted a 3 percent cut for the 1991–92 school year with the promise that the District would repay it and make no further cuts. However, the District's budget deficits kept growing, and it was required by law to balance its budget. The potential for agreement on a contract was very slim, and teachers began the 1992–93 school year without one. The overriding concern for the school board and the District was insolvency and descent into receivership by either the county or state. The stated objective for the teachers union was to keep the gains they had won in the 1989 strike. Believing that the two sides could be brought together through objective evaluation by a third party, LEARN recruited former state attorney general John K. Van de Kamp "to delve into the District's finances and attempt to find an alternative to the deep teacher pay cuts." The commission's recommendations were sensible—incentive plans for student attendance, a reduction in use of teacher sick days, a 10 percent reduction in health insurance costs to the District, and a continuance of a districtwide hiring freeze—but the District and the union were not open to them.[9]

In October, with the funds running short, the school board began to feel the pressure of impending insolvency and felt it had to act. Under labor laws, employers are not allowed to cut wages after the contract year has started, which for the District is July 1, but the school board voted to cut all district employee wages by 9 percent for a total reduction of 12 percent from the 1990–91 school year. The union's reaction was swift. First, they organized a successful strike vote with 89 percent of teachers supporting a walkout on November 24 if pay cuts were not restored. Second, they obtained an injunction on the pay cuts. The school board countered by going to the California Board of Education to obtain a waiver to the labor law that forbade employers to cut wages after the contract year had started.[10]

In the midst of the negotiations, November 1992, Superintendent Anton resigned, and the board appointed Thompson to serve as interim superintendent. Continued negotiations and mediation were unsuccessful, and the

Public Employment Relations Board (PERB) got into the fray to decide the question of whether labor codes had been broken.[11]

Before the PERB hearing took place on January 19, the union once again held a successful strike vote, the District settled contracts with other unions with the caveat that they would be at parity with the teachers once the teachers' contract was settled, and San Fernando Valley–based state senator David A. Roberti began his campaign to break up the District in earnest by getting the Legislative Analyst's Office to write a state report on LAUSD's finances.[12]

Having failed to come to an agreement with a state mediator presiding, the District and the union searched for someone they both trusted to help them negotiate a contract. The one person they could agree on was Assembly Speaker Willie Brown, who had been reluctant to entangle himself in the conflict but was persuaded to by LEARN president Roos, Brown's political ally and protégé. Roos asked him, "As a favor would you come down and do this on your spare time, using your staff, and there's nothing I can give you. Nothing." Roos recalled, "I mean, here he is speaker of the Assembly, he's got plenty to do. He's flying down here every Saturday, pro bono. It's really the great untold story about what real leaders do." Brown had a target to shoot for. Earlier, UTLA president Helen Bernstein had called Roos saying, as he recalled, "Mike, if I can't get this pay-cut below ten percent, I gotta take them out."[13]

On January 12, 1993, district officials met with Brown in Sacramento to tell their side of the story. Two days later, union officials were given the same opportunity.[14] A speedy settlement of negotiations looked unlikely given the situation that both sides had created. While the school board made steps to fund an audit requested by Brown and the union, they had placed barriers to its actual timely commencement by voting to "conduct a public hearing on the selection of the firm." As for Brown's opinion on the matter, he believed that the mediation was moving "sluggishly" because of the "immense gulf between the two sides and their long history of hostility." He also dashed any hopes of a state bailout by stating "under no circumstances will state money be made available to end the stalemate." Two weeks later, he reported that there was continuing progress and that he had come up with a plan for both sides to review.[15] Thompson remembered,

> There was tremendous pressure for a settlement. Brown met with me and Helen behind closed doors. We agree on a settlement. Brown keeps draping his arm around me and calling me "Bro." At one point he does this and says,

"You are going to have to give up some power" [in exchange for the salary concessions]. We gave up assignment of teachers to specific duties. It isn't strictly seniority, but it isn't just the principal's unilateral decision either. It essentially made those decisions negotiable, in an informal way.[16]

Brown had announced the plan on February 20, three days before the scheduled teachers' strike. This gave the District some breathing room because it forced the union to take a vote on the proposed deal. The teachers did not have an easy decision to make. Brown had lowered the cut to 10 percent (a continuation of the previous fiscal year's 3 percent cut and an additional 7 percent for the current year) but was not able to get a promise that salaries would not be cut the next year. He also got the teachers power over grade assignments through seniority and other perks, such as being allowed to use photocopiers and other office equipment. The offer was not good enough to guarantee acceptance, but Bernstein felt that a strike would not be authorized.[15]

Even though teachers were extremely displeased with a 10 percent pay cut, they understood that this was probably the best offer they would get, and the majority accepted it. Others in the District were even more displeased with the results. The administrators' union criticized Thompson because it felt that the contract heavily favored teachers and worried about where the money would come from. Board members had similar concerns, and they were careful to only ratify the agreement in concept, whereas the teachers union had ratified it in full. This left the District some leeway in terms of repaying teachers and implementing the contract. LAUSD still had no idea where the money for the contract was to come from, and the auditing team it had hired had not yet completed its report. Brown appealed to newly inaugurated President Bill Clinton's economic and education advisers to provide aid to the school district, but it seemed that neither state nor federal assistance would be available. So by the second week of March, the contract for the 1992–93 year was still tentative, and the District began sending out layoff notices in order to balance the budget for the next school year.[18]

The approval of the LEARN plan by the school board on March 15 did nothing to ease the tensions between UTLA and the District over the contract negotiations. Despite Thompson, Brent, and Bernstein standing together before the board in order to get a unanimous vote on the LEARN plan, the two unions and the superintendent could not have been farther apart on their views regarding the Willie Brown contract. While UTLA had voted in favor of the contract, the school board and the Superintendent were adamant that the District could not afford the contract and that the state would have to loosen budget restrictions or fund the contract themselves. Without a dependable source of funds, the school board refused to consider finalizing the contract. Still, Brown declared after a closed-door session that the "contract settlement is all but finalized" and that he "hope[d] never to see any of them again."[19]

No matter what Brown had hoped, his duty as a negotiator was not over. UTLA requested his assistance two weeks later to make the school board vote on the contract. Brown sent telegrams stating that the board must vote to ratify the contract on April 5. School officials responded by noting that the contract was not on the agenda for that meeting, and board member Roberta Weintraub said that they "can't approve a deal yet because there isn't money to pay for it." This exchange was preceded by the preparation for widespread layoffs and educational cuts in the District due to the projected $137 million budget deficit. The potential contract had also prompted county officials to block approval because of fears that it would bankrupt LAUSD.[20]

With the District's credit rating and financial stability at risk, Thompson fired back at Brown. Thompson wrote an open letter to the Speaker asking for him to "make good on his promise to waive or change state law to help the District fund the deal." Brown's spokeswoman said that he had never promised to help fund the deal and that the District did not need his help anyway. Thompson insisted in his letter that he and other district officials had understood that Brown "was to identify and secure new sources of funding which would permit a salary adjustment without rendering the District insolvent." Brown's angry reaction revealed that more than school politics was at stake here. He was clearly displeased with the District and accused them of playing politics with Republican governor Pete Wilson and his secretary of education.[21]

Governor Wilson was unhappy with the Brown contract as well, feeling that it was in conflict with LEARN and his recently signed charter legislation. Like most Republicans, Wilson wanted parents to have more control over their children's schooling and more efficient schools. The Brown contract was seen as a concession to unions and a roadblock to the restructuring of the school district. He also supported the District's claim that the approval of the state board of education was necessary to finalize funding for the deal.[22]

Thompson finally relieved the stalemate by presenting the contract for a ten-day public review period. After that, the L.A. County superintendent of education, Stuart E. Gothold, would decide the financial soundness of the plan. Gothold questioned the District's ability to handle emergencies with only $6 million in reserve out of a budget that approached $7 billion. He also felt that the Speaker's deal would bankrupt the District. The Howard Jarvis Taxpayers Association also worried about that possibility and won an injunction against the school district delaying adoption of the contract. The judge agreed that the District could not accept the contract without contingency language. The District was therefore barred from approving the contract unless it included language making payment to teachers contingent on adequate funding. This led to the renewal of the threat of a teachers strike. By the third week of April, the negotiations seemed to be back to square one.[23]

There were, however, others besides Brown, the District, and the county working on a solution to the funding problem. One of Brown's assistants, Rick Simpson, noticed that the District had not applied for all of the grants they qualified for. Brown discussed the matter with State Controller Gray Davis, who agreed to release funds to the District if they applied for the grants. These grants were from the 1991–92 fiscal year and were meant to help defray the costs associated with busing for desegregation. The District had originally failed to qualify because it was unable to raise the $6.4 million in matching funds. Yet, Davis was committed to "assist the District in any legal way possible in recovering money to which they're entitled." It would just take a little time to decide how much that was.[24]

The promise of money from state grants was not enough to stop UTLA's progress toward a strike. Bernstein criticized the District for "dragging their feet in seeking the additional funds" and said that "if they had spent half the amount of energy on getting the money that they spent on trying to undo the contract and change the language, we'd have avoided this court process and all the pain it is inflicting on teachers." The union then set a strike vote for the week of April 26 to decide whether or not they would strike on May 7 if there was no ratified contract. The union's board of directors had recommended that the teachers go on strike instead of reopening negotiations with the District.[25]

The week of the strike vote, Davis revealed that the District had submitted claims for $55 to $65 million in desegregation money. On Monday he told reporters that he expected to release between $25 to $35 million. By Tuesday he had cut a check for $35 million and presented it to the District. Two days later the ballots for the strike vote were counted, and 83 percent of the union voted in favor of the strike. Six days before the planned walkout, the last obstacle to the ratification of the contract was removed when the Howard Jarvis Taxpayers Association dropped its objection to the contract. The union ratified it on May 3, and the board ratified it later that month. The struggle over the 1992–93 contract was over, and the 1993–94 negotiations would soon commence.[26]

So, the launch of LEARN coincided with the teachers taking a 10 percent salary cut, the administrators being unhappy because they thought the teachers broke the bank and impinged on administrative prerogatives, and the school board resenting outside interference. The intervention of educators and politicians over a six-month period only prevented what would have surely been a destructive strike. None of this effort directly advanced education or its reform. It just kept the District going along.

ORGANIZED SUPPORT AND OPPOSITION

The adoption of LEARN and the contract settlement were greeted by both support and opposition. Thirty days after the LAUSD board approved the program in March 1993, a headline proclaimed, "100 Schools Flood District with LEARN Applications." "What this demonstrates to me is that we have many committed school families—parents, administrators and teachers— who sincerely care about restructuring their schools," said assistant superintendent Maria Casillas. "In this atmosphere where everybody is upset with everybody, we still have schools eager to take this risk."[27]

Yet, at the same time, frustration with the salary cutbacks mingled with organized opposition to LEARN. Frustrated teachers at San Fernando High School lashed out at LEARN vice president Mary Chambers, who had been dispatched to persuade a reluctant faculty to participate. The faculty had voted against participating, but the principal called them to a mandatory meeting to provide more information about LEARN. The teachers were furious about the pay cuts and in no mood to volunteer for anything. "We have just been raped and now we're being asked to kiss the rapist," said Sheila Roth, the English department chair.[28] When the first LEARN cohort was created, San Fernando was not among them, and neither was any other senior high school.

The confrontation at San Fernando signaled a much greater divide among teachers. Former teacher union president Wayne Johnson became an implacable foe. UTLA had always had a bloody-minded left wing, and the image of

Helen Bernstein being friendly with Riordan—who personified white male capitalism—fueled distrust. "I think that there was a major attempt on the part of LEARN to reduce teachers' power," Johnson said.[29] By the end of April, "Stop LEARN Now" flyers were being distributed from Garfield High School headed by a quote from Johnson saying, "LEARN will destroy the union and set back teacher rights 25 years."[30] In April 1993, the UTLA House of Representatives voted to withhold support of LEARN by a 2 to 1 margin.[31] Undeterred, Bernstein pressed ahead to recruit schools.

LEARN was also distanced from the heavily Latino schools on the Eastside. Despite the hundreds of organizing meetings held throughout the city as *For All Our Children* was being put together, the perception remained among some sources that LEARN was a movement from the outside, "created by rich, white men who never got input from the grassroots." The LEARN leaders were seen as "racist" ("They don't understand our kids") and as only getting input from the "PTA types."

Vouchers

The school board embraced LEARN in part because it was afraid of something more radical. It was most immediately worried about financial insolvency that would bring on a takeover of the District by the state or county. Following that, it feared legislative or ballot initiative efforts to pass a voucher plan and efforts to break up the District. "With vouchers a year away, we really don't have a choice," said board president Leticia Quezada. "We have one year to prove the L.A. district is really interested in changing itself, revamping itself." LEARN was seen as the last best hope for the District. Quezada said, "If we fail at this, I think all hope will be lost."[32] During LEARN's first summer, education writer Stephanie Chavez framed the issue: "If the LEARN plan succeeds it would offer a national model on how an urban school system can turn itself around. If the experiment fails, it will bolster what critics say is the impossibility of meaningful reform in a giant bureaucracy."[33]

While LEARN required a broad political base, and succeeded in creating one, it failed to create a monopoly on reform efforts in the District or a political umbrella large enough to cover all. Both vouchers and breakup efforts were active in the early 1990s, and they continue in the twenty-first century.

In 1993, Joe Alibrandi, the businessman who had cochaired Kids 1st and was a participant in early LEARN planning, broke ranks with those advocating internal reforms to spearhead a voucher initiative. Proposition 174 would have provided a $2,500 state payment for nearly any student attending a private school in the state. There were some, but few, restrictions. The open-ended, free market approach narrowed the coalition favoring the initiative, and some long-standing voucher advocates, such as UC Berkeley law professors Jack Coons and Steven Sugermann, disassociated themselves. More importantly, few of the state's large businesses joined in support. The California Business Roundtable, which had been a mainstay of support for Ronald Reagan, declared neutrality over the measure. Governor Wilson ultimately opposed the measure. At the end of a lackluster campaign, the initiative was badly defeated. Voucher advocates raised about $3.5 million for their campaign; opponents raised $16 million, about 70 percent coming from the California Teachers Association.

The voucher challenge emerged again in 2000. This time it was backed by Silicon Valley venture capitalist Timothy Draper, who announced his willingness to spend $20 million of his own money on the initiative. He had few allies. In addition to predictable opposition from teacher unions and school administrators, both the governor and lieutenant governor strongly opposed the measure. Even the arch-conservative Howard Jarvis Taxpayers Association announced its opposition.[34] On election day, the initiative fared even worse than its 1993 predecessor, and the prospects for vouchers in California seemed to have ended once and for all.

Breakup

There have been periodic unsuccessful efforts to break up the Los Angeles Unified School District dating back to the 1950s. After nearly twenty years of silence, the idea resurfaced in the early 1990s.

In September 1993, just six months after LEARN was approved, two San Fernando Valley–based members of the State Assembly attempted to bring forward two proposals aimed at breaking up LAUSD. Assemblyman Richard Katz, a Democrat from Panorama City, tried to insert a breakup proposal by Senate president pro tem David Roberti, a Democrat from Van Nuys, into legislation already being considered by the full Assembly. Assembly Speaker Brown effectively killed Roberti's proposal by refusing to allow a floor vote and bottling the bill up in the Assembly Education Committee.

The next day, Brown ordered a similar bill by Assemblywoman Paula Boland, a Republican from Granada Hills, sent to the Assembly Education Committee, which then rejected the bill 11 to 5. Boland's bill would have reduced the number of voter signatures required to put a school breakup measure on the ballot.[35]

There were several more attempts to introduce bills aimed at facilitating the breakup of LAUSD during subsequent legislative sessions. Supporters of the effort finally achieved victory in August 1995, when Governor Wilson signed two companion bills into law. Assembly Bill 107, sponsored by Boland, lowered the threshold of signatures needed to get a breakup initiative on the ballot, removed the Los Angeles Board of Education's veto power over breakup legislation, and lowered the required number of signatures in an area that wishes to create its own district from 25 percent of registered voters to 8 percent of area voters who cast votes in the last gubernatorial election—less than 4 percent of registered voters.[36]

By the late 1990s, spurred in part by this legislation, calls for breaking up LAUSD became more pronounced and less singly identified with conservative forces in the San Fernando Valley, although those forces remained. Organizations were also formed to explore withdrawal in South Central L.A. and the Carson area on the far south side. Though it still lacks a powerful supportive coalition, the notion remains attractive to many.

The Civic Coalition Holds

Through all the disturbance, the civic coalition that fostered LEARN held together. The *Los Angeles Times* continued to support LEARN editorially, and the paper had developed a significant capacity to cover education.

In July 1993, the *Times* editorialized in favor of LEARN. The editorial referenced a new report from RAND which indicated that public schools were failing to educate immigrant children, and the newspaper stated that the report "should serve as further impetus for the important local reform effort lead by LEARN."[37] In August, LEARN was cited as one of the ten reasons that "things are getting better in L.A." in the aftermath of the riots, and education reform was given as an example that the "current period may be remembered by historians less for the economic recession than for the extraordinary period of civic rebirth."[38]

JUDY BURTON AND THE LEARN OFFICE

In May 1993, the board of education approved thirty-four schools to form the first LEARN cohort.[39] But there were no high schools in the group. The

LEARN idea that schools would enter the program in clusters of high schools and their feeder elementary and middle schools was defeated by the voluntary nature of the plan and the opposition to the program that was most pronounced at the high schools. Moreover, the schools ringed the central city, and relatively more schools from affluent areas participated.

The District established an office for LEARN implementation and staffed it with a director and one secretary. Maria Casillas, who was later to head the LAAMP effort, headed the office for a few months before taking an administrative position in Texas. The heavy mantle of implementing the reform program fell to Judy Burton, whose name was to become synonymous with reform efforts within LAUSD in the 1990s. She was an experienced teacher who had risen through the administrative ranks from bilingual adviser to principal when she became involved in reform efforts.

The LEARN office, which was charged with coordinating LAUSD's response to the reform plan, still had only Burton and one secretary. Even at its largest—when the office was charged with implementing LEARN, LAAMP, federal comprehensive school reform legislation, and charter school legislation— the office never had more than eight professionals and three secretaries. In the spring of 1993, however, the task was just to make operational sense out of LEARN. As Burton and LEARN vice president Mary Chambers visited the schools that had applied, they found that "there was a good deal of dissension where teachers felt they had made the decision [to join] and principals decided they didn't want to do it. . . . There were parents who wanted it but couldn't get the teachers and principals to do it."[40] A lot happened before the celebration of accepting the first cohort of schools into LEARN.

The District established seven committees, each charged with implementing the recommendations of one of the LEARN task forces. Burton headed several of them, and others were chaired by other high-level central office staff members.

"Those Will Take a Long Time to Pick Up"

Shortly after LEARN was adopted, the District reorganized itself into clusters with the intent of decentralizing. LEARN and the cluster system were supposed to be compatible, but they were not. The cluster leaders had not been part of LEARN planning, and they were new to their jobs and trying to consolidate their positions. "I think with the cluster leaders, though, the conflict is the same as the conflict or discomfort we had with regional superintendents where they are constantly thinking of having a chunk of schools that is their domain of responsibility and authority, period. When that gets interrupted, that's a major shift in the way people do business. That doesn't create a level of comfort, in some cases for schools as well," Burton said.[41]

Each LEARN school was assigned to a cluster, but they all reported to Burton as well. The goal was to allow them to engage "in the reform effort until there is a critical mass of schools operating in a different way" so they will be "freed up from the system and not contaminated" by it.[42] Despite the support of the superintendent and the school board president, there remained a great deal of uncertainty about, if not animosity toward, LEARN among many cluster leaders.

After the first cohort was announced, Burton met with the cluster leaders and explained that "the LEARN Working Group represents a political reality for all of us." She echoed a growing perception that "it operates almost as if it was another board of education." The Working Group was intent on creating a single reform for the District and on eliminating competing ideas; indeed, doing so was one of the agreements between Superintendent Anton and the group of leaders that formed LEARN. When Anton's successor Sid Thompson would attempt to explain the simultaneous cluster leader reorganization, the response, paraphrased by Burton, was, "Excuse me. LEARN is *the* reform going on" in LAUSD. She added that any time "the direction you might give is perceived as or is different from LEARN, you've got a problem."[43]

An observer at the meeting wrote, "Many of the leaders worried that policies at LEARN schools will prevent them from having any role in or control over the classrooms in their schools, which will in turn prevent them from setting up accountability schemes. They voiced frustration over the fact that many principals at LEARN schools bypass regular channels, and instead go to the Working Group to try to get what they want for their schools. The Working Group in turn goes straight to the superintendent's office, which completely leaves out the cluster leaders and other stakeholders."[44]

In addition, cluster leaders were evaluated on how many of their schools joined LEARN. Burton could remember no dismissals or demotions of cluster leaders for failure to recruit schools, "but if anyone said that they didn't like LEARN or didn't want to support it, you know, it became a problem."[45] Burton along with other top administrators also formally evaluated the performance of cluster leaders.

In organizational terms, LEARN had become an improper coalition where the top and bottom of an organization ganged up on the middle, and the cluster leaders were feeling very squeezed.[46] Cluster leaders had been only recently appointed and had not been part of the LEARN planning, and they had no working relationship with the LEARN Working Group.[47] Perhaps most galling in the low-trust environment that permeated the District was LEARN's association with Bernstein and UTLA. It was said that in LEARN schools, the union ran the place. However, this opinion was rendered only by administrators who had not been part of LEARN. Those who had participated generally said they simply had a good relationship with their union rep.

Many administrators expressed fears that they were being "sold short" by the Working Group and that they needed to be trusted more. "I don't even know if they understand what we're about," one said off the record. As LEARN continued to roll out, resentment toward it continued to build. As one high-ranking administrator remembered, "They understood it; they just didn't like it." Black and Latino administrators were particularly anti-LEARN. "LEARN was perceived as a movement from the outside, created by rich, white men who never got input from the grassroots." Another cluster administrator said the problem with LEARN was largely jealousy on the part of the principals and a feeling of not wanting to relinquish control on the part of the cluster leaders. Except in his cluster, where all the schools were LEARN members, each of the other administrators had clusters that were divided between the haves and the have-nots. Those schools that had joined LEARN got extra funds, and there was active jealousy between the schools that belonged and the schools that had chosen not to join. "Remember, at this time the school district was continually strapped for funds, and so the functions that were provided with the grant monies could not be replicated by the District."

Specialness bred resentment. "They'd come to cluster meetings all smug and open their [Macintosh] PowerBooks like they were members of a special club," an administrator recalled. PowerBooks also became a symbol of administrative dominance and garnered the mistrust of UTLA. Burton recalled, "And one of the first things we do is we give every school a PowerBook and provide some orientation training on how to use it, and we invite the principal and the chapter chair or lead teacher if it's a LEARN school to participate in the training. And with LEARN schools, if both can't come, it's no big deal. Either the chapter chair or the principal comes because they know that the goal is for them to work together." But when they began budget training for non-LEARN schools and sent out a notice saying that either the principal or chapter chair could pick up the laptop and participate in the training, the principals' resistance was so strong that the meeting had to be cancelled.

"You cannot give the PowerBook to the chapter chair; there is not that relationship that exists or any understanding of the need for a working relationship. So the meeting got cancelled until they can both come."[48]

The LEARN office became an outcast within the District administration. A story is told about a secretary from the office tripping in the hallway of the central administration building and spilling a huge pile of paper she had been transporting from the photocopier. No one came to her aid, and one passerby remarked nastily, "Those will take a long time to pick up."

Policy

Besides rebellious cluster leaders, LEARN was troubled by the District's web of rules and policy. As Burton reported, it was so policy driven that she found it difficult to accommodate differences among schools. "[A] district this size is basically run by rules, regulations, guidelines, board policies," she said. Changing policy was not easy. "It takes convincing the office that's in charge that the policy should be changed. It takes that unit of the department researching the impact of the change on the district as a whole, even if it's only implemented in a few schools—the LEARN schools—and then rewriting what the new policy will be. That's time consuming and requires, I guess, a certain amount of collaboration and ability to influence the thinking of others."[49]

It was thought that by the time half the schools had changed to the new mode of operation, the District's system would have changed too. "The system will have changed to allow for that flexibility, and many of those policies will have been tried with a group of main schools in a way that would allow us to expand it to other schools, because that's the way we do things in the District, rather than having to wait for schools to volunteer," Burton told an interviewer in the early days of LEARN.[50] But idea that budding change in the schools could move the central office proved erroneous.

Budgetary Decentralization

In adopting LEARN, the District promised to give schools control over 85 percent of their budgets. Budgetary control was both an incentive to join LEARN and the means through which schools would connect plans to reality. Despite this promise, the District failed to decentralize the budgets and, in so doing, fatally crippled the reform program. The District lacked either the will or the capacity to deliver budgetary autonomy. "It was both," said UCLA management professor William Ouchi. But both the District and LEARN worked very hard on the problem.

In March 1994, as the second cohort of schools was being recruited, Thompson told the schools that an entirely new budget system was being built and that "school stakeholders, not the central office," were the architects of the system.[51] Thompson had established a budget design task force under the direction of district chief financial officer Henry Jones to deal with both revenue allocation to schools and their ability to spend. LEARN also established its own budget task force, and in 1996 the two merged. There was wide representation from UTLA as well as other unions (SEIU and California State Employees Association), teachers, principals, and parents. McKinsey & Company served as advisers.[52] The Mexican American Legal Defense and Education Fund (MALDEF) also watched carefully, in part because a just-settled equity lawsuit depended on a budget system that could deliver equal dollars per student rather than allocating a certain number of teaching and staff positions to each school.[53]

Although there were pilot budget processes, a decentralized system never materialized. A member of the task force recalled:

> LEARN did not die because the District did not try to decentralize the budget. There were rigidities, but the reformers never understood the restrictions of categorical funding and how "all money wasn't really green." But the real problem in implementing LEARN in the fiscal sense is that operating the schools required the District to take funds from most larger schools and give it to smaller ones. We figured that about 750 students was the breakeven point for a school, although this varied by type of school. There were plenty of smaller schools . . . most elementary and special schools, all of the children's schools, and some of the smaller high schools. It was impossible politically to display the extent of the transfers from the so-called rich schools to the poor ones.[54]

To support LEARN, the District decided to continue to subsidize the small schools while moving to a per-pupil formula for LEARN schools, which gave them additional discretionary money, although not the 85 percent the reform plan called for. As more and more schools signed up for LEARN, the small school deficit increased.[55]

William Ouchi, who became LEARN chairman in 1996 when Robert Wycoff resigned, said that the consulting firms that had examined LAUSD financial operations testified that the "accounting systems were completely incapable of implementing a decentralized management system." They recommended that the District abandon its present system and build a new one.[56]

Both at that time and afterward, as the research for this book was under way, there were allegations that District administrators and the school board never intended to decentralize the budget, that they were being clever by feigning cooperation and devious in finding ways not to decentralize the money. However, no data and no on-the-record opinion willing to substantiate that point were found.

LEARN Cohorts

LEARN began as a strictly voluntary program. An application required the consensus of "all stakeholder groups"—parents, teachers, classified staff, administrators—and specifically a 75 percent positive vote from members of the UTLA bargaining unit. Bernstein had insisted on the supermajority approval to ensure that schools entering the program would have solid support.

The prospective LEARN schools had been promised control over their budgets, the curriculum, and a new day in which a community of professionals would run the schools instead of only the principals. To make the transition, LEARN invested heavily in training, and in July 1993 the first cohort of school leaders went to summer camp in the dorms at California State Polytechnic University, Pomona, thirty miles east of Los Angeles. The training, led by the Advanced Management Program (AMP) at UCLA, dealt with the craft skills necessary to run a semi-autonomous school, such as budgeting and putting together an educational plan, and they concentrated on the most difficult of them all: getting adults to work together as a team. "Teamwork is an entirely different way of thinking for them," said Dan Katzir, who directed the program and who would later head education ventures for the Broad Foundation. "This is about unlocking people from their old molds of behavior that have locked them in conflict," said Theodore Mitchell, the UCLA dean who was instrumental in guiding reform plans.[57]

One part of the AMP plan was to get the schools to form a cohesive unit internally, and the other was to get the whole cohort of schools to work with one another as a network of reforming schools within LAUSD. Each of the teams was given its state-of-the-art Macintosh PowerBook and training in how to use a new electronic mail utility that would link the reform pioneers and the budget software that would allow them to control their resources. "This is incredibly important," said Kay Price, a fifth grade teacher at Topanga Canyon Elementary School. "They can share success and failures."[58] "My friends, other principals, ask me: 'Are you crazy? All the pressure. All the work,'" said Claudia Fernandez, principal of San Fernando Elementary School. But she said the laptop computer had already made a dent in her paperwork, and she predicted that other principals would see that she had support in managing the school and they did not. "And they are going to want it, too."[59]

By and large she was right. Participation in LEARN grew in subsequent cohorts, and the training program continued. Some fifty-three new schools, including high schools, joined in 1994, and 101 additional schools joined in 1995. By the fall of 1995, Superintendent Thompson would declare, "We're over the hump."[60]

Early and Late Adopters

The decision that all schools would become part of LEARN clashed with the voluntary nature of the program and led to differences between the early adopters and later ones. The early adopters, as is typical, were true believers. Some of them, like Howard Lappin, the principal at Foshay Learning Center, ran toward the opportunity: "Part of my bent, and the reason for being able to work with teachers, was the more we got the District out of our hair, the better off we were." The teachers, he reported, were willing to be convinced because the school was going to be taken over by the state and the teachers were going to lose their jobs. When LEARN was announced, Lappin talked with his union representative, and they agreed that it would be a good idea. "None of us had a clue of what it meant, but I said to the faculty, 'If you get involved early, you're going to get the most out of it.'"[61]

This experience contrasted with that of schools that joined LEARN later. Evaluators of the fourth group of schools to join, in 1996, noted that "these schools were not basking in the glow of a new initiative. . . . Although each school chose to join, interviews suggest that the choice was not made quite freely. For example, some schools reported being under pressure from other schools in their vertical "cluster" so that the cluster might become a LAAMP family." Some reported community pressure to join what was perceived of as a successful reform movement. Some reported "strong encouragement" from cluster administrators. Many of the votes to join were very close, and several affirmative votes were reached only after several ballots.[62]

The Superintendent's Call to Action

"Over the hump" was a good thing, because the school board had created accountability goals for Thompson, including accelerating the number of LEARN schools so that by 1999 all schools in the District would be a part of the reform program.[63] In the fall of 1995, the school board asked for public comment on the *Superintendent's Call to Action for Improving Student Achievement 1995–2000*. It appeared to integrate LEARN into the standard operating procedures of the District. By November 1995, a "planner" was to be submitted to all non-LEARN schools so that "each school [would] submit a timeline and strategies it will use to come to consensus on commitment to implement LEARN reform principles." Accountability for LEARN schools was to be transferred to cluster leaders, and they were to support and implement the program.[64] The goals were incorporated into Thompson's employment contract and were supposed to be applied to all administrators in the District.

For what appears to be the first time, the District was setting performance standards for all students, and it was doing so three years before California adopted standards and seven years before the federal NCLB Act. The goals were wildly ambitious—test scores would be above the national average by 2000, for example—and most have not been achieved.[65]

CHAPTER 7

LAAMP

Enter Walter Annenberg

In December 1993, just nine months after LEARN was approved, publisher Walter Annenberg announced a gift of $500 million to public education. At a White House ceremony he spoke of violence in schools, but his gift had a broader sweep.[1] Education was the glue that held society together, he believed, and without it we would go back to the Dark Ages. "I wanted to startle our leaders and public and get their attention. I wanted to elevate precollegiate education as a national priority. To do that I felt that I had to drop a bomb."[2] He had used the same strategy in 1990 when he gave $50 million to the United Negro College Fund, by far the largest gift the organization had received and one that was intended as a challenge for them to raise $200 million more.[3] If his goal in making the 1993 gift was to shine a bright light on public education, it did. The challenge generated more than $600 million in matching grants and thus targeted more than $1.1 billion for education reform.

The Annenberg Challenge, in Los Angeles and elsewhere, was panned in many quarters. Conservative friends of Annenberg told him that he had made a mistake, and many writers about philanthropy agreed.[4] Clearly, if the goal of the Challenge was large-scale change in public school systems within a few years, the Challenge was not successful. But the lessons of history have not yet been written. If it is true that public education as an institution is in the midst of historic change, then Annenberg's gift fueled continued attention to education reform and played a major part in keeping the politics of change moving forward. It balanced the libertarian wing of Annenberg's own political party with some very old Progressive Era, American, patriotic notions about caring and responsibility for the less privileged and a belief that none of us thrives while the next generation of children founders.

The announcement was initially received with ambivalence in Los Angeles. With LEARN and a variety of other reforms already established, people wondered whether the city needed an additional reform program, particularly one from out of town. However, when Annenberg's personal friend and adviser, Vartan Gregorian, called University of Southern California (USC) president Steven Sample to ask if Los Angeles would be interested in participating in the Annenberg Challenge, the answer was "yes."

Gregorian, then the president of Brown University, articulated an Annenberg Challenge vision of a public-private collaboration that was consistent with the city's recent history of educational reform. In addition, the ideas of Theodore Sizer, head of the Annenberg Institute and founder of the Coalition of Essential Schools, about school autonomy fit well with broadly accepted ideas about reform in Los Angeles. The Annenberg Challenge also carried advantages not lost on local reformers: linkages to a visible national network and, of course, badly needed financial resources.

Sample assured Gregorian that Los Angeles would indeed be interested, and the effort to form the Los Angeles Annenberg Metropolitan Project began. Several local civic leaders, including some LEARN Working Group members, began the work needed to acquire an Annenberg grant.[5] Although this group was initially led by Sample, he quickly handed leadership to Virgil Roberts, a longstanding school reform activist. One of Sample's concerns was that the LAAMP board be more reflective of the city's diverse racial and ethnic population and that its representation expand beyond what was called the "downtown business elite," even though much of the city's businesses had long before moved from downtown. Roberts, an African American who had a history as a civil rights attorney, previously worked with the Los Angeles Educational Partnership and LEARN. As his first main task, Roberts helped develop a broad-based board to develop and submit a proposal.

The initial idea was to get LAAMP to work hand-in-glove with the existing LEARN project, and, using a phrase that was repeated countless times by LAAMP participants, take existing reforms and "go broader and deeper." One of the initial LEARN ideas that had largely gone unrealized was creating groups or clusters of schools that would operate together so that school autonomy would be joined with a decentralized operating system. So, the proposal designers built the LAAMP plan around what they called "school families," each comprised of a high school and its feeder schools.

The School Family idea was thought compatible with both LEARN's autonomous schools idea and a decentralization plan that the District was adopting. Under the District plan, administrative authority was to be divided into clusters, and substantial operating authority would be granted the cluster leaders. The LAAMP proposal was drafted primarily by Theodore Mitchell, dean of the School of Education at UCLA and his counterpart at USC, Guilbert Hentschke. In December 1994, the Annenberg Foundation announced a $53 million grant to LAAMP that would be matched locally. LAAMP was successful in raising funds, and a total of $103 million was spent over the next five years.

Originally LAAMP was conceived as a way to continue LEARN's work, and indeed LEARN was badly in need of money. The school district itself had never made the financial commitments originally anticipated, and sources of private funding were on the wane. But LAAMP turned out differently.

Three pivotal decisions about the scope of LAAMP—each taken at the strong urging of Sizer and Gregorian at the Annenberg Foundation but with active agreement from the reform players in Los Angeles—stand out as especially important. First, the initial leaders agreed to form a new school reform organization in Los Angeles instead of building on or continuing the work of an existing organization or group. Affiliating with local universities was an available option, particularly because several of the early organizers of the LAAMP effort came from USC and UCLA. Or it could have worked through LEARN. But the Annenberg Foundation had a vision that in many ways extended beyond the scope of LEARN, so they declined to merge the two projects. This decision gave LAAMP the advantages of relative autonomy and a fresh start, but it also substantially delayed implementation of the LAAMP plan because the organization had to spend the time to develop its own board, staff, and program.

In a related decision, LAAMP's early leaders agreed with the Annenberg Foundation that LAAMP would be a metropolitan project. That is, it would invite participation not only from within LAUSD but also from other school districts in Los Angeles County. Indeed, the first headquarters of the new organization was at the Los Angeles County Office of Education in Downey, sixteen miles from downtown L.A. The metropolitan decision recognized both an ideal and a political reality. Increasing numbers of suburban school districts in the region faced "urban school" problems, such as poverty, low achievement, high student transience and attrition, overcrowding, and loss of coherence. More specifically, suburban districts in the Los Angeles region share many of each other's challenges, particularly those associated with great diversity, high proportions of immigrants, and many limited- or low-proficiency English speaking students. By working with a reform effort that spanned the Los Angeles metropolitan area, districts would gain opportunities to learn from each other's ideas and experiences. The political reality was that Sizer's Coalition of Essential Schools already had strong working relationships with several suburban Los Angeles districts, particularly Pasadena and Santa Monica, and that there was fear about putting all the Annenberg golden eggs in the L.A. Unified basket. The metropolitan decision gave LAAMP great sweep, and there were ideas that crossed district boundaries, but it posed substantial organizational problems to the new organization, which found itself an intermediary between the Foundation and fifteen school districts.

A third organizing decision made early on had equally powerful consequences. LAAMP's leaders decided to exclude representatives from the educational establishment, particularly teacher unions and school district administrators, from its board of directors. This marked a sharp departure from LEARN and the 1989 District-developed plan. For the first time, the school district faced a reform agenda almost entirely crafted by outside agents.

MARIA CASILLAS NAMED TO HEAD LAAMP

The LAAMP board cemented its decision to be independent of LEARN when it chose Maria Casillas instead of Helen Bernstein as LAAMP's president. Bernstein, who had served the two terms allowable as president of UTLA, had been at the forefront of school reform efforts in Los Angeles and had shown great ability by leading the teacher union to embrace LEARN. She wanted the job, and Mike Roos wanted her to have it: "It was a very, very sad day for me, because my friend didn't get what I knew she really wanted—she really wanted to do this." The skids were sufficiently greased that Casillas recalls seeing an early LAAMP document in which Bernstein's name was penciled in as president. Recollections vary about why this did not come about. Some say flatly that a union leader was unacceptable to the more conservative members of the LAAMP board, and others say that Bernstein's interview with the board was a disappointment. Roos recalled that "she was double-crossed," that board members who told her they would support her candidacy did not. (He declined to name names.)[6]

Casillas was a near-legendary fixture within the District. She had participated in the two District comprehensive plans of the 1980s, and the LEARN proposal opens with a poem she wrote. She had been a LAUSD teacher, a school principal, and the assistant superintendent in charge of the LEARN office before leaving in 1993 to spend two years as an administrator in El Paso, Texas. In a newspaper interview shortly after her appointment, Casillas characterized herself as a "humble servant from El Paso," yet "one who is comfortable in corporate boardrooms as well as classrooms."[7] Thus, in 1995, she had re-created herself as an outsider and was more than somewhat critical of the school district.

Eventually, LAAMP funded twenty-eight School Families, half in Los Angeles and half in other districts. However, LAUSD's share of LAAMP funds was allocated in a lump sum to the District instead of being allocated to individual School Families. The first $5 million was earmarked to support LEARN training. Thus, LAAMP provided the established reform program with much-needed cash.

CONTRACTING IN, CONTRACTING OUT

LAAMP and LEARN differed sharply in their approaches to influencing the District to take reform steps. LEARN sought to build an unbeatable political coalition, manufacture consent by the school board, and jawbone the administration into following through. In contrast, LAAMP negotiated a Memorandum of Understanding (MOU) with the District in 1995, a quasi-contract in which LAUSD agreed to specific reforms in exchange for LAAMP funds. Disbursements were to be made quarterly, and LAAMP retained the right to terminate the agreement if the District failed to perform.[8] This essentially made LAAMP a "high profile, categorical grants program," said Guilbert Hentschke.

In the MOU, the District agreed to spend specified amounts in support of reform, $8.8 million in the first year. It agreed to make public annual reports and to undertake a comprehensive evaluation of its reform activities. Significantly, the District agreed to extend and revise the student database in order to provide needed information.[9]

Roos thought that LAAMP's MOU approach revealed that organization's discomfort with political solutions.

> I just can't get over—I'll always have a hard time getting over—how uncomfortable people feel with in-your-face politics. And to me, that becomes the great difference between LAAMP and LEARN. They really falsely believed—because I know how much we pounded them, and would threaten them, and love them, and cajole them, and do whatever it took—that you could effectuate change by memoranda of understanding. "If the school district signed it, they must be okay!"[10]

In fact, the contracting idea was being widely used in the corporate sector and was the centerpiece of a 1997 book on "reinventing" public education.[11] Among those who had experience contracting with LAUSD, it was generally agreed that the District was not very adept at working with outside contractors. It was hard to get them to reach an agreement, and they were slow to pay. One of the ideas behind the MOU was to institutionalize the contracting relationship.

How LAAMP Spent Its Money

Some $42 million—approximately 52 percent of its total expenses—went to fund LAAMP's twenty-eight School Families.[12] The Design for Excellence: Linking Teaching and Achievement (DELTA) teacher education initiative spent about $10 million (about 13 percent of the total), and the parent involvement initiative spent about $4.9 million (6 percent). The technology initiative spent approximately $1.8 million (2.3 percent), while LAAMP's public engagement and community involvement efforts amounted to about $1.2 million (2 percent). Its efforts to gather and report data accounted for $2.6 million (3.3 percent, nearly all which went to support the Los Angeles Compact on Evaluation run by USC and UCLA). Program implementation totaled approximately $4.7 million (8 percent), and administration costs were approximately $6.3 million (8.1 percent). Other expenses accounted for about 6 percent.

Under the terms of the grant, LAAMP was required to match Annenberg's $53 million with local contributions. It raised $26.8 million from the private sector and counted $26.8 in public-sector contributions. In reality, local public funds allocated toward LAAMP projects were much larger. LAAMP staff only certified as matching funds those monies that passed the rigorous

Annenberg Foundation audit requirements. In part because the audit costs were relatively high, the LAAMP staff certified only enough matching money needed to meet the terms of the fiscal challenge.

The sources of private matching funds were concentrated. The Weingart Foundation, led by former Lockheed CEO and LEARN Working Group chairman Roy Anderson, dwarfed all others by contributing more than $13 million to the project. As noted below, Weingart joined the Ford Foundation and the California State University system as the principal supporters of the DELTA Initiative, which Weingart funded at $8.3 million. Weingart was also the principal source of funds for the Parents as Learning Partners (PLP) program, at nearly $5 million. The Ford Foundation was the second-largest private contributor to LAAMP, giving $2.3 million for DELTA and other projects. After that, the scale of contributions drops off rather dramatically: The ARCO Foundation gave $808,000, the Mattel Foundation $135,000, the California Community Foundation $134,000, and Bank of America $105,000. No other donor neared the $100,000 mark. (The Stuart Foundation also awarded a $600,000 grant to UCLA to extend the evaluation work of the Los Angeles Consortium for Evaluation, known as LACE, but these funds did not pass through LAAMP.) To put the LAAMP program in perspective, the $103 million raised and spent by the program in its five years is nearly trivial in Los Angeles County, where more than $13 billion is spent each year on K–12 education.

LEARN and LAAMP Operations

LEARN operated with a tiny staff: president Mike Roos, vice president Mary Chambers, and a couple of assistants. "It was really the Wizard of Oz—don't pull back the curtain," said Roos. Because of its small staff, it relied entirely on the District to implement the nine planks in the plan. But LEARN exerted most of its influence at the very top of the system through Thompson, as superintendent, and through training of principals and school-based teams. Mark Slavkin, who was school board president during the first implementation year, believes that the reform organization lost influence by not keeping the large civic coalition together to amass public support for implementation.[13] The small staff approach also meant that LEARN could not aggressively monitor the development of its whole program, and in the end it was perceived largely as a training program rather than a systemic reform.[14]

Conversely, LAAMP grew to a staff of about forty and provided substantial direct service to the School Families it set up. Over the seven years of its existence, LAAMP awarded $77.7 million in grants. The remainder of its $103 million program came in the form of matching grants from the recipient districts. LAUSD got $21 million plus an additional $5 million to intensify work in the North Hollywood School Family.

Parents and Community

In the 1980s and early 1990s, parent involvement in children's learning both at school and at home became a key component of school reform programs, and indeed of education policy at the local, state, and national levels.[15] A body of research had begun to emerge demonstrating a positive relationship between parent involvement and improved academic achievement for students and schools.[16] In particular, some studies noted a positive relationship between parent involvement and the academic achievement of low-income, minority students.[17] In time, some of this academic research made its way into the popular press, including publications such as *Scientific American,* the *Wall Street Journal,* and *Investor's Business Daily,* and references to these articles were found among the materials in the LEARN archives.[18]

While previous school reform plans had given lip service to parent involvement, both LEARN and LAAMP envisioned an important role for parents in the education of their children. Taken together, these initiatives attempted to empower and involve parents as partners, as advocates, and as educators. Although the two efforts varied as to how they defined and structured the role of parents and the degree to which they were successful, both ultimately left a legacy of parent involvement that is still in evidence today.

The LEARN plan emphasized the role of parents as partners in the education of their children. A parent involvement plan was listed as a key component of each school's education plan, and the role of parents figured prominently in the areas of governance and accountability. An annual school report card was to be prepared and an annual stakeholder survey administered to determine "client satisfaction" (including parents)—both ideas that are being utilized today by some charter schools.

The LEARN plan also called for the provision of training, education, and "ongoing support for organizing parents into an effective advocacy group for child welfare and quality schools."[19] However, there is little evidence that LEARN resulted in increased advocacy. Rather, LEARN organized parents to support its plan, and site action plans included parents in school decisionmaking.

An external evaluation of the LEARN planning and implementation processes conducted by the Evaluation and Training Institute (ETI), noted that "LEARN encourages school site personnel to make a concentrated effort to involve parents as equal partners in decision-making. Rather than acting as an advisory group, parents have ample opportunities to work with school staff in making key decisions about budget allocations, staff selection, professional development, etc."[20]

While the LEARN plan emphasized parental involvement in decisionmaking, LAAMP's approach to fostering parent involvement was more program driven.[21] Although parental involvement was to become one of the three strategic initiatives undertaken by LAAMP, some LAAMP board members and staff recounted that explicitly including parental involvement in LAAMP was initially a hard sell for most of the board and that, for the most part, parent and community involvement was "not on their radar screen."[22]

As Ruth Yoon, director of parent involvement initiatives for LAAMP, recounted, a group of LAAMP board members (predominantly female and mostly Latino) had to insist on making parent involvement a priority: "They said 'Your school reform is not going to happen without parents.' And so they pushed it. But it was not a popular notion."[23]

Given the initial lack of enthusiasm, it is not surprising then that LAAMP School Families were not required to include a parent involvement component in their learning plans. Yoon said that it was more of an unwritten expectation: "We couldn't make it say it's a requirement because when you look at the LAAMP proposal, nowhere does it say you shall have a parent involvement action team or anything like that or even a component." Nonetheless, a 2000 report and analysis of LAAMP showed that twenty out of twenty-seven School Families listed included a parent involvement focus in their School Family learning plans.[24] And it was LAAMP's parent involvement initiatives that would yield some of the most positive outcomes in student achievement.

In particular, the Parents as Learning Partners program yielded some of the most impressive results. The program was funded for five years by a $4.9 million grant from the Weingart Foundation. The awarding of this grant raised the profile of the parent involvement initiatives among the LAAMP board members and strengthened their long-term commitment to parent involvement.

The PLP program was implemented in thirty-three schools in three School Families in Los Angeles County (Lincoln High School in Los Angeles, Francis Polytechnic High School in Sun Valley and Long Beach Polytechnic High School) and focused primarily on three elements: parenting, communicating, and learning at home. The program implemented strategies to strengthen each of these areas by providing professional development for teachers and education for parents.

The assumption of PLP and other parent initiatives was that students will achieve more when parents are involved in their children's education, and the program's evaluation supported the conclusion in many ways.[25] A comprehensive 2003 evaluation report on LAAMP published by the Center for the Study of Evaluation at UCLA concluded that, overall, LAAMP had "encouraged attention to parent involvement and increased parents' ability to support children's learning at home."[26] And although parent and community work was only a small part of the LAAMP budget, it may have been the most significant accomplishment.

At the end of its existence, LAAMP fostered a new parent organization, Families in Schools, which continues today and is led by Maria Casillas.[27] After LAAMP closed operations, the Annenberg Foundation supported the founding of the Boyle Heights Learning Collaborative (BHLC) in East Los Angeles, whose design became potentially important as a model for a community-based group that organizes parents both as the "first educators" of their children and as community advocates.[28]

One of BHLC's initiatives, Parent Achievement Academies, has been especially successful in empowering parents to develop productive relationships with their children, their children's teachers, and each other. The academies are rooted in Industrial Areas Foundation practice and in its ideology that grassroots influence springs from interpersonal relationships. As a result, the academies are built around conversation rather than simply "giving parents information." Parents talk to other parents about getting their children through high school or applying to college or getting a scholarship.

The relationships built around helping ones' own children have become powerful in pressuring the school board to make a college-ready curriculum available to all students, and, as this is written, some of these relationships have spilled over into political battles involving housing in the neighborhood, relationships with the police, and the mayor's bid to take over the school district.

Parent organizing is difficult. Many work long hours in multiple jobs and teeter in economic uncertainty. Attendance at gatherings tends to be sporadic; those who attend one meeting may not be at the next. "It's all very retail [i.e., one customer at a time]," said one organizer. It's harder to gather parents than assembling a group of established interest groups together to strategize about a ballot initiative or an election.

Still, the ideal of robust parent participation, particularly among poor immigrant families—a legacy of both LEARN and LAAMP— has grown. The Boyle Heights collaborative has been joined by four others in different areas of the city, and these organizations are beginning to coalesce.

Use of Data and Technology

Even before the details of each family learning plan were set, by the end of 1997 all School Families had embraced a clear commitment to public engagement and reporting. At the urging of the LAAMP board, they agreed that all participating schools needed to communicate with their communities about what they were working on and what kinds of problems and progress they were encountering. By early 1999, many School Families began to share the findings of LAAMP's Data Driven School Reform (DDSR) research with their communities as well.

Part of encouraging schools to use data to drive reform was accomplished through supporting technology initiatives. LAAMP invested $1.5 million, about 2 percent of its budget, in direct technology grants, but several School Families chose technology development as a focus of their work.[29] Most of the money (53 percent) was spent on equipment, with technology related staff (12 percent) and professional development (11 percent) the next largest expenditures.[30] Few of them had long-term impact, and, viewed from a decade after their initiation, the projects seem primitive: for example, training teachers in how to use the Microsoft Office suite or producing Hypercard stacks or PowerPoint presentations of science lessons.[31]

But within these short-lived initiatives were several ideas that would greatly expand through commercial or nonprofit connections. The ability of teachers to put their lessons online for student and parent access, for example, is widely and inexpensively available. The availability of information technology for student portfolios has become commonplace as well, although its use has become less so. Online assessments, which were so rare that they were not even inquired about a decade ago, are now present in about 30 percent of the states.[32] *Education Week*'s tracking of technology use reveals that variables, such as school connectivity to the Internet through broadband connections, are so common that they no longer collect information about them and that the annual technology report is now more interested in whether states support virtual schools and other forms of online education that were hardly known a decade ago.[33] Meanwhile, access to instructional computers has increased rapidly. California, which lags behind the other largest states, reported a computer for every 5.1 students in 2006, compared with 8.1 students in 1999. (The national average is 3.8 students per computer.)[34]

NETWORKS OF SCHOOLS

LAAMP School Families were thought of as a modest and incremental extension of LEARN, but they turned out to be something much more radical.[35] LAAMP introduced a network form of organization into the District and thus challenged its traditional hierarchy, putting the newly formed cluster arrangement to the test. Where the clusters could be thought of as administrative subunits, something the District had ample experience with, the idea of a network of largely autonomous LEARN schools presented organizational problems in the extreme.

The motivation behind the networks, or families, was straightforward enough. Students were getting lost in the system. The transition between elementary, middle, and high schools was often difficult. Students also moved frequently, but they tended to move within close proximity, so the School Family emerged as a means to bridge levels of schooling and as an alternative to the existing bureaucracy. Instead of a strict demarcation between elementary and secondary administrative control, each with its separate reporting arrangements for school principals, schools of all levels would meet together and work on problems of student achievement. Instead of all conversations being hierarchically mediated, teachers and parents, as well as administrators, from different levels would examine student data and craft solutions. In the process, the knowledge of best practices and the definition of what problems were to be worked on moved from the top of a hierarchy to the nodes on the network. LAAMP families represented a power shift.

Where bureaucratic hierarchies looked like tall triangles, with power and authority at the top, networks look like lattices or spiderwebs, with power in the nodes and the links between them. Observers of a network operation wrote:

If you come to visit, you may have a hard time distinguishing parents from teachers and principals. Today, the adults from the area high school and elementary schools that feed into it are bent over computer print-outs of test score data they have assembled in order to determine their students' strengths and weaknesses.

The adults are participating in two days of training about how to use test score data for diagnosing student needs. They are divided up into five groups, each of which has a representative from all three levels of schooling and the three stakeholder groups. One group is baffled by a dip in reading scores between the eighth grade and the ninth. Another group compares reading test scores of English Language Learners and English-speakers and is surprised to find that they were all performing at low levels, regardless of whether they were tested in their native language.[36]

At first glance, this description seems innocuous. But consider the breaks with standard bureaucratic operating assumptions.

- Parents, teachers, and administrators have equal status; and depending on the training they receive, expertise may rest more heavily with the teachers, and maybe the parents, than with the principal.
- Printouts of test scores are the artifact of achievement, not the assessments of individual teachers or the observations of the principal.
- Representatives of the different levels of schooling, once sequestered into different organizational divisions, are mixed.
- Teachers operate as something other than deliverers of instruction.
- Data that reveal weaknesses in the system are openly shared with nonprofessionals, and they are supposed to participate in generating solutions.

Later on in the narrative, it is revealed that these descriptions link to how resources are to be distributed.

LAAMP believed that if it could get people from different levels in the system to meet and talk together, they could begin to solve their problems. A LAAMP staff member recalled how "the relationship between high schools and elementary schools was non-existent, and the relationship between high schools and middle schools typically was that the high school told the middle school they weren't doing a good job."[37] However, "just putting people together doesn't necessarily lead to that kind of systematic planning about instruction and assessments."[38] Expertise is dispersed, and operations depend on the information linkages between the one node on the network and another.

Most of the LAUSD cluster leaders did not take to the idea. They understood, as did LEARN president Mike Roos, that "the families of schools idea is a good way of breaking up the structure. One of the things that the family system does is to hold the elementary school accountable."[39] But some administrators saw advantages in the family structure. District administrator Richard Alonzo, whose cluster included the North Hollywood Family, was among them.[40] He considers organized parent involvement and professional development one of the legacies of the Annenberg grant, and the North Hollywood Family first used several of the techniques that are now widespread, among them the use of specialist teachers who acted as coaches for other teachers.[41]

The School Family pioneered development of what has become the District's longitudinal student information system. Perhaps the kindest assessment is that in 1999 data gathering and analysis in the LAUSD was in a very primitive state. High schools could download some data and perform their own analyses, but elementary schools could not.[42] Very little of the information was of much use to teachers or principals looking for clinical information to improve instruction. The School Family data analysis project produced disquieting information about achievement. Only 35 percent of ELLs were designated as English proficient by the end of the fifth grade. There were huge unexplained gaps in the performance of different classrooms. The system had virtually no information on what happened to students once they left school. Students and parents could not access much information at all. Even such basic questions as "How am I doing towards graduation?" or "How many college prep classes have I taken?" required a trip to the counselor's office, a data query, and a wait for results.[43]

Merle Price, who was the principal at Palisades High School and later a cluster leader, was also an early supporter: "LEARN was part of a quick turnaround."[44] The high school was in danger of closing because of declining enrollment, and most of the students were bused in from other neighborhoods. The School Family process injected both professional energy and community support into the high school and its feeder schools. The schools now operate virtually as a charter district. The high school and several of the elementary schools have charter status, and they consciously operate as a network. There is no superintendent or overall administrator, but there is a great deal of communication among the schools.

The Palisades is an affluent area and thus atypical for Los Angeles, but the story Price tells of what it took to make a School Family successful was not unusual. It started with a belief: "Because the first thing you have to create is hope and a vision that we can get beyond where we are today and there's a new tomorrow, as corny as that is." It was hard work, "fifteen hours a day, sometimes six or seven days a week; it was a mission." It required active discontent with the status quo. "People had sort of circled the wagons and saw all these district policies as disenfranchising and contrary to the local needs." It required people who had resources and were willing to be organized. "I cultivated parent and community leaders as well as faculty leaders. I had eight or ten people who were designated lead teachers in addition to department chairs." They had good tools to work with, "processes so that people felt valued as participants, owned the changes that were being proposed and then committed to the next steps and actual tools." Among these was a new labor contract (teachers remained members of UTLA but developed their own work rules). Using these, they created a curriculum they liked, "completely transforming mathematics instruction, science instruction, English language arts; we were pioneers in benchmarking outcomes and backwards planning designs."[45]

The School Family network idea was particularly problematic with the high schools. "If you're in a room and you've just got twelve elementary principals in your [School] Family and it's just the one middle school and the one high school, it was never about them or anything of substance about their instructional practices."[46] Even supporters, such as LEARN administrator Judy Burton, felt that "we were not paying sufficient attention to secondary schools," and after Roy Romer became superintendent in 2000, he actively discouraged the School Family structure because it did not seem to positively impact the high schools and hence the District's most visible achievement problems.[47] But one of the goals of the family structure was to connect low achievement problems, which became most visible in middle and high schools, to their roots.

LAAMP funded twenty-eight networks, or School Families: fourteen inside LAUSD and fourteen in other school districts in the county.[48] As was the case with LEARN, participation as a School Family began with what was called a "learning plan." The goal, which was the most visible of the seven LAAMP action principles, was to create what were called stable learning communities in which students were known by adults, there were committed and coordinated approaches to teaching, and there was a smooth transition between levels of schooling. The plans focused on different activities, although most were built around improving results in English language arts and literacy. Eleven of the fourteen LAUSD families also focused on working with parents, and ten focused on using educational technology.

IT'S A PROBLEM OF WILL/CAPACITY

LEARN set out to build a systemic reform, and LAAMP sought to make that reform "broader and deeper." However, both assumed that the school system was stable and capable. If sufficient political and organizational will could be generated, the District would follow the reform plan. LEARN assumed that if the school board agreed to a reform plan, they had the will and capacity to follow through. LAAMP assumed that if the District signed a contract in which they pledged to undertake reforms in exchange for millions in philanthropic dollars, they would honor the letter and spirit of the contract. The school board assumed that when it hammered out a *Call to Action* with the superintendent, the schools had the capacity to deliver on those goals.

In reality, the system was changing under the feet of both the reformers and the District. The federated nature of LAUSD's governance was displayed throughout the reform. State-level intervention was necessary to kick-start LEARN as Assembly Speaker Willie Brown brokered a labor agreement and persuaded the state to find $35 million to make the settlement possible. During the reform operations, the District faced constant border wars with the legislature and against initiatives trying to break up the District. The operating system of the District became increasingly networked, relying on outsiders for professional development and coaching. Most importantly, the momentum for change was coming from the outside, not the inside, of the District.

Fear and uncertainty took hold. One principal whose school was not in LEARN said, "It is just frightening that we know that we many times are not making the difference, but we don't know how to make that change in the reform path."[49] There was almost a tone of desperation among the participants. A teacher union chapter chair said, "If LEARN does not take hold and show results, the District is dead."[50]

CHAPTER 8

Implementation

Excitement and Challenge in the Schools

"It was Castro's strategy. You organize the countryside, and move in on the capital. . . . That was clearly the idea. And the capital would fall. Underestimated that one. You know? [*laughter*] I really did."

—*Mike Roos*

LEARN and LAAMP assumed they could channel pent-up grassroots demands for improved schools into powerful support for educational practices that would better connect the schools with the needs of students. However, the countryside proved less enthusiastic and the capital more durable than expected. There was often a loneliness among the pioneers who first implemented LEARN. As a teacher said, "I'm glad my school became LEARN, because it has created a renewed spirit on campus. . . . Perhaps it will spread to others, but not without lots more support and a plan from the top. I don't see it yet, but I know it could get done if there were the will."[1]

LEARN and LAAMP illustrate the difficulty of implementation and the extent to which it was underestimated. The large body of research on public policy implementation begins, as LEARN did, with a legislative perspective.[2] Someone in authority makes a decision, other people implement it, and the project is evaluated according to the fidelity of their adoption. The blinding insight of the implementation literature is that people did not always do as they were told. Sometimes the proposed program was too complex; sometimes it required a long chain of decisions before action could be taken. The probability of successful implementation declines rapidly when the number of decision points increases. Sometimes people are afraid that they can't do what is required, or their status or even their job depends on not changing.

All these aspects of implementation are fodder for the standard conclusion that reform projects do not work.

But in its most fundamental sense, LEARN and LAAMP were not projects to be implemented; they were innovations to be developed and adopted. The founders of LEARN and LAAMP wanted to set the schools free to audition new ways of operating. Virgil Roberts said, "We had the freedom to fail, which venture capitalists can do, professional managers can't." But with public money, he said, "if somebody has an idea for a reading program, or a Saturday school, or something, and it doesn't work, then you know, you could be subject to an editorial in the *Los Angeles Times* saying, 'Our hard-earned taxpayer dollars were spent in this failing effort.' And we have the freedom to pursue ideas we think will work, so don't be afraid to say, 'It doesn't work.' It's okay to say, 'We failed.'"[3]

The venture capital innovations approach posed problems, however. Good ideas didn't necessarily spread. Roberts had thought that new ideas tried out in small scale by teachers would be integrated into the system. "We couldn't get them to pick up anything, not anything."[4] In addition, the public spotlight was on LEARN, LAAMP, and the foundations that supported the reforms. In some ways the reform projects they had inherited became the object of derision and delegitimation, just as LAUSD had been.

Thus, the analysis of LEARN is much more like an innovative process or product that appears in the marketplace of ideas than a legislative mandate. Innovations are more rapidly adopted when they have a clear relative advantage over existing practices, when they are simple to adopt, and when the superior results of are easy for all to see.[5] Innovations are grabbed by prototypical early adopters, who, as a type, are eager to try new ideas. If successful, the innovations eventually work their way to more cautious and traditional practitioners until they reach a tipping point where adoption becomes nearly universal.[6] But LEARN was a complex innovation. The schools were not so much being asked to implement a prepackaged program as they were asked to design their own school. As a teacher noted, LEARN "does not have a blueprint for success. That is for each school to discover. . . . In other words, it is the process, not the plan that makes LEARN successful."[7]

THE SITE ACTION PLAN

The primary mechanism by which a school joined LEARN was through the creation of a Site Action Plan, which was to be devised during a school's first year of participation. LEARN's underlying theory of action was that when teachers, the principal, and the surrounding school community had a sufficient grasp of their own needs and were given the necessary planning tools, they could create orderly plans for their own transition into productive self-governance. The Site Action Plans, whose design originated with Dan Katzir at UCLA, were to be the equivalent of corporate strategic plans.[8]

There was a template for the plans, including mission and vision statements, a section on school governance, a personnel selection procedure, achievement and accountability, a section on mandated programs such as special education, a section on parent participation, a section on staff development, and a section on waivers of district or state rules for which the school would apply. At the Camellia Avenue Elementary School in North Hollywood, the mission was to "educate children to excel academically, be problem solvers and effective communicators with respect for themselves and all people."[9] The Robert Frost Middle School in Granada Hills "will provide an innovative instructional program, which will develop literate, self-motivated, physically fit students with strong critical thinking and academic skills, who will contribute positively to a highly technological and multicultural society."[10] Equally flowery but vague language was found in other plans, leading one school board member to say, "It all sounded like [President] Clinton, 'over the bridge to the twenty-first century.'" Roberts remembers that the plans were "universally awful" and that early in its existence LAAMP had to shift gears to provide technical assistance in creating them.

But in time the plans did get specific. Although student achievement goals began with expansive language, they ended with measurements. In addition to doing well on state-mandated tests, some plans called for local measures. For example, at Camellia Elementary effective communications was to be measured by "teacher-developed assessments requiring students to teach/present information to peers."[11] Respect was to be measured by a school-wide conference of teachers and families that would review pupil suspension and referral records, their own observations, and the results from a student survey.

Frost Middle School targeted two goals: respect and reading. They argued that reading well was the key to all learning and thus concentrating there was the key to raising the school's behavior overall. They wanted state test scores to increase but did not specify by how much; more books would be checked out of the library and students would be observed reading in their free time.[12]

All the plans included a governance council including teachers, parents, classified employees, and the principal. The UTLA site representative, or designee, was always included. But as the plan at Frost illustrated, representation was no simple matter. Each of the schools had existing bodies; some of them, such as the bilingual education council, were required by statute and had preexisting budgetary authority. Others, like the school parent organization, were longstanding. The planners at Frost were mindful of the need to get all the organizational gears to mesh. Their LEARN council consolidated a contractually established Shared Decision Making Council and an existing School Improvement Council, "plus necessary department and volunteer participants" on an ad hoc basis. "The various Councils make decisions and recommendations solely by the consensus process," the plan said. "It is imperative for success that decisions have basic unanimity of support by all concerned."[13]

The Frost plan illustrates the long decisional chains and uncertain conclusions that Aaron Wildavsky warned about in his studies of implementation.[14] Issues, concerns, ideas, and suggestions were to flow from the existing councils and committees to the new LEARN council, which would in turn appoint a committee to come up with a proposal that would be submitted to the LEARN council and then to the standing committees for their consideration returning to the LEARN council for ratification.

A NETWORK OF EXPERTS

Each of the LEARN and LAAMP schools found itself a part of a network of support. Thus, for schools, and particularly principals, the known—comforting and frustrating—hierarchy was replaced by a web of relationships in which a principal could be in the middle but not at the top. What was happening to these principals was emblematic of the shift between hierarchy and network as the fundamental form of school organization.

LEARN schools reported to the school reform office headed by assistant superintendent Judy Burton and to their local cluster leader. But reform support and direction came from a third source: the network of support and training that LEARN put together. When LAAMP began operations, it added to the web of associations by grouping schools into School Families of high schools and elementary and middle schools.

Each LAAMP school was assigned a consulting agency or partners to assist in planning and implementation of what was called the Learning Community

Program (LCP). The LCP was loosely modeled on the idea of a producer's cooperative. Hierarchical authority would recede into the background, and the school's strong culture would come to the forefront. A program announcement says, "The Learning Community concept is built upon the work of Milbrey McLaughlin and Joan Talbert at Stanford University. [They] examined schools nationwide and found that the schools making significant improvement in student learning had a common theme—their faculty members were actively involved in professional teacher networks that stimulated and supported the implementation of effective, new teaching practices."[15]

Evaluators called the LCP "a collection of meaningful relationships in which teachers participate in significant collegial activities such as curriculum design, peer observations, standard setting, and the sharing of instructional strategies."[16] The report continued, "In such professional communities teachers are able to reflect on their instructional practices, explore new pedagogies, examine their assumptions about teaching and learning, and adopt new innovations in their classrooms. It is in this environment that teachers are able to make significant progress in reforming their teaching."[17] Thus, the role of individual teachers was to change substantially from the compliance-driven hierarchy, which the Los Angeles public schools typified. In this type of organization, teachers may have had substantial discretion, but it was because their work was underinspected despite being subject to regulation and rule-making to the smallest degree.

The idea of learning communities also grew from work that the Los Angeles Educational Partnership had been doing for over a decade. LAEP had been formed in 1984 after a group of forty community leaders, business people, and educators decided to form an intermediary organization.[18] Peggy Funkhouser, who had cut her teeth on business-community partnerships in Pittsburgh, and David Abel, a young civic activist, convened a mostly business-leader group to talk about what could be done to improve the local schools. "We had no agenda, no plan, and generally not a clue about how to intervene," Funkhouser remembered. But the general idea was to "bring the community to the table around educational issues." LAEP grew from these conversations. Superintendent Harry Handler supported LAEP "because he felt the District couldn't accomplish all that was needed on their own."[19]

LAEP knew that it could not gain leverage over the system, so it adopted a strategy of working with teachers in the hope that *they* could become the engine of change. They began with $400 grants to teachers. "These teachers became our window—our intelligence—into the reality of life in their schools," Funkhouser said.[20] In the months after its founding, LAEP launched a fellowship for math and science teachers and highly popular small grants program.[21] LAEP got high marks from teachers and from UTLA, because Funkhouser "believed and trusted teachers. I mean, she just gave them a check if they, you know, wanted one of these little project grants."[22]

By 1986 LAEP had won a $500,000 grant from the Rockefeller Foundation to begin an interdisciplinary humanities program, named Humanitas, which remains in operation in thirty-nine high schools.[23] Humanitas became organizationally important because it symbolized the movement of pedagogical and academic reforms away from the school district's central office to persons and locations outside the bureaucratic control.

LAEP also introduced the idea of connecting reforms in Los Angeles with those taking place throughout the country. It became a Public Education Fund member and received its initial support from that organization. Its design for the Los Angeles Urban Learning Centers program became one of the New American Schools designs, and the Elizabeth Street and Foshay designs remain in existence.[24]

Funkhouser was a consummate diplomat who never openly challenged the superintendent, staff, or school board. Yet, by the 1990s it became clear that LAEP was an important private center for innovation and advocacy directed at the District. Maverick administrators and teachers found ways to work through LAEP to accomplish what they could not through the school district directly. LAEP became the structural prototype for lodging reforms in external private organizations. To some extent, LAEP had become the professional and curriculum development department for the school district.

The Professional Learning Community Model of Change

Although these organizations differed somewhat in their approach to assistance, all subscribed to the notion of bottom-up change, a view captured by the phrase "you can't mandate what matters," a perspective on change popularized by education professor and dean Michael Fullan.[25] As the program continued, Fullan's statement was taken as something close to revealed truth. As the Stanford evaluators were to say, "The program's focus on teacher learning community builds upon experience with planned change and education reforms that demonstrates in clear terms that reforms can neither be mandated nor imported from experts or agencies outside the school."[26] This was directly counter to the work lives experienced by LAUSD teachers and administrators.

The baseline assumption was that schools wanted to change, that principals wanted independence from the district, and that teachers wanted to create a professional practice of shared norms and expectations built around collegial relationships. As the evaluation report put it, "As [a] medium for reforming teaching and learning [the LCP was] grounded in the principle that teachers are 'agents of change in their own classrooms.'"[27] The language of job roles changed markedly from the traditional rank-and-file nomenclature of principal, assistant principal, department head, and teacher. Into this structure came a new set of job roles.

School Change Consultants (SCCs) were assigned by one of the five assistance organizations to each school. As the number of schools that signed on for LEARN increased beyond LAEP's capacity to provide assistance, four other organizations were commissioned to provide assistance, each using a their own modification of the Learning Community Model: The Achievement Council, Action Learning Systems, The Coalition of Essential Schools, and Educare. Typically, one consultant would work with about four schools.

They would work with the Instructional Transformation Team (ITT) at each school, which were to be the agents of change within the school. "The primary task of the SCC was to build capacity for meaningful educational change by developing skills in problem solving. The strategy assumed that SCCs would be trusted partners and thus able to assist schools in collaboratively creating the Site Action Plans focused on student achievement and reduce the barriers to implementation."[28]

The ITT design was based on the popular diffusion model in which a few members of a school learn about an innovation and "bring it home" to their school.[29] Particularly at the beginning of the program, training the ITT focused on interpersonal skills: building their capacity to conduct efficient meetings, building trust, and carrying on focused conversations.[30]

Professional Learning Communities were to "encourage teachers to change classroom practices in order to find more effective means of improving student learning and achievement." Professional communities would be brought about through study groups, cross-school networks, and the use of teacher practitioners and technical advisers. Teachers would learn new instructional strategies through "study, action research, and interaction with their peers at other schools." These forms of professional development would integrate the content and process of teaching into the whole school's strategy, thus enhancing "the teacher's role as a change agent."[31] Yet, about two-thirds of the School Change Consultants came from business or business consulting organizations.

AMP Training and Other Professional Development

The District, along with LEARN and LAAMP, made a substantial investment in leadership training, mostly though a contract with the Advanced Management Program at UCLA. AMP-training, as it was called, became a ritual for all LEARN schools, and by the end of the program nearly 1,000 participants in 374 schools attended. A leadership team usually included the principal and the school's teacher union representative and they all attended a three-week summer institute held in Palm Springs.[32]

The institute helped participants develop skills in a variety of business, management, entrepreneurial, and collaborative leadership techniques. It provided a problem-based learning environment with case examples, hands-on demonstrations, and "real world" situations. The AMP faculty consisted of university professors, business trainers, and well-known field practitioners. Course modules assumed that the leadership team would be running a small, autonomous organization and thus included topics such as strategic planning, marketing, finance/accounting, computer modeling, management communications, organizational behavior, human resource management, entrepreneurship, and instructional leadership.

The summer institute was also intended to jumpstart work on a school's Site Action Plan, which was to link a school's mission and goals with resources and desired educational outcomes. Principals learned basic accounting, operational budgeting, and cost-benefit analysis. Although there were sample school plans, each school was strongly encouraged to build a plan that reflected the specific needs of its students and community. "The fact that we spent so much time developing a vision provided us with the insight we needed," one principal said. It allowed the school to question any decision in terms of "how will this help us meet our school vision or specific goals."[33]

Because the summer institutes assumed that leadership teams would be running semi-autonomous schools, it was a powerful, even revolutionary, experience for them. One LEARN principal recalled the training with fondness. "I absolutely loved the training. It was current, cutting edge and relevant. Even the homework was very good. It was a big commitment but it really helped. In many ways I already used many of these strategies in the school and it was easy to continue."[34]

Another former LEARN principal recalled, "They made me feel optimistic, empowered and hopeful." Dan Chernow, director of the UCLA School Management Program said, "AMP had the best and newest research to what was effective in making change. The fact that the participants wanted to be there and were eager to learn was a big plus." The training experiences created esprit de corps. "The best thing about [LEARN] Phase II is the camaraderie of the other educators committed to restructuring."[35] A top administrator who was skeptical about LEARN's "white-guy" business-oriented origins, lauded the training: "The trainings were mostly regarded as positive. Many of the process strategies for conducting meetings, consensus building, etc., had never been seen before by the principals. They were also held in plush hotels and treated like professional business people. However, many felt that the trainings lacked substance in terms of curriculum and instruction. Upgrading instruction and data assessment came much later."

Yet, participants in the training were painfully conscious of who was not at the table. "The Board and Top Staff is who needs to get the training now, and walk the talk immediately," said a participant in a LEARN school. "Without that, change will not be pervasive, and there will still be plenty of places for resisters to hang out waiting for this 'fad' to pass."[36] Another participant said, "Middle and upper middle management should have been trained with us, as Judy Burton was. Maybe then they would know what education is all about these days."[37] An independent contractor wrote, "From my experience to date, I think the most serious unresolved issue in district reform today is staffing and training cluster leaders who understand and support the LEARN reform process. The greatest danger is that these clusters emerge as mini-bureaucracies that stifle energy and innovation in the same way that larger bureaucracies are capable of doing and have done. The District is beginning to address this issue in the form of a two-day training seminar for the cluster leaders."[38]

"The training was strong on many fronts," said Ronni Ephraim, who was appointed deputy superintendent in 2007 and who attended AMP training as an elementary school principal. "It provided lots of opportunity to think together about how we used our money to meet goals. Gave us time to think about our school story . . . . and it put us in an environment with other people who were interested in leading change."[39]

AMP training did not ignore instruction, but to an extent it treated it as an organizational problem rather than as a pedagogy or instructional strategy. "There was more emphasis on the big picture, but we needed more specifics about better teaching techniques and instructional practices," one principal recalled.[40] The slowness of coming to grips with instruction was apparent, and may have been a design contradiction. Those who were working with teachers felt that LEARN had underestimated the problems of implementation and was too focused on principals and district leadership. Judy Johnson, who had led training at LAEP, recalled her disagreements with LEARN leadership and what she perceived as a belief "that if they just changed leadership and got a vision for leadership, and gave people the freedom to muck around with budgets and choices of teachers and some things like that, then everything would be okay." Instead, the key was in "teacher knowledge" and building a community of teachers. "And you have to do that by having them look at the performance of kids, and making decisions about where to focus their attention for a while."[41]

CHANGE IS HARD

As an innovation, LEARN suffered from several characteristics that made its adoption difficult. The pace of change was much slower than external expectations. LEARN was a complex innovation and hard to adopt for schools that were not already headed toward self-sufficiency. The advantages of participation were not always obvious, and the results that would have allowed participants to claim victory were not always apparent. But time was the most obvious difficulty.

The Problem of Time

Time was a problem in two ways. First, LEARN was an intensive innovation that challenged the schedules of those involved, and the adoption process was slower than the political coalition that founded LEARN would endure. LAEP, in articulating its theory of action, said that "school change leading to improved learning and achievement is a 3–10 year process."[42] One of the school change consultants said, "It takes about three years for any of this to get into the classroom," to which the Stanford evaluators added, "Our analysis of teaching and learning suggests that this time frame is realistic; most schools do not even begin to delve into issues of teaching and learning until after their Site Action Plans are complete."[43] Virgil Roberts, the LAAMP board chair, came to a similar conclusion: "We have been in existence about five years, but most of the schools have only been working at doing school reform for maybe two at the most, because there was a year we spent organizing ourselves, then there was a year spent getting the schools to understand how they needed to implement their plans and then it was almost the third year when they started implementation. And then by the time they did a mid-course [correction] at the end of the third year, we're into the fourth year and talking about winding down."[44] A LEARN principal said of reform, "It should be fed like baby food, a little at a time. We didn't make this monster overnight and we are not going to correct it overnight."[45] A teacher leader also felt the time crunch, saying, "The biggest problem is enough time to share all of the information, and to do the planning. The problem is tremendous, if we are going to meet any of our major expectations. Even the leaders at UCLA and LEARN do not appreciate the size of the task."[46]

Second, LEARN was wearing out those who tried to adopt it. "What we lack is the time for them to reflect more on what changes need to be made," said Maria Casillas.[47] Reform activity "just sucks up so much of my time where on any given week a LEARN principal is gone two days . . . they've got those meetings with the cluster where they're doing stuff, they've got meetings for the district, they've got these AMP columns of excellence things, they've got their residentials, they've got the ITT training things that we do . . . . whoever has time to do anything back at the school?"[48]

LEARN had profound implications for principal time. Virtually all principals grow frustrated by the time demands of their jobs, but the layering of time demands and a near-desperation about finding time was especially felt by LEARN principals.[49] The literature on management activities in general speaks of "work at an unrelenting pace," and the literature on the principalship documents 149 activity days, a virtual time famine.[50]

One principal said, "But there is an attitude that permeates LEARN and the Advanced Management Training program that has always bothered them [the principals], and that is the issue of time. Because they do not have a grasp, no matter how much we've told them, about this, they do not grasp that what they talk about cannot be done on top of everything else."[51] Another said, "There is very little acknowledgement that the job is not doable as it stands, and then you bring LEARN in on top of it . . . and they now expect you to do another 80 hours a week without compensation. . . . I sensed a disquietude associated with acceptance of the monumental importance of time, and therefore a near paranoid distrustfulness of any activity or event that threatened to waste it."[52]

The "Trainer of Trainers" Model of Change

It was generally conceded that the Instructional Transformation Team (ITT) did not work as well as hoped.[53] The ITT design was based on a well-established theory of diffusion in which a few members of a school learn about an innovation in workshops and training sessions and take it back to their own school. "During the first two years, the Learning Community Program focused almost exclusively on developing the leadership capacity of the ITT." The basic markers of a good ITT is its ability to conduct efficient meetings, build trust, and carry on focused conversations.[54]

The shortcomings of this model became apparent early on. "In the words of one teacher, 'The ITT seemed like a good idea, but it was not workable for us. Instead we have all the faculty work together.'"[55] Despite modifications, the ITT model was judged "a weak tool for the actual amount of change that we'd [LAEP] like to make."[56]

Evaluators noted that the ITT faced three problems. Sometimes the ITT was composed of the "same old people" signaling the rest of the school that no real change was afoot. Sometimes a whole school strategy worked better. And sometimes the ITT made communications within the school worse because information and ideas are not shared with the whole school.[57] In other words, it became another layer of bureaucracy.

"However, in some cases, the ITT can have the effect of alienating the rest of the faculty. In some schools, faculty members not on the ITT perceive the extra training and resources received by the ITT as inequitable." In another school the SCC said that the ITT really was elitist, remarking, "The faculty still was very angry about LEARN because . . . they didn't know what it was about and they thought that a handful of people were making decisions."[58]

Lack of Progress Benchmarks

LEARN promised increased student outcomes: "Every student will be expected to master a 'core of learning' . . . [which] promotes learning as a thinking, problem-solving process. . . . Instead of regulations and procedures, Los Angeles schools will create a culture that . . . . emphasizes successful learning experiences for *all* students."[59] But it did not have control over an assessment system that would indicate whether or not students were learning, much less one that would actually help them.

LEARN's designers had hoped to create instructional and pedagogical coherence by linking accountability, student testing, and the curriculum. The primary vehicle for this effort was to have been the California Learning Assessment System (CLAS), which was developed beginning in 1991.[60] In addition to tightly linking assessment to curriculum frameworks, CLAS was designed to be a more thorough performance examination. It had longer writing assignments and presented problem-solving situations and holistic scoring as opposed to right or wrong answers. CLAS was an almost perfect example of professionally driven reform. Test creation involved some of the best-known subject matter specialists and testing and measurement experts in the country. Teachers were involved in every stage of the design and administration; more than 400 English teachers scored the exams.[61]

But CLAS was only administered in 1993 and 1994 before Governor Pete Wilson vetoed its budgetary reauthorization (SB 1273). Professional competence clashed with political common sense.[62] Religious groups complained that the writing prompts asked students to reflect on their home lives and on moral dilemmas that should not be the province of the public schools. Others objected to the holistic scoring techniques and the lack of "objective" scores. An investigation critical of the sampling procedures claimed that some 11,000 sampling errors produced results that invalidated any cross-school or cross-district comparisons.[63]

Regardless of the politics, the effect of the CLAS test veto was to leave the school reform effort in Los Angeles (as well as the rest of the state) without an anchor assessment, particularly one that worked at the individual level. To be sure, there were still other indicators available, but neither LEARN nor the school district had invested in a comprehensive indicator system that would connect changes in classroom practice and school organization with measured cognitive assessment or any other forms of student output. Some LEARN schools became proficient at tracking their progress, but this did not become widespread.

The District's own data system and a don't-ask-don't tell academic performance culture inhibited data feedback that assisted instruction in LEARN schools. "Test scores came out late this year and LEARN schools still have trouble knowing how to use them to look at improvement," a LEARN consultant said in 1995.[64] "You don't call up [the District] and ask for your data unless you're a really astute person," said Judy Burton. "Not that you can't. People don't. They don't because they don't know that they can. Even if they knew they could, they wouldn't know what to ask for. The other thing, too, is that what we have available is lots of summary data, and that doesn't really help you out at school, getting down to individual classrooms or individual students."[65] Linking data and instruction began in LEARN, but "we didn't have as much data as we do now," said Ephraim."[66] During the LEARN years, reform participants said that most principals got their school rankings from the *Los Angeles Times*.

By 1997, LAAMP had homed in on organizing around achievement, much to the consternation of some of the schools and districts who had been attracted to participate because they thought that LAAMP would embrace the ideas of Theodore Sizer's Coalition of Essential Schools, which generally held that comparative measures of cognitive achievement were shallow and inauthentic. But the LAAMP board insisted on quantifiable measures of student achievement.

LAAMP, in particular, pressured schools to attend to their achievement data. At first, the schools (both those in LAUSD and outside) didn't take very seriously what was becoming an accountability mantra. "Everything was very abstract like 'can't we just have a handshake and a wink and give us the money,'" a staff member recalled. Some principals actively resented LAAMP for pursuing hard questions that were not being asked by their hierarchical superiors.[67] "What we really didn't talk about was district accountability," said Ephraim. "We all went [to the training], but whether we implemented what we learned was left to the individual. In my case I took it very seriously."[68] LAAMP's response was training in data-driven school reform and the use of external data teams to assist schools.[69]

Only in 1997 did the state create a testing system for grades two through eleven that was linked to a public reporting system.[70] Gray Davis, a Democrat, succeeded to the governorship in 1999 with education as a prime goal. He called the legislature into special session with a package of bills all aimed at increasing accountability and focusing reform. Through an Academic Performance Index (API), at first based largely on the Stanford 9 test, schools would be ranked, and those that scored poorly or which failed to improve would be subject to intervention. Although other indicators, such as graduation rates, were supposed to be attached, a school's index score was virtually determined by its standardized test scores. Those that increased test scores would be eligible for monetary rewards. Social promotion was also eliminated. Schools were forbidden to pass students to the next grade unless they had demonstrated proficiency. One of the immediate results was an upturn in summer school enrollments for makeup or catch-up work. The legislature also authorized a high-stakes high school exit exam. The effective date of the test was delayed twice, until 2006, largely in response to the large numbers of students who did not pass. In L.A. Unified, 86 percent of the Class of 2006 had passed the exit exam by the time of graduation; statewide, the passage rate was 91 percent.

The state system was joined by the requirements of the federal No Child Left Behind Act, whose definition of Adequate Yearly Progress is different from the state performance index targets, although efforts are being made to reconcile the two. NCLB has greatly affected the District. In 2005, more than a third of elementary schools (184), including seven charter schools, had been labeled as Program Improvement schools under the federal law, and almost all the high schools fell under its sanctions.[71] The District labors under the possibility that it will be declared as failing and subject to a state takeover; however, there is reticence in Sacramento about exercising this power.

The Conflicted World of LEARN Principals

Principals of LEARN schools existed in a shadowy borderland, a little outside the territory of the school district but still subject to most of its laws and cultures. LEARN, its training, and an entrepreneurial spirit that infected those early adopters who eagerly joined the reform pushed them further away from historic behaviors and beliefs. District procedures, rules, and, in the end, the incentive system pulled them back.

LEARN was supposed to shift responsibility for budget, staff selection, and teaching methods to the school. Site Action Plans were to specify how students would be taught and how the school would be run and achievement targets.

In some ways, LEARN opened up new vistas for principals. They would get more control over resources, and they would gain exposure to the latest thinking about leadership. In an early LEARN training session in November 1993, UCLA professor Jack McDonough, spoke of "dedicated behavior . . . the willingness on the part of the individual to do whatever it takes to advance the interest of the wider organization regardless of the internal organizational boundaries."[72]

As the LEARN plan said, "Principals' roles will be redefined. Principals will be become more effective educational leaders accountable for school performance. They will be collaborative team builders, good managers, inspiring leaders and enablers."[73] And they would be evaluated according to "the school's record of achievement; and the principal's record of collaboration with the stakeholders in the school: parents, students, teachers, staff and community members."[74]

However, the blunt edge of the evaluation was an annual "position review" in which a simple majority of either the school's teachers, parents, or classified personnel could vote to have the principal removed. Although there are no records showing how many principals were removed, Judy Burton, who headed the LEARN office, recalled that it was "more than a few."[75] If there was friction in a school or a complaint, the LEARN office was supposed to intervene. Sometimes teachers were dissatisfied with the principals, and UTLA would rather have the central office intervene than file a formal grievance; sometimes it was dissatisfied parents, and intervention "was a huge part of the contention," Burton said. "The problem was having it be me, a district employee who's also an administrator listening equally to people who reported to the principal or who were community members, and that's just probably what annoyed people more than anything else."[76]

Many principals said there was "a questionable logic of such a provision in light of the often unpleasant and unpopular duties which a principal must perform. Others believed that principals may be tempted to act to garner the popular vote as opposed to doing the right thing."[77] Although the provision was designed to keep control at the local level, it often divided the staff, and some said it hurt more than it helped. As one teacher explained, "It put the principal in the uncanny position of having to do the popular thing and made them question their instincts."[78]

Dorothy Jackson, a LEARN principal herself, studied the perceptions of reform by other LEARN principals and those whose schools did not adopt the reform.[79] Jackson, like her fellow principals, "became secretly resentful of unions, local leadership councils, school based management, community advisory committees, every variety and stripe of group that I perceived as placing obstacles in the path of my doing what I believed I was hired to do: to use my best analysis and judgment in running a safe, efficient and stable school. Although I considered myself innovative, I entered a subliminal complicity with the nay sayers to restructuring and transformational practices."[80] Like other LAUSD principals, Jackson was the product of a selection and training system that emphasized fidelity to rules and the maintenance of a stable and orderly school environment. Los Angeles, like most large public bureaucracies developed during the Progressive Era, had an elaborate examination process that served as a rite of passage into administration. What was known in the District as "the test" consisted of a 150-item multiple-choice exam and a training-and-experience essay.[81] If candidates were successful, they faced an oral interview panel that would determine if they would be placed on "the list" that insured initiation into the exclusive society of school principals. Being listed and gaining a first assignment was cause for congratulatory phone calls from other administrators throughout the city.

"The test" was a big deal. Principals described it as nerve-wracking, and for some it was the biggest turning point in their careers. Exams were given in highly structured settings, sometimes in hotel ballrooms, with proctors and specific instructions and time limits: training and experience essays could only be written in twelve-point type, single spaced, and the margins must be one inch all round. Passing the exam involved extensive preparation. Months before the test was administered, study groups were formed. Experienced principals led practice sessions, provided participants with district memos that were likely to be subjects of questions, provided practice exams, and offered opportunities to read the training-and-experience responses and provide feedback.

Most of the exam questions tested highly specific knowledge about procedures and regulations, knowledge of the contract with UTLA or regulations about categorical programs. For example, prospective principals were asked about who could authorize the closing of a school campus, how many shortened or minimum school days were allowed each year, and what the contract with UTLA says about assigning duties to "roving" teachers.

The training-and-experience part of the examination served to reinforce a decades-old tradition of internal sponsorship and promotion. The exam questions allowed candidates to describe instances in which their work displayed exemplary behavior in such areas as analysis, judgment, planning and organizing, and instructional leadership. However, in order to answer the questions, a candidate needed actual experience, which required that their supervisor or some other administrator viewed them as a potential principal and provided them with what was the equivalent of an internship.

After the exam was written, a candidate's current and former supervisors scored the papers based on *their* recollection of the events a candidate had described. "This was the most dangerous part of the process," a former administrator noted, "because someone who did not like you or someone you had a disagreement with, could put an end to the candidacy by grading you down." Most principals knew at least one candidate who did not pass the exam because a previous supervisor had given them a less-than-glowing report, and it was customary for candidates to obtain the blessings of their supervisors before applying to take the test.

Researchers who investigated leadership training and selection, commented: "It is important and interesting to note that in light of all the reforms that the District went through, including LEARN, School Based Management, and Shared Decision Making, none of the multiple-choice questions, written exam prompts, or interview questions measured the candidate's capacity for collaboration, vision, or bringing about a change in a school. The emphasis was in knowing district rules, following those rules, and managing personnel without breaking the contract."[82]

Conflicting Programs

LEARN was not the only plan in town. Said one teacher and school change coach, "One of the issues facing the LAUSD is the problem of several different directives coming from the Hill [the central office] and the Board at the same time. For example a LEARN school needs time to concentrate on restructuring, but we are inundated with more 'plans' i.e. the 'plan' to raise CTBS scores, the Cluster 'plan' etc. Administrators are also inundated with directives from the Hill. Where is the continuity, the support, the time for restructuring, rather than the hindrances?"[83]

These seemingly competing plans and directives led some to wonder if the District was intentionally trying to undermine LEARN, or at the very least not allowing LEARN to gain traction. Said one LEARN participant, "I think LAUSD has loaded the schools down with cluster formations, accountability studies for the state . . . so that LEARN just gets lost in the daily manic fury of looking busy, and looking like we are trying as hard as we can. Are we promoting sustainability?"[84]

And each program, especially those with special funding attached, needed tending. As a lead teacher pointed out, "Each program has to be administered. And at the district level, to get money from those programs, we have to have someone to write grant proposals, administer, distribute funds and evaluate them, etc. This is all lost money from the classroom. I don't know how many state programs there are, but the Hill is full of administrators, coordinators, secretaries, clerks, accountants and auditors taking care of those funds."[85]

Most significantly, the problem was not that the money ran out. The evaluators reported that the School Change Consultants cost between $24,000 and $30,000 a year.[86] This is substantially less than LAUSD schools spend now on assistance and less than schools spend currently for the Open Court reading program, so it wasn't a lack of resources that caused LEARN to wither and die. In addition, the District and the state used the flush times in the late 1990s to adopt very expensive changes in school operations, including reducing class size and adding time to a teacher's instructional day for before- or after-school meetings. All in all, it purchased most of the big-ticket items recommended in the 1989 *The Children Can No Longer Wait* reform report.

And finally there was anger—at the District because it continued to take principals for granted without providing what they needed and at the reform program itself because it had not managed to make LEARN capable of implementation. Said one, "I do know that I don't want to go away for two months for training. I really don't. I think that is infringing on my time and space—my personal life."[87] The principal's remark echoed another more generalized feeling: Since the pay cut, there was such animosity that even dedicated people thought twice about putting in extra time.

AT THE END OF THE DAY

In the end, it wasn't student achievement results that caused LEARN's demise. It was a series of political events and administrative decisions. However, even as the politics was playing out, several evaluations sought to determine whether an achievement effect could be attributed to LEARN or LAAMP.

One of the earliest and most visible was carried out by the *Los Angeles Times,* which compared 1997 and 1998 scores on the District's norm referenced test.[88] LEARN schools gained two percentage points against national norms while other schools in the District gained just one.[89] No one considered the result impressive.

Earlier reports compared LEARN schools to others in the District between 1992–93 and 1994–95. Phase I LEARN schools had increased the percentage of students scoring above the national average in grade four CTBS-U, where other District schools showed only modest improvement. LEARN schools also showed improvement on the Aprenda exam that was given to Spanish-speaking students. Other schools showed none.[90] A second report done a year later indicated small but statistically significant differences between LEARN and non-LEARN schools in CTBS-U reading and language, Aprenda math, and school attendance.

LEARN itself did not commission a comprehensive final evaluation, but LAAMP, which in L.A. Unified included only LEARN schools, commissioned an extensive external evaluation that was carried out primarily by researchers from UCLA and USC.[91] Their final report, issued two years after the program ended, found no significant difference between schools in the program and those not in the program. "Looking at test scores, LACE [the Los Angeles Consortium for Evaluation] researchers saw improvement at LAAMP schools over the 3-year period from 1997–1998 to 2000–2001. However, there was no statistically significant difference between LAAMP schools and non-LAAMP schools with regard to student performance on the state's Stanford 9 standardized test."[92] The report cautioned that the SAT9 did not measure the actual curriculum taught in classrooms, and it said that "it seems premature to expect to find LAAMP effects on student achievement."[93]

By 2002, there were four years of data available from the state's Academic Performance Index, and a LAUSD evaluation compared with others in the same socioeconomic bands showed LEARN schools ranked higher than their nonparticipating counterparts, but the differences were minor.[94] Some 54 percent of LEARN elementary schools, 56 percent of middle schools, and 59 percent of high schools were ranked above the median of their comparison groups.

A 1998 evaluation found that virtually all the site action plans targeted a much broader spectrum of student achievement than that reflected on standardized tests. The majority of the schools were committed to a "student centered educational philosophy aimed at boosting academic achievement and preparing students to function in a more technologically and culturally diverse world." However, the

> measurability of the goals identified in the [site action plans] could be significantly improved upon. . . . Concrete plans for collecting, analyzing, and sharing data with local school stakeholders are rare. In many cases they are absent altogether.

For example, the performance-based assessment tools and strategies (e.g., rubrics, portfolios, etc.) cited by many of the LEARN schools in Phases 1–3 as the means to measure student progress in communications and problem-solving skills either do not exist or they are not implemented in a rigorous manner that would allow local school stakeholders to evaluate whether or not the instructional program or strategy being used is, in fact, yielding gains in student achievement.

Responding to a survey, teachers and administrators from LEARN schools gave themselves a solid B on how well they followed through on their plans overall. Student learning and assessment received a self-rating of B+, as did governance, budget decentralization, facilities, and professional development.[95]

Former associate superintendent Merle Price, an early LEARN principal, summarized:

> In a few places it transformed instructional practice but not in enough places, so that allowed it to have a label of a failed reform. And even as recently as two weeks ago when I met with 50 or 60 of the union chapter chairs here in District 6, and we were having a dialogue about instructional reform and their roles as teacher leaders, one of the chapter chairs who was a product of the LEARN reform challenged me about why LEARN doesn't have the role that it had in the past. And I had to be honest, and I said, "Even though I come from that background and tradition, and there is a lot that we learned and a lot of people who are still using many of those ideas, frameworks, practices, tools for collaboration, etc., in many places it was a failed reform because people didn't get beyond the governance issues into the transformation of instructional practice."[96]

There was very little encouragement in the evaluations for continuing large-scale reform efforts, and the civic coalition that supported LEARN knew this well before the reports were issued and had already moved on.

Part of the problem was project execution, but a part of the measure of disappointment came from setting unrealistic goals in the first place. When LEARN and LAAMP started, the District's data about itself was rudimentary at best. As a former assistant superintendent put it, "Before LEARN there was no accountability." Thus, both the outside reformers and the school board were given to expansive goal statements. Consider the Superintendent's *Call to Action* adopted in 1994 during LEARN's first year. Table 8.1 paraphrases some of the goals and the status of their achievement more than a decade

TABLE 8.1
1994 Superintendent's Call to Action and Results

Call to Action Goals[1]	*Results in 2005–07*
Identify districtwide learning standards.	In place. District standards were superceded by state standards.
All students will meet District's reading standards by the end of the third grade.	In 2006, 27 percent of third graders scored at the Proficient level or above on the California Standards Test in English language arts; 31 percent scored above the national average on the California Assessment Test of reading.[2]
All schools will establish annual targets and report progress.	In place. District standards were superceded by state and federal standards and accountability measures.
Raise student performance on norm reference tests to meet or exceed the national average in key areas by 2000.	Results against national norms in 2007: *3rd grade* *7th grade* Reading 26% 31% Language 37% 31% Math 48% 35%[3]
80 percent of English Language Learners entering middle school and high school would be prepared to move into an all-English program of instruction.	In 2005–06, 52 percent of sixth graders and 63 percent of eighth graders in English language development programs were considered English proficient.[4]
Every high school student (including limited–English speaking students) will be enrolled in four or more college preparatory courses.	In 2005, about 48 percent of graduates had completed a course of study that would make them eligible for University of California or California State University admission.[5]
Increase student enrollment in AP classes and the numbers taking the examinations by at least 25 percent.	In 1997–98, the earliest year we have data, 22,205 students were enrolled in AP classes; in 2005–06 the number was 39,800, an increase of 79 percent.[6]
Make substantial progress toward 100 percent high school graduation.	In 2005–06, 86 percent of the class of 2006 had passed the exam by the time of graduation.[7]

Call to Action Goals[1]	Results in 2005–07
By July 1, 1996, there will be no remedial courses for ninth grade students, and in subsequent years all remedial courses will be eliminated.	As of March 9, 2007, the District's summer session featured more than 100 "Remedial/ Proficiency Courses," which it describes as "repeat courses for students who have received a grade of D or Fail or have not passed [the California High School Exit Exam]."[8]
All senior high schools will evaluate success of graduates through a follow-up study and set targets to increase the transition rate to postsecondary education, vocational training, or employment.	As far as we can tell, virtually no progress has been made toward this goal.

1. *Superintendent's Call to Action*, Appendix A.
2. Accessed on June 10, 2008, from www.star.cde.ca.gov/star2006.
3. Accessed on June 10, 2008, from www.star.cde.ca.gov/star2007.
4. Based on the California English Language Development Test, California Department of Education (CDE) Dataquest (accessed June 10, 2008, from http://dq.cde.ca.gov/Dataquest/CELDT/CELDT03_Dist.asp?cTestNumber=3&RptNumber=01&cSelect=1964733%5E--%5ELOS%5EANGELES%5UNIFIED&cYear=2005-06&cChoice=Celdt3&cCharter=0000).
5. CDE Dataquest (accessed June 10, 2008, from http://dq.cde.ca.gov/Dataquest/Cbeds3.asp?Grads=on&Uccsu=on&cSelect=1964733-LOS+ANGELES+UNIFIED&cChoice=DstProfl&cYear=2005-06&cLevel=District&cTopic=Profile&myTimeFrame=S&submit1=Submit).
6. Accessed June 10, 2008, from Dataquest at cde.ca.gov.
7. Carla Rivera, "More Effort to Pass Exam Urged." *Los Angeles Times*, July 22, 2006, B3.
8. Accessed June 10, 2008, from http://www.lausd.k12.ca.us/lausd/offices/btb/summer/Mem_3588/MEM-3588.0%20Attach%20P.pdf.

later. Generally, the *Call to Action* reflected the rather imprecise goal setting and accountability system that was in place in the mid-1990s. Lofty goals and imprecise measurement was the norm nationwide, not just in Los Angeles. When more precise measurements were applied, the goals LAUSD set for itself were much more difficult to achieve than it had thought.

WHAT KIND OF SYSTEM?

As LEARN and LAAMP were being implemented, they were beset by sometimes voiced and sometimes silent differences about what kind of school system the reform was trying to create. The Professional Learning Community model originated with the Los Angeles Educational Partnership in the 1980s and found full-flower with the network of school change consultants, critical friends, and ITTs. It was both practically and philosophically poles apart from the more corporate vision of many LEARN and LAAMP board members.

William Ouchi was LEARN's chair in its final years. A confidant of Richard Riordan, who drew together many of the program's founders, he was also deputy mayor and an experienced scholar of large organizations. To Ouchi, LEARN was an example of a decentralized multidivisional structure (M-Form), the organizational form pioneered in the 1920s that allowed such giants as General Motors, Sears, and Standard Oil to rise to prominence.[97] Ouchi's writing about the effectiveness of these organizations that promote autonomy and flexibility for managers had gained him an international reputation, and he had studied the Tokyo school system that followed the same organizational pattern.[98] He brought this experience to the early meetings of LEARN planners. Ouchi's vision was decentralized, but it was profoundly managerial. The first of his seven keys to school success was "every principal is an entrepreneur." Principals may delegate power because it is good management practice, but it is theirs to distribute.

> It is true that systems that grant budgetary and personnel control to committees of teachers and parents rather than to the principal are unlikely to work well. That's because parents and teachers aren't accountable for either student performance or budget performance. It's the principal who is accountable, and it's the principal who should have the final say in these decisions. As we've pointed out, though, that doesn't mean that the principal should be allowed to become an emperor or empress—he or she should be expected to consult with and listen to all parties.[99]

Teachers in this model are professionalized in the sense that they have high skills and advanced education and need autonomy to do their jobs, but they are individually professional. Formal authority rests with the bureaucratic hierarchy.

The LAEP version of LEARN looked more like a producer's cooperative: the collections of family citrus groves that dotted Southern California (before smog and sprawl) where collaboration was necessary to water and market the crop, the Israeli kibbutz, or the worker-run factories in northern Italy. Those involved in producing education would have a decisional stake in the design and execution of schooling. Teachers in this model strive for collective responsibility. They are trained as and work in teams. They criticize one another's work and hold themselves accountable for results.

Variations of these two views of the school system in the making created both philosophical differences and different assessments of the implementation process. For Ouchi's M-Form decentralization to take place, money and authority had to be moved into the hands of the principals, especially money: "Ignore everything that you hear about local control. Follow the money—that's where the control lies."[100]

LEARN's legislative approach to implementation assumed that if the school board ratified the plan, district management would implement it. When budget decentralization didn't take place, "our response was we thought they were being deceitful, and we became angry. Not a constructive response, but understandable."[101]

The business-oriented LAAMP and LEARN participants were particularly edgy about the teachers' union, as was the District central administration. The LEARN Working Group was able to accept Helen Bernstein as the "good unionist," and in the same fashion the UTLA leadership was able to accept some of the administrators. "She used to call me her oxymoron. I was the good principal," said Howard Lappin.[102] But UTLA as a union was a different matter. Ouchi understood that union protection was necessary for teachers. "In fact, we have experience with this particular LAUSD hierarchy, and we know that it's capricious, and we know that it can be deceitful, and we know that it is self protective, and we know that it can be harmful to human beings, toxic to them."[103] But the union only had two ways of shielding teachers from the LAUSD hierarchy, he noted: "Either we're going to have a very thick rulebook that protects them, or you're going to give us decision making rights."[104] LEARN was supposed to slim the rules and provide flexibility at the school level by giving decisionmaking rights to the school. But the idea that a committee of teachers, including the UTLA chapter chair, would control those resources was not what the business executives had in mind. As Ouchi said, "So when we both said we agreed on school autonomy, we were thinking about two very different implementation models."[105]

For those doing the grassroots training and implementation, the key was getting action focused on instruction, and this required that the adults in the school get beyond "their adult agendas" and focus on instruction and learning. But that was slow in taking place. As the program evaluators wrote in 1998, five years after the LEARN plan was adopted, "next year we need to look at some bottom-line stuff—teaching and learning outcomes."[106]

The difference in perspective was also present within the Annenberg Foundation and the Annenberg Institute at Brown University. Theodore Sizer, who was the first director of the institute, was a passionate believer in school-based change. His Essential Schools program, which predated the Annenberg funds, was built around what became known as *authenticity*. Teachers would push aside mandates for covering an impossibly long list of topics and encourage depth and understanding of a few essential topics and questions. In L.A. school reformer argot, this became known as "going deep." Students would progress from year to year and graduate by presenting an exhibition of their work, a public presentation of written work, critical thinking, and research. In contrast, Vartan Gregorian, who was the president of Brown and the principal adviser to Walter Annenberg, favored systemic reform, which in practice looked a lot more top-down or at least more structured. Gregorian's interchanges with Virgil Roberts and others during the formation of LAAMP were efforts at negotiating this difference between school and systemic philosophies.

Finally, it became increasingly apparent, at least to the women involved, that there had been a division of labor between the mostly male LEARN Working Group, which was to think big plans and negotiate deals at the top, and the mostly female providers of coaching and education. There was quiet resentment of what were called "the boys down at the ARCO Towers." At one point, LEARN president Mike Roos referred to the organizations providing implementation assistance as "contracted vendors for services," something far less than the partnership these providers thought themselves belonging to. The remark incensed Peggy Funkhouser of the LAEP, and the organization's vice president Judy Johnson wrote Roos a "you're-not-thinking-about-this-straight" memo.

> It is inappropriate to describe the work in the trenches of changing schools and "pilots" as going nowhere. I believe that it is also not well advised to assert that systems change alone will be a great benefit to our students in L.A. School change is an essential part of systemic change. Research tells us that great teachers in fully-functioning schools will abandon their district, and even their careers, if the district climate does not support and reward them in their efforts to make changes that allow students to achieve at higher levels. We need both.
>
> [Reforming schools] is a tough job and it should not be done alone (and LAEP as well as other organizations serious about reforming schools do not

appreciate being relegated to "unimportant" back-up service to LEARN's agenda.)[107]

By 1998, the LEARN leadership began to despair about the possibilities of long-term success, and an organizational crisis developed. As LEARN chair, Ouchi asked the board, "Should we declare victory, strike our tents, and go home?" As he recalls, every board member said "no." But there was no clear sense of direction.[108]

Ouchi found himself at a meeting of the New Schools Venture Fund in Redwood City and remembers one speaker saying that multischool brands will appear for charter schools. "And I heard that and this light bulb went off in my head, ding! And I said, branded charter schools, federations of autonomous schools under a loosely knit central umbrella. That's an M-form structure. That's the LAUSD [as] we would like it to be. That's the LEARN plan."[109] And what had been a parallel universe of charter schools began to converge with ideas about reforming LAUSD.

CHAPTER 9

Permanent Crisis

A "Failing School District"

D uring the 1999 school board election campaign, the *Los Angeles Times* asked candidates whether they thought Los Angeles Unified was in crisis. Most incumbent candidates responded defensively. Barbara Boudreaux, for example, said, "Not really, not in crisis." Jeff Horton said, "Performance has not been that disastrous." George Kiriyama said, "Well, I don't know. I think we have turned it around the last two years." Of the incumbents, only David Tokofsky responded with an unequivocal "yes."[1]

In stark contrast, their challengers and the general public were brutal in their assessment. Genethia Hayes responded, "Absolutely. And it needs triage work." Caprice Young said, "I don't think people on the board really, fully comprehend the depth of the crisis." Yolie Flores Aguilar said, "Severely in a crisis." Mike Lansing's "yes" was unequivocal as well. And the views of the general public were closer to those of the challengers. In response to a *Times* poll, 63 percent rated the local schools as fair or poor, and only 27 percent approved of the school board's performance.[2]

Three of the four challengers won.[3] Only Tokofsky survived.

The declaration of crisis as a school board election issue foreshadowed a series of events that led to labeling the entire District a failure by 2006, despite a huge building program and test score gains that outstripped most other large California city districts. However, the crisis was not a turning point. LEARN, like other reforms, was categorized as a failed project, and the crisis appeared to be permanent.

"LEARN IS DEAD"

The declaration of crisis came on the heels of LEARN's effective demise. By the summer of 1998, it was clear that LEARN had run its course. After 104 schools embraced LEARN in 1996–97, extending the program to nearly half the schools in the District, Superintendent Sid Thompson announced that he would retire in June 1997. In part, he made the decision because storm clouds were gathering, and sources outside the district were looking fondly at how Chicago mayor Richard Daley gained control of that city's schools and ousted the top leadership.[4] That summer, Helen Bernstein, who had stepped down from the teacher union presidency after completing her second term, died tragically, struck by a car as she crossed Olympic Blvd. The departures of Thompson and Bernstein, both strong and long-term LEARN insider advocates, left little high-profile support for the program within the LAUSD establishment. Judy Burton, the assistant superintendent in charge of LEARN, was isolated from the rest of the District's structure, as were the LEARN schools. LEARN vice president Mary Chambers, who had been the seven-days-a-week operating arm of LEARN, resigned to take another job. Said Roos, "When you take the aggregation of those events, along with everything else, it isn't the same for me. I've gotta wake up. You know, I was tired, too."[5]

The school board further undercut LEARN when it promoted Deputy Superintendent Ruben Zacarias—never a strong LEARN supporter—to replace Thompson as superintendent. Before becoming deputy superintendent, Zacarias had been in charge of the schools in the heavily Latino Eastside, where LEARN had been denounced as a takeover by the white business elite. Zacarias began his term in the summer of 1997 with his own initiative. Called "Hundred Low Performing Schools," it combined publicly "naming and shaming" the schools thought to be the least productive with a revitalization of technical assistance. That school year only twenty-nine new schools entered the LEARN program, and the school board cut the LEARN budget by millions of dollars the following year. In his initial year, Zacarias got high marks from the school board, which announced, "We believe the superintendent is moving in the right direction," in its official evaluation.[6]

At the same time, relations between Richard Riordan, who had become mayor of Los Angeles, and the seven-member school board reached a nadir. Though he lacked any formal authority over the District, the recently reelected Riordan continued to use the mayor's office as a bully pulpit to challenge district officials and advocate reform. He openly sought to toughen accountability, fire bad principals, and reconstitute low performing schools. "We need a revolution," he was quoted as saying. Board members resented his intrusions, and mutual public recriminations grew increasingly common and ugly. Riordan publicly ridiculed board members and questioned their competence to pursue any coherent agenda.[7]

The growing dissatisfaction rose to the surface in the 1999 school board election, but dissatisfaction was not the only thing bubbling up. Methane and other toxic gases were rising to the surface of the Belmont Learning Complex, a $200 million combined high school and retail site under construction near downtown. Belmont became the symbol of the board's ineptitude. It was big, it was bad, and it was unfinished.[8] The criticism of it may well have been overdrawn. The school district had been encouraged to be more innovative in its land use and acquisition, and the mixed-use retail and educational site was its response. Much of Los Angeles sits on a pool of oil and gas, and in Beverly Hills the school district pumps and profits from oil on its high school site. Still, the symbolism of an exploding high school was headlined for months.[9]

Attention that had been focused on comprehensive school reform through the LEARN and LAAMP coalition moved away. In some cases, people faded from the scene. Robert Wycoff, who brought business leaders into LEARN, retired, remarried, and wanted to attend to family matters. Roy Anderson, who had initially spearheaded school reform in the late 1980s, retired and was in failing health. Peggy Funkhouser was retiring from the Los Angeles Educational Partnership.[10] Many of the key businesses that had supported reforms ceased to exist or were merged into other corporations. Even the venerable *Los Angeles Times*, which had shaken off its deep provincialism to become a widely respected newspaper, was sold.[11]

There was concern that the entire civic infrastructure would collapse. What did collapse was the belief that the District could heal itself, even with external assistance. When LAAMP board chair Virgil Roberts was asked what he had learned over the last fifteen years, he replied quickly, "That Los Angeles Unified as a school district is totally dysfunctional, and you probably can't fix it."

> I think what really led me to that conclusion was the experience that we had with LAAMP. . . . It was eye-opening to work with other [than L.A.] school districts that had the same population of kids, but different approaches to what they were going to do. I think the thing that stuck in my mind most was when—there were two meetings that I did with Maria [Casillas]. One was

when we were working with Pasadena, and we went to meet with the super-intendent. [He] was able to get all the principals in one office from all the schools. The other meeting was when we met with Santa Monica. We were able to get all the principals and the entire school board and the superintendent in one classroom. Now the thing that came home to me was in each of those meetings the superintendent [and the chair] of the school board could say, "This is what we're gonna do," and get buy-in from everybody that was leadership in the district essentially.[12]

If the former reformers and their newfound colleagues didn't believe that the school district could reform itself, what did they believe? Attention bifurcated into two somewhat contradictory paths. Practitioners and philanthropists transferred their affection and attention to the charter schools sector, and attention directed toward the District was aimed at creating coherence and centralized control. In addition to the belief that LEARN wasn't moving schools fast enough, there was a belief that the theory of action was wrong: An idea started in a few schools would not ripple out to the rest of the District; the virus of reform is not very catching.

In 1999, decentralization and LEARN were declared dead. Principal Howard Lappin announced the demise during a group interview with the *L.A. Weekly*. "That's not true," said Mike Roos, to which Lappin replied, "I'm sorry, Mike, it's dead. . . . As a LEARN principal who has been at it for a long time, I can say that everything is returning to the way it was."[13]

That same year, four of the seven school board seats were up for election, with all the incumbents running for reelection. Riordan and several of his business colleagues formed a political action committee called the Coalition for Kids and recruited a slate of challengers, in effect creating an opposition or reform party in this nonpartisan election.[14] The election was punctuated by a combination of a reform vision and the political clout of a civic coalition with roots in Riordan's 1980s Kids 1st effort. While the mayor and his friends raised and distributed cash for the campaign, some of them joined with other reform activists to form the Committee on Effective School Governance (CESG), which was technically an informational campaign but which advocated policies embraced by the opposition candidates.

Several members of CESG supported Riordan in his efforts to recruit and finance the campaigns of challengers to three of those members—President Barbara Boudreaux, Jeff Horton, and George Kiriyama—whom they viewed as ineffective in reforming the school district. Riordan and several CESG members endorsed challengers Genethia Hayes, Caprice Young, and Mike Lansing, as well as the fourth incumbent, David Tokofsky. Riordan and his allies raised more than $2 million for the reform slate.

Twenty-one of the twenty-six CESG members had been associated with LAEP (including Chair Doug Brengal), LEARN (including President Mike Roos and Chair Robert Wycoff), or LAAMP (including President Maria Casillas and Chair Virgil Roberts).[15] CESG published its views through LAAMP, which contributed $147,000 to the reform group.[16] As the election campaign was beginning in 1999, CESG issued a stinging indictment of the school board and, in effect, a code of conduct for board members to which it challenged candidates to subscribe. Its report attacked both the board's micromanagement of the District and its lack of a coherent strategy.[17] "Board members tend to see their primary role as satisfying the day-to-day requests of individual constituents rather than representing the community's long-term needs," it noted.[18] Pointing out that the District had set more than twenty priorities in recent years, the report offered that "having so many priorities really means having none."[19]

In a series of recommendations that would have been welcomed by the administrative progressives of the early century, CESG endorsed a strong, independent "superintendent as chief executive officer," a clearly defined set of priorities, measurable pathways to student achievement, and accountability.[20] It set up four candidates' forums during the campaign and undertook mass mailings urging substantial reform in the way the District was run.[21] Attendance at the forums was light, the largest at about 150 people—this in a school board district of 230,000 registered voters. But the press and cable television attention to the reform agenda was substantial and so, too, was the attachment of the reform label to the three challengers and one incumbent who had won the electoral support of Riordan and his friends. All the candidates pledged independence from the mayor but fealty to reform.[22]

It was a very ugly campaign. The contest between incumbent Barbara Boudreaux and Genethia Hayes, who was the executive director of the Southern Christian Leadership Conference, was particularly bitter. Boudreaux repeatedly attacked Riordan's support for Hayes as "plantation politics," and her supporters punctuated candidate forums by waving pictures of the mayor and twenty-dollar bills.[23] After a contentious campaign and a runoff to decide the Hayes-Boudreaux race, the entire CESG slate won and took office in June 1999, immediately electing Hayes as the new board president.

In her installation speech, Hayes pledged to help Superintendent Zacarias "to soar and to fly and to, unfettered, lead this district into the next millennium."[24] But within weeks there was talk of the superintendent's ouster. The new board understood well its mandate to "kill the culture of the District," as one CESG member put it. It first hobbled Zacarias by placing real estate attorney and former school board member Howard Miller in charge of construction. Riordan openly began discussions about a new superintendent, and after negotiations as ugly as the election, Zacarias resigned.[25] His flight into the new millennium lasted only two months.

Then the board brought in as interim superintendent Ramon Cortines, recently resigned chancellor of the New York City school system. Cortines, who said he would only serve six months and was as good as his word, famously pledged books and bathrooms—students would have textbooks and the toilets would be cleaned.[26] It was a measure of how far the school district had fallen, that a blunt, pragmatic interim superintendent could garner positive press from a pledge to undertake so basic a task.

Within two months, he and Miller had produced a plan to divide the District into eleven subunits, each with a semi-autonomous superintendent. Each of these subdistricts would be sizable in itself, approaching twice the size of the Boston or San Francisco public school systems. As the announcement was made, Cortines promised that the new superintendents would have autonomy: "The only responsibilities that will be directed by the central core will be those things required of us by the state and federal government, and things like the busing system."[27]

The plan was notable for what it did not say. There was virtually no detail about how much fiscal autonomy each subdistrict would have or how fiscal or operating autonomy would be made possible. The District would continue to have a single labor contract, all its schools would be owned and maintained by the central district, and it was apparent that at least some curricular decisions would be made centrally. (Shortly after the decentralization plan was adopted, the school board voted to require a single highly prescriptive phonics-based reading program, Open Court, for all elementary schools.)

While the District was trying to reorganize itself, it was also searching for a new permanent superintendent. Following a pattern in other big cities, the board hired a noneducator, former Colorado governor Roy Romer. Romer, who had also been chair of the Democratic National Committee and head of the National Goals Panel, brought a reputation for settling fights and building coalitions. While he had won widespread praise in the 1990s for intervening in Denver's public school system, he had no experience running an educational organization, and he got a rough welcome to the District. The *Times* called Romer a "71-year-old, well-intentioned but limited Democratic Party boss" and editorialized that the appointment was "ill-considered and seriously undermines confidence in the board's ability to set a sure course for the public schools."[28] The press warmed to Romer as time passed.

The "reform" board lasted one term, after which a slate supported by UTLA defeated all the members that Riordan had supported. But Romer survived. He centralized control of the District and launched a massive school building program. With its budget of $15.2 billion for new construction, repair, and modernization of existing facilities, LAUSD's building program exceeds that of Boston's "Big Dig," which, at $14.7 billion, has been described as the largest civil works project in U.S. history.[29] The eleven subdistricts, later reduced to eight, never gained the autonomy foreseen and promised by Cortines and functioned much more as administrative subunits. Although a workhorse with enormous energy, Romer never possessed the professional politically neutral competence ascribed to Progressive Era superintendents, and even after five years in office he was still considered an outsider by district principals and most of the central office staff.

Romer declared LEARN a failure and proceeded to promote centralized control and "managed instruction" of what was to be taught and how it was to be presented. To support Open Court Reading and a companion math program for elementary schools, Romer recaptured much of the compensatory education money from school site control, placed it in a single program, and made schools adopt it. In many ways this action is reminiscent of the victory of the administrative progressives over the pedagogical progressives in the early twentieth century. Managed instruction recreates the best and worst aspects of hierarchical control of the classroom, which historian David Tyack called "the one best system" that dominated school organization up until the 1960s.[30]

New computer capacity made it possible for the administration to monitor classroom outcomes closely, and the legion of language arts and math coaches directly examined instruction more closely than principals ever could. Test scores effectively replaced teacher judgment as the measure of achievement. Scores on each unit of instruction were captured about every six weeks; they were analyzed and feedback was provided to teachers. The system was supposed to foster a professional community. Romer hired University of Pittsburgh professor Lauren Resnick to help create substantive interaction among teachers.

But Romer's recentralization raised UTLA's ire, which particularly objected to the practice of having groups of teachers visit other teachers' classrooms. The practice was initiated as part of creating what were called professional learning communities, but teachers and the union saw "that Learning Walks were being used as a tool by administrators to mandate procedures, monitor their use, and evaluate teachers. In spite of frequent reminders that Learning Walks were non-evaluative, teachers' experience spoke otherwise. Many teachers felt patronized by the unwelcome visitors, who without ever addressing the teacher wrote down secretive comments, looked through teacher materials, and whispered to students."[31] UTLA pressured the District until Learning Walks were outlawed in the 2005 teacher contract.

"IT'S A FAILING DISTRICT"?

When Republican Arnold Schwarzenegger led a successful recall campaign to replace Democratic governor Gray Davis in November 2003, one of his first acts was to appoint Riordan his secretary of education.

Ideas for reform continued to percolate in Los Angeles, however. Early 2005 saw the emergence of the Small Schools Coalition led by charter schools entrepreneur Steve Barr. The coalition championed the conversion of Los Angeles to charter schools, or at least smaller conventional schools, and they challenged all of that year's candidates for mayor to get on board.[32] Nobody took them up on the offer, so Barr and the group began campaigns at individual LAUSD high schools to convince teachers and parents to petition for charter conversions.

Meanwhile, former Assembly Speaker Bob Hertzberg, a Democrat from the San Fernando Valley, tried to revive the decades-old idea of breaking up the District into several smaller districts.[33] Though he had some support in Sacramento, he finished third in the mayoral primary, and the idea of breakup once again died.

The winning mayoral candidate, Antonio Villaraigosa, was a former UTLA organizer, and with the union's endorsement his campaign made bland promises to champion improvement in LAUSD. Shortly before he was sworn in on July 1, however, Villaraigosa abruptly changed course and endorsed a legislative proposal by state senator Gloria Romero to give the new mayor the power to appoint the school board.[34] The idea lingered without much public discussion for months, and then in his first State of the City address Villaraigosa announced his intention to assume full control of LAUSD through a bill passed by the state legislature. The District was failing, he said, and needed clear, accountable leadership like the mayors were providing after similar takeovers in New York and Chicago.

Villaraigosa's plan sparked vociferous objections from Romer in his own State of the Schools address in July 2006. Villaraigosa's labeling of the District as a failure was nothing more than "propaganda," Romer said. On the contrary, "This is a district that has more success than any other metropolitan district in California in the last six years. This is a district which has been driving up some of the scores of the whole state." He made a detailed presentation of data on the District, explaining dozens of charts and graphs and particularly emphasizing research showing LAUSD to be outperforming other urban districts in the state. "If I were buying stock, that's a company I'd buy into because the lines are going the right direction." Romer added,

> The mayor made a fundamental mistake. He came in and said "I want to be a great city mayor," and he looked around and said, "I have to run the schools to do that." I wouldn't even argue with him on that point, but he should have said the following: "You've made some real progress. I can help you make that progress faster. Let's build on what you've done. I'll join you and here we go." If he had said that, we would all be here applauding.[35]

Romer was the first person in years to raise a serious challenge to the now-established view that the District was failing and in crisis. But no one outside the Central Office believed him. He left the District the next year.

Villaraigosa and Romero pressed on with their takeover legislation. After weeks of heavy lobbying with his old friends in the legislature, where he had once been Speaker of the Assembly, Villaraigosa brokered a compromise in August 2006 that allowed the mayor substantial control while retaining an elected school board and providing for input from surrounding cities. California State Assembly Bill 1381, also known as the Romero Act, passed overwhelmingly, and Governor Schwarzenegger signed the bill into law in September 2006. The LAUSD board immediately filed suit to block the law, claiming that it violated the state constitution by allowing a local government to take over an educational agency. In December 2006, the Second District Court of Appeal ruled AB 1381 unconstitutional.

The school board, seeing the writing on the wall, allowed Romer a graceful exit and appointed former Navy admiral David Brewer as the new superintendent. Brewer tried to hit the ground running. He commissioned a Florida-based management-consulting firm called Evergreen Solutions to write him a report explaining what was wrong with the District. Not surprisingly, they reported that the District was a mess, and in response Brewer pledged to clean it up.[36]

Villaraigosa remained undaunted, however. He shifted gears again and adopted Riordan's approach, recruiting or endorsing a slate of school board candidates who would support his approach to the District. "Among those struck by the similarities was Riordan himself. The plucky former mayor had an explanation, one characteristically his own. 'It's because I was right,' he said. 'And because he hired all my people.' For example, Riordan's chief of staff, Robin Kramer, is now Villaraigosa's chief."[37] Like Riordan, Villaraigosa raised money from his own campaign supporters to fund the slate, but this time the teacher's union was ready. UTLA set up the most expensive school board election in history. Candidates in two of the four races spent more than $1 million.

Villaraigosa's candidates prevailed in May 2007, bringing him a working majority of four "allies" to the seven-member board. Villaraigosa announced that he would not appeal the judge's ruling of his takeover plan, and soon afterward the new superintendent and the mayor negotiated a partnership between the city and the school district. "It's time to get out of the courtroom and into the classroom," Villaraigosa said.[38] "With this superintendent and this board in place, I am confident that we can forge the partnership envisioned by the [law]," he told the press.[39]

Throughout the process, Barr has emerged as the lightening rod for the charter operators, both because of his willingness to publically engage the mayor and because of his efforts to take over Jefferson and then Locke high schools. Both Barr and the mayor recognize the shifting alignments of federated school governance in California; both are willing to go to any arena in which they have an advantage and both have returned to Sacramento multiple times.

Meanwhile, Villaraigosa appointed former interim superintendent Ray Cortines as deputy mayor, and Cortines assembled a team to plan operational takeover of at least part of the District. Their plan, *The Schoolhouse*, borrowed heavily from LAAMP and LEARN's ideas.[40] The plan itself was not greeted with acclaim, or much attention, but the ongoing efforts to take over two or three clusters of schools continued to move forward. In spring 2008, Cortines was named deputy superindendent of LAUSD.

PERMANENT CRISIS

The word "crisis" connotes a turning point. The patient recovers or dies. A marriage is saved or dissolved. In what is remembered as the Cuban missile crisis, the confrontation between the United States and the Soviet Union lasted for twelve days in 1962, and during that time a small council of advisers to President John F. Kennedy steered the country though the problem and the crisis was declared over.[41] But public education exhibits no such turning points. "This place has been in crisis for a decade," a high-ranking LAUSD administrator said as this book was being written, and other crisis declarations go back forty years.

That declarations of crisis are not followed by rapid resolution has been a source of controversy and frustration in public education. Crisis is supposed to interrupt a stalemate.[42] From *Priorities for Education* in 1986 to *The Schoolhouse* in 2007, a declaration of crisis was supposed to create a call to arms, a coming together of people to work urgently to solve the problem. But the problem doesn't go away, and the crisis calls are repeated. In situations such as this, people and organizations exhaust their resources and patience. Individuals tire and turn their attention elsewhere. In Los Angeles, civic attention moved from being focused on the school district to being focused on the growing charter school sector. Meanwhile, policy scholars and political commentators declared both reform projects and the LAUSD to be failures.

Where crisis compels action, the declaration of failure connotes uncertainty, not knowing what to do next. People do not know what to think or how to act.[43] Often, they don't know where their own best interests lie. New ideas, such as those auditioned in LEARN and LAAMP, reduce uncertainty by explaining in a normative way what went wrong and how to organize anew. These same ideas become resources in organizing and coalition building, and they become weapons to delegitimate the old institution. They also act as blueprints for a new institution. When existing institutions fail, or appear to fail, "it is ideas that tell agents what to do and what future to construct."[44] New ideas (not old institutions) reduce uncertainty and lead the way to future action.

CHAPTER 10

Charter Schools

A Parallel and Converging Universe

PARALLEL TRACKS

On September 22, 1992, just as the LEARN plan was being developed, Governor Pete Wilson signed SB 1448, the Charter Schools Act of 1992, a charter schools bill sponsored by Democratic state senator Gary K. Hart of Santa Barbara. The legislation provided for the establishment of up to 100 charter schools that would be freed from most district and state education regulations by granting them special "charter" status.[1] That very same day, LEARN president Mike Roos met with the Los Angeles Chamber of Commerce Education Committee. It would later be reported that the Chamber of Commerce had sent a letter to state senator David Roberti urging support of both LEARN and charter schools.[2] The two reforms marched on parallel tracks.

California's charter school law was the second in the nation, following the passage of Minnesota's earlier in 1992. The threat of school vouchers in the form of the impending Proposition 174, and the debate over them in the state legislature, created the political climate for the bill's passage.[3] Hart said that he envisioned the proposed charter schools to be "where only the academic basics are taught; students and teachers do the work of custodians, and parents and children go to school together on Saturdays. . . . We are certainly going to get some innovation and variety in the schools that I think is way overdue. We are trying to break out of the bureaucratic, legalistic mode that is so frustrating to so many people."[4]

The text of the legislation said that it was the intent of the legislature to allow for the creation of schools that "operate independently from the exist-

183

ing school district structure." As specified in the California Education Code (EC) 47601, the purpose of the law is to:

- Improve pupil learning.
- Increase learning opportunities for all pupils, with special emphasis on expanded learning experiences for pupils who are identified as academically low achieving.
- Encourage the use of different and innovative teaching methods.
- Create new professional opportunities for teachers, including the opportunity to be responsible for the learning program at the school site.
- Provide parents and pupils with expanded choices in the types of educational opportunities that are available within the public school system.
- Hold the schools established under this part accountable for meeting measurable pupil outcomes, and provide the schools with a method to change from rule-based to performance-based accountability systems.
- Provide vigorous competition within the public school system to stimulate continual improvements in all public schools.[5]

In California, charter schools operate under a five-year renewable contract negotiated with a school district, county office of education, or the state board of education. Like noncharter public schools, charter schools are expected to demonstrate adequate or improved student performance under state and federal accountability systems. If a charter school does not meet specific achievement goals, the charter-granting agency can refuse to renew the school's charter.

Public funding for charter schools in California can come directly from the state or through the chartering district. Rather than applying separately for certain categorical programs from the state, charter schools currently receive a block grant that encompasses more than forty categorical programs. Moreover, charter schools are not bound by the specific requirements that school districts must follow for the categorical programs included in the block grant and can spend these funds at their own discretion. Charter schools may also access additional funding for students who are English learners or who are eligible for free or reduced-price lunches, and they may also apply separately to several state categorical programs and all federal categorical programs that are not included in the categorical block grant.[6]

Charters began as heresy, the product of strong-willed and entrepreneurial individuals looking to escape the clutches of the district bureaucracy. But by the turn of the century, people began to speak of charters as a "parallel universe." Charter schools are now often described as the idea that everyone likes. Although still opposed by some in LAUSD, and particularly UTLA, the idea of charters has gained acceptance as a means for public school reform rather than a method of escaping them.

Charters schools have bipartisan support, and advocates can be found among free market economists, civil rights leaders, religious fundamentalists, advocates for the poor, and public educators.[7] Such broad support is possible because the charter school structure brings together various combinations of autonomy and freedom from bureaucracy, the introduction of variety and choice or market mechanisms in public schooling, accountability and high standards, and parental involvement.

CHARTER SCHOOLS IN L.A.

In 1993–94, the first full school year after the passage of the Charter Schools Act, LAUSD had a total of fourteen charter schools enrolling nearly 13,000 students.[8] By 2006, LAUSD had 103 charter schools enrolling more than 33,000 students.[9] As a local newspaper described it, "If there is a center to the fast-expanding charter universe, it is the Los Angeles Unified School District, which is home to more charters than any other district in the country."[10]

The growth in numbers of charters in Los Angeles follows the trend in the state as a whole. In 1993–94, California had thirty-one charters enrolling 10,761 students. By 2006, there were 574 schools and 102,683 students, comprising 3.2 percent of the state's total enrollment.[11]

Charter schools in Los Angeles also parallel those statewide in the proportion of ethnic populations they serve. As a whole, charter schools in LAUSD and throughout California enroll greater percentages of white and African American students and smaller percentages of Latino students than do noncharters. In 2005–06, 23 percent of students enrolled in LAUSD charter schools were white, while only 8 percent of students attending LAUSD's noncharter schools were white. African American students made up 17 percent of the enrollment in LAUSD charter schools versus 11 percent in noncharter schools. Conversely, Latinos students made up 53 percent of student enrollment in LAUSD charters and 74 percent of the District's noncharter schools.[12]

The earliest charters in LAUSD were "conversion" charter schools: existing public schools that converted into charter schools. Under the charter school law, for an existing public school to convert into charter status, a petition must be signed by 50 percent of the permanent-status teachers at that school. Most conversion charters in LAUSD initially operated as "dependent" charter schools and, after 2002, as "affiliated" charters. Affiliated charter schools retain both a fiscal and a service relationship with the District, purchasing services, utilizing district teachers, and participating in collaborative programs and professional development.

In contrast, independent charters are legally independent entities and are fully autonomous from the district. Employees in independent charter schools are on charter school leave from the district for a period of five years, at the end of which time they either resign from or return to the district.[13] The great majority of charter schools in LAUSD operate as independent charters.

These early conversion charters may be regarded as a natural outgrowth from the earlier SBM and LEARN models. Certainly that was the thinking of Mike Roos, who remembered, "I didn't say it at first, in mid-1991, but I certainly was saying it by 1994, that our end game is you move these schools up with some level of quality control, and then you take them charter. That LEARN was a staging ground to convert them to charter schools. And that really was the end-game of LEARN, as we began to enunciate it in Working Group meetings."[14]

School board president Mark Slavkin also saw a natural connection between LEARN and charter schools, commenting at the time that charter schools were "the ideal model" for giving the local school site responsibility and a sense of ownership. He noted that "we're trying to duplicate that in LEARN, but I think charters in some ways are a more pure sense of how it ought to be done."[15]

Merle Price provides a career example of the interweaving of SBM, LEARN, and the charter school movement. As an assistant principal, he and the UTLA chapter chair at Jefferson High School wrote a school-based management plan in response to the SBM clause in the 1989 teacher contract. As the principal of Palisades High School, he was recruited by UTLA president Helen Bernstein to bring his school into LEARN. The autonomy offered worked for "Pali" High because it provided the opportunity of "creating a common vision of how we could utilize diversity for the benefit of all, improving instructional programs, having much more ability to determine our destiny. People had sort of circled the wagons and saw all these district policies as disenfranchising and contrary to local needs."[16]

The school had fallen on hard times. Enrollment had fallen from 2,600 to 1,500 as a result of demographic shifts, and resources had become tight. LEARN provided the opportunity for entrepreneurship within the school district. "LEARN had a whole marketing plan for how you changed community perceptions and we took that step farther" by transforming the school into a charter. Rather than hunkering down with the effects of low enrollment, "we went out and said, 'we have space for 1,000 more kids, let's go market that.'" Using curricular innovation and the school's location in the affluent Westside, Pali became an attractive school of choice and within two years had a waiting list of more than 500 students.[17]

As deputy superintendent for instructional services, Price coauthored the LAUSD policy document for charter schools. The charter policy brought forward many of the LEARN and LAAMP operating ideas. As did those two programs, charter policy requires a specific local school plan.[18] Price noted that experience with the reforms in the 1990s allowed Palisades High School an easy time writing its charter application: "LEARN helped with putting some more specific defining elements into the plan and that also set the stage for making it very easy to write the 13 elements of a charter petition, because the planning had already been done, the benchmarks were set."[19]

Charter plans must be specific, thus avoiding the problem of high-flown language that plagued many of LEARN's attempts to get schools to write Site Action Plans. Charters must include descriptions of the instructional methodology to be used and how the school plans to embed professional development in the work schedules of teachers. Measurable student outcomes are required, as well as a governance process that includes parent involvement—all LEARN ideas.[20]

It took nearly ten years for LAUSD to develop and approve its "Policy for Charter Schools in the Los Angeles Unified School District," which the Board did on June 25, 2002, under the leadership of board president Caprice Young. Young was elected to the school board as part of a reform slate in 1999 and was heavily supported by former mayor Richard Riordan and CESG, which was largely made up of LEARN and LAAMP board members. She was defeated for reelection four years later in a campaign in which her opponent, Jon Lauritzen, was heavily supported by UTLA. Young went on to become the president and CEO of the California Charter Schools Association.

The District's charter school policy was developed through the collaboration of three groups: a newly formed Focus Group of Charter School Developers, which consisted of leaders of both conversion and start-up charters; the long-standing LAUSD Superintendent's Charter Advisory Committee; and the staff of the LAUSD Charter Office. According to the policy's vision, LAUSD viewed charters as representing "the opportunity to examine practices and develop structures that can help solve the many challenges facing schools in the Los Angeles Unified School District and the greater educational community."[21] However, the District policy also sets up what is a highly regulated charter school market. There are specific criteria for entry, elements of due process for deciding whether to approve a charter, and an explicit set of steps in the approval process with appeal rights.

In addition to outlining the charter development process, the policy also called for the development of a "Community of Practice," which was to create "a network of support, accountability and dissemination of best practices for continuing and newly established charter schools."[22] Along with sharing information and resources, this network was charged with recommending policy to the District. In turn, the LAUSD Charter School Office was to convene a yearly conference or symposium "dedicated to the meaningful sharing of best practices."

The policy also identified a list of ways in which charters might "provide possible solutions to urban school challenges," including:

- Easing the shortage of school facilities and seat space
- Narrowing the achievement gap among students of various backgrounds
- Increasing responsible parent and student involvement in learning
- Improving teacher quality and performance evaluation systems
- Providing data to help identify and evaluate issues that affect quality educational programs and student learning and achievement
- Serving as laboratories to test, demonstrate and disseminate ideas that can promote better educational practices
- Providing an additional educational option for parents[23]

In reality, LAUSD sees charters as both threat and opportunity. The District has adopted a small high schools policy requiring its large comprehensives to subdivide themselves into smaller "houses" or learning communities, and it has embarked on a large building program that will introduce many physically smaller high schools. It is presumed that many of those will be operated as charters.

At the same time, piecemeal chartering is troubling. Three of the District's highest performing comprehensive high schools operate as independent charters: Palisades, Granada Hills, and San Fernando Valley. "I take this present method as a very serious threat to the whole district," former Superintendent Roy Romer said in 2003.[24] Likewise, some school board members resent the amount of time spent approving and monitoring charter schools. In fact, the District allocates twenty-seven employees and an annual budget of nearly $4 million to provide oversight and support for charter schools.[25] Caprice Young recalls one board member complaining that "we don't even look at our own schools with this kind of rigor."[26]

NO LONGER MOM-AND-POP: THE RISE OF CMOS

By 2005, the charter movement had matured, and it was said that the era of independent "mom-and-pop" schools was over.[27] The rise of Charter Management Organizations (CMOs) has put increased pressure on school districts throughout the state and especially in Los Angeles. CMOs operate as not-for-profit organizations. In some states, for-profit school management companies have been established to take advantage of the nationwide charter school business opportunity. However, in California the average per-student funding is so low (thirty-second in the nation in 2005, and more than $4,000 less than funding in New York state) that most companies have chosen not to operate schools in California because they would most likely prove to be unprofitable.[28] CMOs are centrally managed systems of charter schools that can leverage the benefits of scale and experience. California is home to a number of CMOs, which take a variety of different approaches toward organizing and managing their education programs, governance, and business functions.

The first CMO to operate in California, and the first to develop and implement a not-for-profit CMO business model, was Aspire Public Schools, headquartered in Northern California. Founded in 1998 by former public school superintendent Don Shalvey and Silicon Valley entrepreneur and Netflix founder Reed Hastings, Aspire opens and operates public charter schools throughout California with an emphasis on serving low-income communities. Aspire's business model combines principles of entrepreneurship and standardization. Shalvey likens it to the notion of the Starbucks model, where a cup of coffee at 6:00 A.M. tastes the same as one at 10:00 P.M. Consistency is key, Shalvey said: "It's where the Starbucks inside me comes out. It doesn't mean you can't be creative but it means you have to have a strong tool kit and then get creative. So we're doing what I think are innovative practices around getting better at commonplace things."[29]

Like many charters, Aspire pays close attention to student outcomes. It uses what it calls a "balanced scorecard" to evaluate its effectiveness and to hold itself accountable for results: "The Balanced Scorecard, a tool developed in the private sector, is a way to ensure an organization is measuring all the important factors that contribute to success. In Aspire's case, that includes measures related to students, staff and community. The organization has set goals for each metric. Measures are taken at the individual and site level, and 'roll up' to provide a complete picture of the organization's effectiveness in meeting its goals."[30]

Compared to many charter schools, Aspire takes a somewhat more circumscribed approach to parent involvement. Aspire schools involve parents in decisionmaking at the school site through participation on School Advisory Councils and Teachers Hiring Committees and in yearly "grading" of the schools. However, unlike many charter schools and even private schools, parents and students are not represented on Aspire's board of directors. Shalvey explains: "In a business of choice, if they don't like the way you're running business, they'll go to a different business. And if we are a true school of choice, then that's the rule we have to play by. So that's why there aren't parents or students on the Aspire board of directors. We've been very true to that operating principle . . . and it's just the opposite in school systems."[31]

As of the 2006–07 school year, Aspire was serving more than 6,000 students in grades K–12 at twenty-one locations throughout the state, with plans to open three to four new schools each year.[32] They are also exploring opening charter schools in Los Angeles in the near future.

While Shalvey and Hastings were forming Aspire, Shalvey was also working as a consultant for the Santa Monica–Malibu Unified School District. The district had received a LAAMP grant to establish Critical Friends Groups, and Shalvey was the "critical friend" for Malibu High School and Lincoln Middle School. It was also during this period that an important friendship between Shalvey and future Green Dot Public Charter School founder Steve Barr was solidified. As Shalvey tells it, Steve "basically shadowed me for about a year-and-a-half when we were developing Aspire. Steve would pick me up at the airport, drive me to Lincoln, I'd work there, and he'd pick me up at the end of the day. . . . I was one of the three founding board members of Green Dot."[33] And three of Lincoln Middle School's teachers would go on to assume senior leadership positions at Green Dot.

Green Dot, founded in 1999, describes itself as "the leading public schools operator in Los Angeles and an important catalyst for education reform in the State of California." It states that its mission is "to transform public education in Los Angeles so that all young adults receive the education they deserve to be prepared for college leadership and life. Green Dot's work is directly focused on influencing LAUSD to transform its failing high schools into clusters of small successful schools and helping the District reinvent itself as one of the best school districts in the country."[34] As founder, Steve Barr said in a 2007 interview with the *Los Angeles Times*, "My mission is systemic change. . . . I don't want to be building charter school No. 49."[35] By 2007, Green Dot had opened ten charter high schools in some of the highest-need areas of Los Angeles and had announced plans to open twenty-one new high school campuses by 2010.

Often called brash and confrontational, Barr has deep roots in Democratic Party politics as a fundraiser and campaign organizer. Jaime Regalado, the director of the Edmund G. "Pat" Brown Institute of Public Affairs at Cal State Los Angeles, describes Barr as having a "take-no-prisoners style" and observed that "he's channeled the outrage of African-American and Latino parents into the public space in a way that's new."[36] In 1990, Barr cofounded Rock the Vote, which led the way to the first upward surge in eighteen- to twenty-four-year-olds voting since the passage of the Twenty-sixth Amendment, and he led the successful effort to pass the Motor Voter Bill, which was signed into law in 1994 by President Clinton.

And while most charters have nonunion teachers and are often called "union busters" by opponents, Barr supports organized labor, and teachers at Green Dot schools are unionized, although their contract is less rigid than those at other L.A. schools. Green Dot's teachers are represented by Association de Maestros Unidos. Their union contract is thirty-three pages long and offers competitive salaries but no tenure. It also allows for class schedule and other instructional flexibility outlawed by the 330-page contract governing most LAUSD schools.[37]

Green Dot is one of approximately six major CMOs operating schools in and around LAUSD. These include the Knowledge Is Power Program (KIPP), a national CMO started in 1994 that operates two schools in Los Angeles;

Partnerships to Uplift Communities; the Accelerated Schools; Inner City Education Foundation; and the Alliance for College Ready Public Schools. Combined, in 2006–07 these CMOs operated thirty-two schools within LAUSD and enrolled more than 8,000 students.[38]

THE ALLIANCE

The Alliance is the organizational descendant of LAAMP and LEARN. As LEARN and LAAMP shut their doors in 2000, they formed a new organization, temporarily called L3. Its board of directors was almost entirely composed of veterans of the two older organizations. Early on, the new board decided it would no longer be engaged in large-scale systemic reform projects; the appetite for that had simply run out. The new organization took on the mantle loosely defined as "advocacy," but it was unclear what was being advocated. The name was changed to the Los Angeles County Alliance for Student Achievement, or simply the Alliance. Within its first year, the organization declared itself to be in the charter school business as the Alliance for College Ready Public-Schools.

Alliance board member Virgil Roberts recalled that the origins of the group as a charter school operator began with a simple question: "What's the best way to educate the kids?"

> Let's not start from how we change the system. Let's look at it the other way around. What does it take to educate the population of kids that we have and to achieve the standards that we want them to achieve? Because I think when you start off by asking, "How do we change the system to make that happen," you are starting off with the wrong assumption. Rather than asking "How do change our Model T factory to make Ferraris," let's talk about how we make Ferraris. What's the best way of doing that? And then figure out how to modify our system to do that. So that was our charge. . . . And what we came back with was charter schools, because it gives you the opportunity to do all the things you want to do with public schools, but you're able to create your own culture and climate for success without buying into any of the history of the past. [39]

Another Alliance board member, William Ouchi, first heard about the concept of "branded charters" at a conference hosted by the New Schools Venture Fund.[40] The idea of charter schools as "federations of autonomous schools under a loosely knit central umbrella" immediately appealed to Ouchi, who remembers thinking, "That's what we would like LAUSD to be. That's the

LEARN plan." He continued, "We didn't know we wanted it, because when we created the LEARN plan there was no such thing as a charter school in America. They didn't exist. But our idea was to turn the LAUSD into a network of charter schools. And I said to myself, if we can't fight them and win, we can compete against them and demonstrate by our example that this idea works. This is what we have to do."[41]

The Alliance mixes the unabashedly corporate with the educationally interesting. It has a business plan and corporate-sounding titles. Judy Burton, who headed the LEARN office, was hired as the president and chief executive officer. Howard Lappin, who transformed a moribund South Central L.A. middle school into the celebrated Foshay Learning Center, became the chief academic officer.[42]

Simultaneously, the Alliance carries forward some of the educational practices ideas that were found in LEARN and LAAMP: great autonomy for schools, the idea of small learning communities, critical thinking skills, project-based learning, high expectations, staff development embedded in the school day and year, and technology integrated into teaching.[43] Lappin says that the idea that developed in the 1990s "was that the school would, in essence, be what have become charter schools."[44]

Lappin believes that LEARN could not have survived inside the District. "The deputies and the assistants and the mid-level bureaucrats—and I'm not going to name any more names, because I know them all—just hated the idea that principals could make decisions, that schools could make decisions for themselves."[45] Charter schools may have started as an escape from a smothering and frustrating bureaucracy—which Caprice Young likened to "swimming through stinging jellyfish-infested molasses"—but they have become a parallel and sometimes intersecting model of reform.[46] Much of the personal energy and sense of excitement attached to LAAMP and LEARN now flow through charter school formation and operation; charter schools are an outlet for philanthropic instinct and civic engagement for mavericks and entrepreneurs, for the visionary and driven.

Charters in Los Angeles compete with the school district, but not in the way that free market advocates suggest. Thus far there is only a single case in which a charter operator has caused the closing or reorganization of a traditionally operated neighborhood school (Locke High School by Green Dot in September 2007), which suggests the good-drives-out-bad market logic has, as yet, little influence in Los Angeles. Instead, charters have been winning the competition in ideas and political organizing. Most of the LEARN-like ideas about school autonomy and operations have persisted in charters, not within LAUSD. Most of the LAAMP-like ideas about parent involvement and grouping schools into families are found among the charters. But where LAAMP created geographically contiguous organizations, charter operators are creating a network of schools based on a particular theme or idea.

This dynamic may change, however. First, declining enrollment caused by population exit from Los Angeles and a decline in births is pinching LAUSD finances and causing staff reductions at many elementary schools. In this environment, movement of children to charter schools is directly and immediately felt inside conventional LAUSD schools.

The second recent change is a renewal of interest in decentralized management in the area surrounding Belmont High School, in Superintendent David Brewer's Innovation Division, and in Mayor Villaraigosa's Partnership for L.A. Schools. In what is called "the Belmont Zone of Choice," for example, seven small schools are being developed as essentially in-district charters modeled after the Pilot Schools in Boston.[47] These schools remain fully LAUSD operated, and the teachers stay in the UTLA teacher bargaining unit under a shortened contract. Such innovations increasingly take on the qualities of charter schools yet under a different name.

MISSION AND METRICS

The charter school world in California has also become increasingly sophisticated in terms of development and operations and the formation and utilization of expert networks. Through the establishment of networking, advocacy, and support organizations such as the California Charter Schools Association, charters have essentially created a parallel universe. Membership in the California Charter Schools Association (the Association) offers "an array of products, services, expertise and financing tools to strengthen our member schools and allow them to focus on what matters most: educating students."[48]

Most recently, the Association launched the nation's first Certified Charter Schools Program. Participation in the program includes commitment to high-quality academic, fiscal, and governance standards along with an independent peer review.[49] According to the Association, certification means "parents can choose a charter school with confidence, authorizers can renew a charter with conviction and participating schools can show their continuous improvement towards their mission and goals."[50]

The Association also helps to connect charters with a range of vendors who can provide everything from school construction and back office support to curriculum and special education services. In fact, an entire industry—both for-profit and not-for-profit—has sprung up to support charter schools. One charter provider has even begun its own graduate school of education in order to train teachers and school leaders.[51]

One of the leading providers of development, business, and management services is the nonprofit ExED. ExED, which stands for "excellent education through charter schools," was founded by William E. B. Siart in 1998. Siart, the former chairman and CEO of First Interstate Bancorp, was a finalist for the job of LAUSD superintendent in 1997.[52] ExED has had particular success in helping finance charter schools, including applying for and being awarded a $36 million allocation of the New Markets Tax Credit (NMTC) from the U.S. Department of the Treasury, which will be used exclusively to create facilities for charter schools in low-income Los Angeles communities. ExED has used these tax credits, coupled with grant funds, to provide below–market rate loans for charter school operators, and it expects to make five to seven charter school facility development loans with these funds.[53]

Another nonprofit, Pacific Charter School Development, based in Huntington Park, was founded in 2003 by former corporate executive Glenn Pierce and New Schools Venture Fund executives Kim Smith and James Willcox. According to its website, Pacific Charter School Development was formed to "address the single greatest hurdle that high-quality charter schools face in educating urban children—securing adequate academic campuses."[54] Their business model is designed so as to "marshal the resources of the leading members of the philanthropic community and socially-conscious lenders to produce new school seats in low income communities with the greatest need."[55] In 2008 they were the recipients of a no-interest $6 million loan from arts and education philanthropist Eli Broad's foundation to help jump-start the development of at least seventeen new campuses in the L.A. area.[56]

The California Charter Schools Association's stated goal is to enroll more than 10 percent of California public school students in charter schools by the year 2014. This goal is echoed by other charter school advocates and is viewed as an important tipping point toward achieving broader public school reform. As Reed Hastings explains, "One way to permanently impact the system would be to have 10 to 20 percent of California schoolchildren enrolled in charter schools. That would be critical mass, and enough of a force to induce a competitive dynamic in the system."[57] And Shalvey believes that they will succeed: "I believe we're succeeding and we'll succeed at scale, like [Green Dot] is succeeding at scale and KIPP is succeeding at scale. All with different theories of action."[58]

Young describes the charter school world as falling within three distinct categories: those who are "rescuing kids" and creating an elite; those who see themselves as creating "replacement schools" while the "public school monopoly" continues to fail; and those who are trying to create systemic change. It is this last category that has captured the imagination and support of venture capitalists and philanthropists as well as a variety of charitable foundations, including the Bill and Melinda Gates Foundation, the Broad Foundation, and the Walton Family Foundation.

Organizations like the New Schools Venture Fund or the Charter School Growth Fund[59] typify the approach of venture philanthropists in supporting charter schools. Committed to expanding high-quality K–12 educational opportunities for the underserved (and in some cases to transforming public education more broadly), these organizations hire staff with business, venture capital, and philanthropic experience and invest in new charter schools and provide them with financing and hands-on management assistance.

The New Schools Venture Fund was founded by entrepreneurs and venture capitalists on the premise that just as the power of entrepreneurship can create new and visionary organizations in sectors such as technology, so too can education entrepreneurs bring about dramatic change in public education if they are given strategic, hands-on support in starting and growing their organizations. The New Schools Venture Fund is headed by Theodore Mitchell, one of those former L.A. school reformers who is now an active supporter of the charter school movement both in LAUSD and throughout the state.

California's charter school law specifically states that charter schools are to be held accountable for meeting "measurable pupil outcomes." In reality, achievement outcomes for students attending charter schools both in California and nationally are mixed. In 2004, two contradictory studies on charter schools and student achievement and the resulting controversy made front-page news.[60] Most researchers agree that measuring and comparing the performance of schools is "always a complicated endeavor."[61]

After controlling for differences in enrollment and student characteristics, a 2007 report on California charter schools concluded that:

1. Elementary charter schools did not perform as well as elementary noncharters;
2. Charter middle schools significantly outperformed noncharter middle schools;
3. Charter high schools scored higher than noncharters on the API, but the results were not stable over time; and
4. Charters run by management organizations scored significantly higher than other charter schools. [62]

In fact, some charter schools in LAUSD are struggling to meet the requirements of NCLB, and in 2006–07, more than half a dozen charter elementary schools were designated as Program Improvement schools.[63] California Charter Schools Association CEO Caprice Young does not worry about the rigor of state standards or NCLB: "It's okay if schools go out of business and assets are reallocated."[64]

Despite the rhetoric of charter schools having more flexibility for creativity and innovative instruction, what sets charter schools apart from traditional public education is not necessarily their innovative educational methods. Young describes charter schools as "the traditional model of education done well." Or as Aspire's Shalvey puts it, "We are trying to do the common thing uncommonly well."[65]

For Young, one of the major differences is a simple matter of paper. She points out that the entire California Educational Code for charter schools is only forty-five pages, as contrasted with the tomes of code for noncharters whose numbered sections exceed 100,000. Charters also have a much more simplified financing structure. In addition to giving greater budgeting flexibility and control at schools sites, this allows opportunities for outsourcing of business functions, professional development, and even more specialized educational services.

A CONVERGING UNIVERSE

Charters have carried forward many of the ideas from the earlier reform efforts of LEARN and LAAMP and continued to audition them with increasing effectiveness. They offer parents choice and involvement, smaller personalized settings, administrative autonomy, and a high degree of accountability.

In Los Angeles, charter schools have also become a powerful interest group with powerful allies in the mayor's office and on the school board. Green Dot's president and chief operating officer, Marshall Tuck, was appointed in January 2007 to direct the Mayor's Partnership for School Excellence, which will help the mayor implement reform efforts in three clusters of LAUSD schools. Green Dot also convinced the Los Angeles school board to let it take over Locke High School, one of the lowest-performing schools in LAUSD and in the state.[66] Outside of L.A., the Green Dot model has gained national prominence and made inroads with the powerful United Federation of Teachers, as it entered into a partnership with the New York City teachers' union to jointly run a New York City charter high school in the South Bronx.[67]

Charter schools may also be redefining the role of school boards. In the process of developing the Alliance charter schools, Virgil Roberts remembered thinking, "maybe we don't need school boards. I mean, the money comes from the State, textbooks come from the State, professional development standards are set by the State. Why do we need school boards?"[68]

In comparing his experience as a public school superintendent answering to an elected school board with that as a CEO reporting to a board of directors, Don Shalvey says that it is much easier to work with a board of directors: "The Aspire board of directors comes for only one reason and that reason is to make sure Aspire leads its mission and its metrics. And there's no other reason why they would come." Board members also can be selected for particular talents or experience, allowing the organization to "identify the resources you need to really get the job done," as Shalvey recounts. "The best example I can give you is that we had to get through this decision of whether we're going to open schools in Los Angeles or not. And as a board we looked at it as a team. We looked at it and we made the decision that we would not seriously consider going to Los Angeles until we had brought on a board member who understood multi-regional retail, because [at the time] we had no one on the board to do that." Moreover, Shalvey believes that "an elected board of education has built in flaws that keep the organization from moving forward."

> The special interest aspect of elected boards erodes some of what you need to get your job done. The short life span of a school board and of many school board members who see this as a career ladder for public service and there-

fore make decisions either based on their constituencies or based on the next best thing coming up. And in California, school boards are asked to do an almost impossible thing in my mind, which is to essentially govern a school district without the ability to raise revenue. What a crazy situation when your only option is a school bond.[69]

Perhaps most significantly, charters are creating a competitive idea of what a school district should be, and they are moving the dividing line between public and private. *Public school* in Los Angeles as elsewhere meant publicly owned, operated, governed, and staffed. Teachers were employed by the District, they organized themselves into unions, joined a pension plan with other public workers, created careers based on the internal labor market of the district, and formed professional relationships and often deep friendships— all based on the membership-by-employment that working for the district afforded. Now, *public school* is coming to include organizations operated by nongovernmental organizations in which the teachers may or may not be public school employees and in which allegiance and professional identity may be more centered around the particular style or identity of the charter school operator rather than the school district. Ideas about what constitutes good teaching, acceptable behavior, and other professional norms and values are more the creatures of the charter network rather than district culture or policies. Conspicuously, charter school operators have appended the words "public school" to their names, as in Green Dot Public Schools.

The very idea of a public school district is changing gradually. The district has a contractual relationship with the charters rather than a managerial one. Among metropolitan-sized school districts, LAUSD may be closer to the contracting-out model proposed by policy scholars Paul Hill, Larry Pierce, and James Guthrie than any in the country.[70] The district has become partly operator, partly contractor, and, through its choices of charter operators, partly the holder of a portfolio of schools.

Yet, just as the identity of public schools has changed, so has the meaning of "private." Under California law, an existing private, independent religious school or for-profit organization cannot become a charter school. But in their entrepreneurialism and their operations, charters act more like private than district-run schools. This essentially private instinct has been brought under public regulation and thus brought the not-so-invisible hand of government deep into the nonprofit and philanthropic world. Along with the growing body of charter school law and regulations, the district in its oversight role strongly influences which charter school providers are allowed and whether or not they will continue to operate.

Since the initial charter school legislation was passed in 1992, California lawmakers have passed a number of laws that affect the governance, accountability, and funding of charter schools. In 1999, legislation (Senate Bill 434) was passed to require a specified minimum number of instructional minutes, the maintenance of written attendance records, and certification that students have participated in the state's Standardized Testing and Reporting (STAR) program. Also in 1999, the passage of Assembly Bill 544 included, among other things, a provision to compel school district governing boards to approve charter petitions unless they make specific, valid written findings that the proposal is unsound or otherwise fails to meet specified standards of law.

Four years later, in October 2003, Assembly Bill 1137 put into effect a series of specific accountability requirements with regard to oversight and outcomes. Districts were now required to conduct annual site visits and to ensure that "the charter school complies with all reports required by law, that the fiscal condition of the charter school be monitored, and that timely notification be given by the charter authorizer to the California Department of Education in cases where renewal of the charter is either granted or denied, the charter is revoked, or the charter school is to cease operations (regardless of reason)."[71]

In turn, new reporting requirements were placed on charter schools:

> Specifically, charter schools must submit a preliminary budget on or before July 1, an interim financial report on or before December 15, a second interim financial report on or before March 15, and a final unaudited report on or before September 15 for the full prior year. Reports are to be submitted to the charter authorizing entity and the county superintendent of schools, or only to the county superintendent of schools if the county board of education is the chartering entity.[72]

But perhaps most significantly, this legislation requires specific student performance outcome measures for charter schools in order for their charters to be renewed.

> Commencing on January 1, 2005, or after a charter school has been in operation for four years, whichever is later, a charter school's charter may not be renewed unless specific performance standards have been met. Among the

performance standards that may be used to satisfy this requirement are: (1) attainment of the school's Academic Performance Index (API) growth target; (2) an API decile ranking of 4 or better; (3) an API Similar Schools decile ranking of 4 or better; (4) documented evidence that the charter school students are performing at least equal to that of the students in schools of the district that the students would otherwise be attending; or (5) the school qualifies for participation in the Alternative Accountability System Model.

While charter school advocates such as Caprice Young support regulations aimed at ensuring the fiscal soundness and academic success of charter schools, there is also concern about encroaching bureaucracy. She observed in the press that the petitions required to start a charter "have gone from 75 pages to nearly 500."[73]

The convergence of charter schools and reform ideas within LAUSD strongly suggest the form of the new institution. If history is a guide, two possible institutional reforms have already been politically eliminated. California voters have defeated voucher initiatives, and a reprise of the idea is garnering very little support in the current policy environment. At the same time, maintenance of the existing school district in its current form is proving not to be very politically exciting. All the reform auditions suggest that the new institutional form is some combination of decentralization to somewhat autonomous schools within the district and charters or charter management organizations. In many ways, LEARN, LAAMP, and the charters follow the same developmental path: moving operating authority away from the central office and vesting much greater decisional power at the school level. At the same time, both district-run schools and charters have bowed to the power of the state to set outcome standards and to test students in their achievement.

CHAPTER 11

Beyond Crisis

Structuring Politics for a New Institution

"There's *puro canto y nada de opera* (much singing but no opera)."
—*Maria Casillas, LAAMP president*

The process of institutional change lies in developing and enacting new ideas, not in recreating or defending the old ones. As suggested at the end of the last chapter, the transition from a massive hierarchy to a network of schools is already under way. But the process is stifled in part because there is a strong instinct, particularly among the business elite, to recreate Progressive Era professional dominance and the politics of quiet elite influence that accompanied it; and there is an equally strong instinct among teacher unionists and administrators to protect existing turf.[1] In Los Angeles, policy entrepreneurs are equally drawn to seeking a czarlike superintendent and to the charter schools sector. The more open system of decentralized operations and community-based schools appeals to many businesspeople and community activists. The tension between those who would recreate the old system, only make it better, and those who would follow the reform pathway has produced a state of "permanent crisis."

In Los Angeles, crisis mongering has not enabled anyone to gain the necessary political legitimacy or operational capacity to quash opponents and successfully restructure politics. Instead, education in Los Angeles is in a period of great uncertainty and political churning even though the ideas about reform have proved remarkably stable. All proposals from the District-generated plans of the 1980s to Mayor Villaraigosa's *Schoolhouse* plan in 2007 have proven to be variations on the same themes.

Moving beyond permanent crisis first requires realizing how much things have changed already and how substantively different the ideals about the future are than those from the past. Then, it requires structuring politics to make the new ideas work.

It is clear that LAUSD operates within an institution that has been radically altered from the ideal of a school district that the Progressive Era reformers put in place a century ago. The dimensions of the emerging institution seem clear. Instead of a district run by a local elite, there is one whose board is at once the creature of and the target of multiple interest groups—from business groups and the mayor to organized parents and a teachers union powerful enough to turn board members out of office. Instead of a locally controlled district, authority and influence are scattered from Washington to Watts, from capitols to neighborhoods. The District no longer sets tax rates, picks the course of study for students, single-handedly controls the curriculum, or manages the testing of students. Instead of a single hierarchy commanded by a professional educator as superintendent, there is a complex web of experts—both employees and contractors—who create curricula, advise schools, and provide direct services to principals and teachers. Instead of a high-trust environment of confidence about school operations, the District is subjected to a low-trust environment of compliance and consequences.

This reality clashes with the ideal embedded in LAUSD by the early twentieth century reformers who "wanted to buffer schools from lay influence, to eliminate ward school boards, to consolidate small districts, to restructure city schools as hierarchical and specialized bureaucracies, and to differentiate the curriculum to fit the presumed abilities and needs of students. They sought to reorganize schooling systematically on principles of business efficiency and educational science."[2]

In the place of the old institutional ideas, reforms and political change have given us four new ones:

Pluralistic politics: Activists, governing bodies, interest groups, parents, and voters now compete for control of virtually everything that happens within public education.

Federated governance with multiple levels of control: From site councils to the central office to Sacramento to Washington, D.C., and everywhere in between, dozens of governments make policy for the district, its schools, and its teachers.

A network of experts instead of a hierarchy: While remnants of the old command-and-control hierarchy remain, educators and administrators more often find themselves working across the boundaries of the organization with colleagues, consultants, and contractors.

Accountability with consequences: The performance of students, teachers, schools, and districts is more transparent than ever, and they are rewarded or punished on the basis of data about tested outcomes.

NEW IDEALS WITH UGLY FACES

Each of these four ideas is recognized as an ideal, something that a new institution of public education should be built around. (See Table 11.1.) But each is Janus-like, and the ugly frowning face is all too apparent. In reality, the democratic practice of pluralistic governance is conducted through aggregations of people into interest groups, and the image of interest groups is not nearly as appealing as that of a can-do executive who stands tall and shoots straight. The ideal of grassroots democracy morphs into the reality of school board meetings packed with angry parents agitated by professional community organizers or parent coordinators, who are actually on the payroll of the school district. Political theorists, policy scholars, and reformers alike shied away from the reality of strong teacher unions or the messiness of vocal parents. Ironically, it has largely been the much-maligned school administrators who have attempted make a badly defined environment work.

Similar tensions arise for each of the other ideas as well, presenting tremendous challenges to reformers who want to make the best of this new reality. These four ideas are inescapable features of education policymaking, but they do not necessarily make for successful reforms. Are there ways to channel these ideas, to structure reform politics in ways that advance the best of these ideals without letting their destructive sides make things worse? To date, most attempts to do this have proven incomplete and inconclusive.

Pluralistic Politics and Self-Interest

Americans count schools among our most basic democratic institutions, and we demand that they be responsive to our demands and aspirations. The problem is that others we disagree with want them to be responsive as well, and those others often organize into interest groups to advance their causes. Political competition among these organized interests can paralyze schools or, worse, lead them to do things we may not like.

TABLE 11.1
Old and New Institutional Ideals

	Characteristics of the Progressive Ideal	*Characteristics of the Emerging Institution*	*The Ugly Face of the New Ideal*
1.	Apolitical Governance *The Ideal: Clean and visionary* • Nonpartisan elections • Civic elites govern	Pluralistic Governance *The Ideal: Representative and responsive* • Powerful interest groups • Strong alliances to local and national political parties • Shifting civic coalitions	*Narrow Self-Interest.* • Tendency for representation and advocacy to descent to narrow self-interest. • Short-term calculation of interest. Uncertainty about one's real interests.
2.	Local Control *The Ideal: Civic pride and community values govern* • Finances and educational policy • Policy momentum through a national network of superintendents	Federated Control *The Ideal: Distributional equity* • Increased state and federal government influence • Policy momentum through state and national policy networks	*Gridlock* accompanied by competing claims and jurisdictions between levels of government. • Hollowing out the ability for independent action. • Complex and lengthy decisionmaking processes. • Tendency toward single issue politics.
3.	Professional Hierarchy *The Ideal: A professional civil service* • Operational control by professional administrators • Access to positions by specified education and licensure • Internal labor markets • Vertical integration of functions	Expert Networks *The Ideal: "Close to the customer" expertise and decisionmaking* • Operational control not limited to experienced educators • Hybrid models of administration combining career professionals, managers imported from other sectors, and external operating organizations • Chartering and contracting out	*Lack of Competency* in decentralized operations. • Lack of technical knowledge and ability. • Loss of coherence in the system. • Tendency toward process paralysis.

4.	A Logic of Confidence	A Logic of Consequences	*Limited System Capacity:*
	The Ideal: Independence of action and flexibility in the bureaucracy	*The Ideal: "All children can learn"; universal high expectations*	the lack of a known technology to produce the results demanded by accountability systems.
	• Loose coupling of allocation and oversight decisions to the technical core	• Direct internal and external oversight of results	• Tendency to recentralize.
	• Incentives based on organizational loyalty	• Linked with (largely negative) incentives for individuals and schools based on student results	• Emphasis on an industrial division of labor.
	• Bell curve expectations in which noncompletion represented student failure or lack of ability or motivation	• Externally created, near-universal standards in which dropping out represents system failure and discrimination	• Narrowing of instructional mission to match tests and sanctions.

There are two common policy responses to political conflict among powerful interest groups in education. The first is to try to make the groups go away or dampen their power, as Governor Schwarzenegger tried to do in 2005 when he advanced unsuccessful ballot initiatives to limit the influence of public workers' unions. The second is to try to channel the energy of interest groups in constructive ways, which appears to be what Mayor Villaraigosa is trying to do in his efforts to influence the District.

As everyone since James Madison in 1787 has recognized, it's hard to make interests go away.[3] The teacher unions—object of most anti–interest group efforts—survive and gain influence even in states such as Texas, where collective bargaining is not mandated. But American history demonstrates that the participation and power of interests can be structured and channeled, both in the range of what interest groups can be allowed to influence and in the ways they are allowed or encouraged to pursue their goals. The Progressive Era founders understood this. When they called for apolitical governance—taking the schools out of politics—they meant taking schools out of the partisan and demonstrably corrupt municipal politics of Los Angeles and California and creating and sustaining governance by a civic elite. Elite politics eventually collapsed, and even the efforts of LEARN, whose leadership included corporate heavyweights, could not reconstruct them. Meanwhile, the school board became more explicitly representational.

This breakdown of elite politics ushered in a period of domination by interest groups, and, as in most cities, the strongest interest group in Los Angeles is the local teachers union. It is easy to characterize UTLA as big and bad, an organization whose power far exceeds the responsibility it takes for the school district's outcomes. The collective bargaining contract it negotiates effectively governs how the district spends its operating budget and its personnel policies. It contributes hundreds of thousands of dollars to school board and other elections, and it heavily lobbies school board members.

Like many stereotypes, the "big and bad" characterization contains partial truth. However, the history of UTLA's participation in school reforms is much more subtle. LEARN as a reform probably would not have been possible without the leadership of Helen Bernstein. But her participation in LEARN made the reform suspect among school administrators, and it probably strengthened their determination to strengthen their own union. UTLA negotiated strong incentives for teacher professional development in the form of a hefty $15,000 pay raise for teachers who become nationally board certified, and it runs one of the largest programs in the country that prepares teachers to take the National Board for Professional Teaching Standards examination. Its organizing strength was vital to the success of the District's bond election campaigns to build new schools.

The current political environment challenges UTLA in many ways. Its strength exists largely within the boundaries of the existing District, and thus the shifting politics threaten the union as much as the District. Nowhere is this more apparent than the emergence of the charter sector. Both Mayor Villaraigosa and Green Dot Public Schools present a particular hazard. Green Dot's schools are unionized, but its teachers have organized a separate union local. Both the mayor and Green Dot founder and CEO Steve Barr are experienced organizers with impeccable union credentials and ties to the Democratic Party, so conflicts with the union occur within the political party traditionally supportive of the union.

UTLA is also challenged by the politics of accountability and consequences. So far it has been able to fend off calls for linking teacher compensation and student outcomes. But the union has not put forward a coherent way of linking collective bargaining and other teacher advocacy with student outcomes, and thus they allow themselves to be vulnerable to successive policy entrepreneurs.

UTLA is, of course, far from the only interest group. Particularly over the last decade, interest in education policy has spread to the charter schools sector, which has organized rapidly and effectively.

Parent and community-based organizations have coalesced less rapidly and with less strength than charter school operators and supporters. But one of the legacies of LAAMP was a spin-off organization called Families in Schools. In its startup it was largely apolitical, providing books and backpacks to students and encouraging parent participation. In recent years, the organization has been run by former LAAMP president Maria Casillas, who has given a sharper edge to the group's work. By 2007, a number of community organizing efforts were ongoing in Boyle Heights, the Belmont area, and North Hollywood. The Annenberg Foundation heavily supported the Boyle Heights Learning Collaborative that seeks to activate parents both as their children's first educators and as public voices. Alliance for a Better Community is active in Latino neighborhoods and was instrumental in lobbying for completion of the Belmont High School construction and the issuing of Latino Scorecards in 2003 and 2006.[4] Another Los Angeles–based community organization, New Schools Better Neighborhoods (NSBN), utilizes a mix of public and private funding to serve as a "catalyst and third-party intermediary to front-fund, convene, and manage collaborative, stakeholder master planning of joint-use, community-centered pre-K facilities, schools, parks, and family resource centers in Los Angeles County and throughout California."[5] NSBN offers a unique combination of master planning, advocacy, and community engagement strategies to meet their goals of raising student achievement and revitalizing neighborhoods.

Given the proliferation of interest groups and the political clout attributed to them, it is surprising that there are not more clear winners among them.[6] One can argue that UTLA has been successful in protecting member's jobs and that the contractual web of work rules hobbles principals from harsh discipline. But the big payoff for teachers seems elusive. In 2000, California teachers ranked thirty-second among the states in inflation-adjusted salary, and teacher salaries overall have not kept pace with inflation.[7] Vigorous union representation has not replaced industrial-era workplace routines with those resembling a professional community. One can ask similar questions about parents or civil rights advocates, politicians, or business interests. If someone is winning big, the prize should be more visible.

Broader participation in politics is the contemporary ideal. Unions, charter schools, parents, and scores of other interest groups make up the real face of broadened participation. The dilemma is that broadening participation requires structuring participation to make it productive. LEARN tried to do this by creating a classic big civic coalition and unitary politics in which the things that drew people together were stronger than those that separated them.[8] LEARN's failure to keep a coalition together underscores the difficulty of banking on subordination of self-interest. Instead, picking potent, central issues to fight about may better advance the necessary task of making varied interests productive.

Federated Control and Gridlock

The early Progressives believed in local control. They recognized that school systems were creatures of the state, and their intention was to increase state oversight of the many rural and small-town school districts that were seen as hopelessly backward. But city schools were a different matter. They were of sufficient size to be professionally efficient and to have a citizen-elite enlightened enough to provide forward-thinking control. Local control was critical, in part because school building and operations rested largely on the local property tax, and school board members were supposed to be among the opinion leaders that could convince their friends and neighbors to tax themselves to support schools. Local elites could also see that their mores and cultural values were supported by the curriculum and evident in school operations.

As we've seen, local control dissolved. The symbolism of local control of schools, like states' rights in general, shifted from benevolent paternalism to bigotry and racism: a white establishment illegitimately protecting its interests. Civil rights cases and legislation were an explicit attack on local control, as were the categorical programs initiated during the Great Society programs of the 1960s. In the aftermath of these successful challenges, LAUSD is now effectively governed through a multilayer federation.

But federated governance is subject to deadlock, complex decisionmaking, and protracted inaction. While efforts have been made to simplify the arcane reporting requirements of categorical funding, it is clear that the reporting and accountability requirements of federal NCLB legislation are driving behavior in the school district. Initiative and referendum have proven extremely disruptive to school operations. Even Proposition 98, which was supposed to lift California school funding to the level of the other large industrial states, has been "a sausage of unintended consequences."[9] Rather than increasing funding, ten years after it was passed in 1998, schools were getting less in inflation-adjusted dollars than they were before the measure was approved.[10] Even though direct democracy did not solve the school's financial problems, the shift in the political process meant that "real policy decisions are now being made in the plebiscitary process and not in the halls of the legislature or the office of the governor, much less at the school board or city council."[11]

Authority over California schools has shifted dramatically to Sacramento, but the state governmental structure is wildly incoherent. California elects a state school superintendent who heads the Department of Education. The department, however, answers to a state school board, which is appointed by the governor, and many board members have themselves become policy entrepreneurs rather than trustees. For example, Marion Joseph, who served on the board for five years at the turn of the twenty-first century, campaigned for a phonics-based language arts curriculum, and she remains an advocate.[12] Netflix founder Reed Hastings, who served as board chair for two terms, is an advocate for charter schools and was one of the early investors in the New Schools Venture Fund. The legislature, of course, has active education committees, and legislative initiative was responsible for charter school laws. But in California the governor holds the fiscal trump, the right of line-item veto over appropriations that would fund the legislature's policies. Historically, the governor had an education adviser, a staff member who modulated educational issues for the chief executive's ears. In the last decade, this position has become a cabinet position, and the governor's appointed secretary of education is seen as the conduit to power at least equal to the elected state superintendent of public instruction. Former Los Angeles mayor Riordan briefly served as education secretary in 2004, and he was followed by former San Diego superintendent Alan Bersin, who also had a brief and unhappy tenure.

Streamlining this system is not a short-term task. But the history of reform inventions shows that more sensible alignments are possible. State charter school policy has already produced potentially useful new ways of moving both money and authority to individual schools. Layers of regulation have been removed. Categorical funds have been bundled so they can be used without as many cumbersome reporting and accounting procedures.

The role of the school boards (both state and district) has been clarified so that boards do not micromanage the charters, although charter advocates complain about increased regulation. Much of what schools sought under the LEARN and LAAMP reform efforts has in fact been delivered to the charter sector but not to regular District schools. Given these examples, at least a partial approach to the problems of federated governance can be found in applying some of the regulatory logic and ethos found in the charter sector to regular LAUSD schools.

Expert Networks and Operating Competence

The early-twentieth-century Progressives made their ideas work by professionalizing school administration. The superintendent of schools became the unquestioned leader of the district, and the district and state invested in the infrastructure to legitimize a new profession of school administration. This new model borrowed heavily from business practices, which at the time included a heavy dose of vertical integration. Just as a steel manufacturer would purchase iron mines, a city school district, and particularly a big one, would bring under its direct control the design of curriculum and pedagogy, the training of teachers, and a host of ancillary services, from nursing to running mammoth kitchens. Former superintendent Sid Thompson recalled his introduction to the school district when he started as a teacher in 1956. His first impressions were more about scale than purposes: "Of course, I didn't know how the District operated then, I just knew it was massive amounts of ice cream, and massive amounts of hamburgers, because they took us on tour to show us the warehouses."[13]

To enable productive control over such huge organizations, the structures of a profession were created for school administrators. Training programs were established for teachers and administrators, licenses were created. Professional norms and standards were attached to school accreditation. School superintendents' voices dominated the discussion about educational policy in the state. Although the trappings of professionalism were created for teachers as well, it was clear that one side effect of this managerialism was the subordination of the role of teachers and teaching.

Over the last forty years, the ideal of a vertically integrated professional hierarchy has been seriously challenged and compromised. The persuasiveness of the Progressives' call for professionalism and independence, and thus an end to political interference in school operations, rested on their demonstrated ability to design and deliver the core functions of schooling. Particularly within big cities, the curriculum (and its delivery) was generated within the district. In the last decade, however, the instructional design of primary elementary education in particular was outsourced to two corporations, McGraw-Hill and Houghton Mifflin. Unlike book companies, which had sold school districts texts for generations, McGraw-Hill markets the Open Court system as an entire integrated instructional machine. It offers stories, problems, end-of-unit tests, and feedback to teachers. LAUSD coaches critique lessons, how classrooms are organized, and what is displayed on bulletin boards. They run feedback exercises at the end of units in which teachers are required to write down what they could do differently in the future, an exercise that teachers interviewed in this research have found degrading. At the same time, teacher-generated innovation has become increasingly the function of external organizations, such as LAEP.

In the former world of professional domination, the central ideas flowed from within a rather tightly bounded system known as the "iron triangle": influential superintendents mostly from big cities, deans of education at leading universities, and the National Education Association (in its pre–collective bargaining days). Within the last twenty years, idea generation has broken out of such tight boundaries to the point that virtually any area of education is politically contested terrain. Most visibly, the internal career ladder to the superintendency was broken. In this century, two noneducators have become superintendent of LAUSD: a former governor of Colorado and a retired U.S. Navy admiral. Noneducators were hired at lower positions as well, particularly in finance and construction. More importantly, the vertical integration between educational design and curriculum and its pedagogy that characterized LAUSD and other big city school systems was compromised.

LEARN and LAAMP auditioned expert operating networks as alternatives to the old system of insular, top-down control. The LEARN model created an internal network of teachers, committees, and parents, and it created an external network of advisers, coaches, and access to knowledge. LAAMP created families of schools in which the points of tangency between one campus and another were not necessarily through the school hierarchy but through the expertise of teacher leaders and what LAAMP called "critical friends."

Those auditions did not always go well. Some self-designed network operations were extremely cumbersome, and schools somehow forgot to design in the extra two days a week it would take to attend the meetings and gain the consensus necessary to keep the network operating. LAAMP families resembled human families: Some were sources of strength and ambition; others were dysfunctional.

Both reforms demonstrated the problems in building competence for a network of schools. Even though upward of $10 million in foundation funding was devoted to professional development during the 1990s, the amount proved to be nearly trivial in the context of a school system with a multibillion dollar annual budget. Reformers also discovered that it was surprisingly difficult to create school staffs confident and competent enough to examine how their schools operated and the relationship between how they used resources and the results they were seeing from students. The irony is that the more schools are decentralized, the more sophisticated the professional infrastructure needs to be in order to provide the necessary craft skills and analytic ability.

Competence in network operations was also harmed by the shortness of the LEARN and LAAMP trials. Most schools had three or fewer years of operation, not nearly enough time to establish a track record and to start to internalize the lessons of operating in a mode other than that of a conventional public bureaucracy. Network competence requires experience over decades, not months.

Logic of Consequences and System Capacity

Most significantly, without recognizing it, or organizing around it, public education has taken on the expectation that a very large percentage of students will be educated to a high standard. This is a far different goal from what the Progressives gave the schools in the early decades of the twentieth century, and a far different goal from that LAUSD was organized around in its glory day. As the work of various scholars and advocacy groups illustrates, there are individual schools that successfully educate poor and minority children to high levels. There are, however, no districts that can replicate this performance across a large number of schools. In late 2007, the California Department of Education named ninety-nine (out of about 1,000) school districts as "failing" under the requirements of NCLB and thus subject to state intervention.[14] Other states had similar experiences.

Intervention only works if those intervening have a sure knowledge of how to set things right. Few do. Intervention in LAUSD schools by the state, county, or the District itself has a long and largely unsuccessful past. In California, the use of detailed intervention protocols extend back at least twenty years, well before the current federal mandates. Some LAUSD schools have been subject to four or more attempts by teams of outsiders to set things right. It should be reasonably obvious at this point that the entire system lacks the capacity to produce the results sought and that the adoption of any particular packaged program will not save the schools or the District.

Instead, schools and districts will need to find their way to what educators might call a new technical core: new ways of providing and managing instruction, new ways of coordinating operations. By looking at school districts around the country and state, it is apparent that innovation and improved performance are possible, but not by obvious means. There are quite different results being achieved from similar levels of resources, and there are quite different processes being used to produce similar results. No one has yet figured out how to capture in a bottle the lightning of dramatically improved school performance. Relatively more freedom and experimentation are needed, rather than a broader application of some agreed-upon standard operating procedures.

EVOLUTION AND INTELLIGENT DESIGN

Institutional transformation that can accomplish such sweeping goals requires a mixture of long- and short-term thinking and action. Short-term action is necessary because activists, from parents to philanthropists, are drawn to education reform by the promise of results: They feel an urgent need to make a difference for children currently enrolled in schools. Long-term thinking is necessary because it will take perhaps a quarter-century to get all the pieces in place. The political process for both the short and long term is a mixture of experimentation with explicit systems thinking—or, in other words, a constructive combination of both evolution and intelligent design.

Combining evolution with explicit design would mirror the efforts of the early-twentieth-century administrative progressives, who, as historian David Tyack noted, "had a clear vision of how to reform American school systems. . . . Their reforms were not piecemeal ones but a package they considered coherent."[15] The vision guided their day-to-day actions, even as it guided their slow creation of organizations and practices that would advance their goals of educational improvement.

In seeking to achieve institutional transformation comparable to that of the Progressive Era, one is tempted to advocate a grand design strategy something like a city charter commission or a state constitutional convention. But there is not a comparable vision of what the new institutional order should look like, nor do we share their confidence that we can come together and agree on one. Given the relative lack of success of past blue ribbon commissions, investigative grand juries, consulting reports about the District and, indeed, LEARN and LAAMP, attempts to forge consensus on some specific, comprehensive reform program seem likely to lead to additional frustration and disappointment.

Likewise, wishing for an end to day-to-day partisanship and interest group politics is bound to lead to dashed hopes. California has prospered during shining moments of unitary politics. The phrase "the Party of California," was coined to describe the high levels of cooperation fostered in Sacramento during the post–World War II era when the state grew spectacularly, and commentators frequently wish it to return. Even though the phrase was given new currency by Governor Arnold Schwarzenegger in his 2007 second-term inaugural speech—"The people are disgusted with a mindset that would rather get nothing done than accomplish something through compromise"—politics as usual followed.[16]

Both long- and short-term perspectives are necessary to move beyond a state of permanent crisis. The Los Angeles reform experience should amend the political theory that change will occur rapidly when the old equilibrium is disturbed.[17] The problem for public policy is not simply getting problems and proposals on the agenda and disrupting the existing system but figuring out how to sustain attention to the issue and direction over a quarter-century, a constructive contribution to evolution and intelligent design.

Evolution is found in the day-to-day policy of experimentation and best practices, conscious attempts to try alternative ways of teaching and learning and to extract a set of practices from experience. It was also part of LEARN's implementation design: Schools would consciously learn from their experiences and from those of other schools in the program. Both the federal government and numerous foundations follow this path. Evolution is also consistent with the new breed of philanthropists and foundations that want to try new ideas now and see if they eventually pay off rather than continue investing in the existing institution.

One might add that the evolutionary approach has deep roots in public policy. Political scientist Charles Lindblom observed decades ago that even in cohesive policy domains, policymaking is usually done on a day-to-day, year-to-year basis by trial and error.[18] Economist Anthony Downs showed that shifting coalitions and a fickle public made for incoherent environmental policymaking, for example, and yet in the middle of this incoherence the Environmental Protection Agency was created.[19] If successful policy is seen as progressing from agenda setting to legislation or mandates to implementation, scholars agree that this process almost always brings constantly vexing political challenges. The problem of implementation is nearly universal.[20]

The evolutionary approach of experimentation and slow, adaptive change is consistent with what happens in classrooms and schools every day. Most of what educators do with children is built around what might be called a weak core technology: Only rarely is it possible to specify what teaching and learning approaches lead to a desired outcome for any particular child on any particular day. Yet children *do* learn, and society continues to demand more. The all-children-can-learn slogan of the 1960s and 1970s became a social expectation and then a legislated standard. It no longer counts that the District graduated most of its students, or even that many of them went to college. Neither the labor market nor an increasingly demanding critical public is satisfied with a system that graduates fewer than 20 percent college-ready students from many of its schools. The conditions of poverty and race, which were given as justification for meager results forty years ago, are no longer acceptable.

However, evolution and incrementalism have their limits. The search for powerful pedagogical or programmatic remedies has proven elusive. While there are vigorous debates about the value of different pedagogies and approaches to learning, there are no off-the-shelf answers to the problem of educating large numbers of English-language learners to a high standard, filling them with a sufficient love of learning and appreciation about the stakes involved that they persist in high school and graduate ready for college. LEARN and LAAMP bundled best practices from Los Angeles and around the country in the 1990s but failed to produce rapid achievement gains. Centralized control and curriculum coherence in LAUSD began to produce achievement gains that outpaced other California districts with similar demographics in the first years of the new century, but hundreds of schools were still labeled as failures by state and federal testing programs. The challenge is to produce continuous incremental improvement while creating and sustaining practices that encourage continuous vigorous searching for more systematic alternatives.

This combination of short-term and long-term effort would require reimagining the notion of systemic reform in a more thoroughgoing way.[21] At its best, it would enable a reworking of the entire education system from the individual child up to the national level, rethinking the work and responsibility of every participant as well as the division of resources, authority, and labor. This reworking would drive not only longer-term reform efforts, but it would also shape the daily decisions of everyone in the system. This is the polar opposite of what our current state and federal policies encourage.

An evolutionary approach to institutional change can also take advantage of the information technologies that have emerged in the last decade. When LEARN started, the Internet was still exotic, and only a small percentage of households were connected to it.[22] Since then, the power of its connections has changed how business is done and how people collaborate to get work accomplished. The idea of open source learning is exemplified in such massive collaborations as Wikipedia, the online encyclopedia, and in the development of computer languages. The most powerful, and largely unrecognized, change in education is the ways in which students access information and the ways in which teachers collaborate to change how they teach. Thus far, these experiments have seldom been encouraged or been able to bubble up to affect the system.

Simultaneously, long-term attention provides an opportunity to soften up the political landscape so it can accept change.[23] Sustained attention allowed the charter school idea to move from political backwater to generally accepted public policy, but that process took nearly a quarter-century. Interestingly, twenty-five years was about the span of time between the pioneer urban superintendents of the nineteenth century and the writing of the first texts about how to operate professionalized schools in the Progressive model. Thus, building a civic infrastructure around a new ideal requires a willingness to keep long-term goals in mind every day, to keep the central ideas alive while waiting for or creating political opportunities to carry them out. This strategy paid huge dividends for conservatives, who turned the politics of ideas into real political power beginning with a range of think tanks, some of which operate in California and participate in the ongoing delegitimation of public education.[24]

Long-term attention also may provide ways around contemporary political gridlock in Sacramento. Making a solution for Los Angeles contingent on finding a solution in Sacramento invites despair and inaction. But presenting institutional change as a long-term goal may make it more politically attractive in an environment where relatively small revenue infusions can sometime set more significant change in motion and where a political constituency for larger change can grow over time.

Governments are not good at long-term attention, and California, where term limits virtually erase the institutional memory every decade, is worse than most at sustained attention. Interest groups excel at long-term attention, but they tend toward narrow-gauge objectives and short-term definitions in their own interests that make it difficult for them to understand institutional change, much less operate as its effective agents. This leaves three potential groups, either individually or in combination: universities, foundations, and individual policy entrepreneurs. Of the three, individuals have the most freedom of action, but foundations have the resources. In the past decade, California has been in the forefront of venture philanthropy that is in some ways reminiscent of steel magnate Andrew Carnegie's giving during the last gilded age.[25] Venture philanthropy has a decidedly entrepreneurial bent. There is an appetite for risk but also an expectation of results. Whether foundations become sufficiently long range in their attention or systemic in focus remains to be seen, but the door of political opportunity is open.

WRITING A NEW INSTITUTIONAL TEXT

One way to know that a new institution has taken hold is to find that someone has written a textbook on how to operate within it.[26] When the administrative progressives took hold of public education in the early twentieth century, their activities were followed by texts written by the reformers themselves, such as Stanford University professor and dean Elwood Cubberly, whose 1916 *Public School Administration* became a touchstone for a generation of school administrators.[27]

Such textbooks come in two kinds. Operational texts such as Cubberly's and the scores that have come since provide concrete guidance about how to organize a system and how to conduct oneself as a leader. These spawn craft knowledge and lore among those doing the work and make possible formal training programs. The new institution does not yet have an operational text, although there is a great deal of operating knowledge and manuals exist for parts of the institution, decentralized schools, for example. But there is another kind of text presented here, a text about political organizing. If one subscribes to the belief that institutions don't just happen, that they are caused by deliberate political acts, then it becomes imperative to think in institutional terms and to plan actions accordingly.

CHAPTER 12

Five Policy Levers

What We Learned from L.A.

In various ways, all the past reforms have auditioned a network form of organization. Where bureaucratic hierarchies look like tall triangles with power and authority at the top, networks look like lattices or spiderwebs, with power in the nodes and the linkages between them. At the center of the network, a small core staff provides strategic direction and support. Because each of the operating nodes works independently, networks can respond more quickly and are considered better than traditional hierarchies when customization or task complexity is required. Their relative isolation allows more experimentation and learning from mistakes. In a well-designed network, if one part fails the remainder is not compromised.

In a network form, the smaller scale of and substantial autonomy in individual schools would simplify the managerial structure and reduce the diseconomies of scale that have plagued LAUSD. In the charter sector, firms have already appeared to provide services that central administrations now provide, or sometimes notoriously don't.

A network of high-capacity schools would re-center authority on the school and focus on the educational work that happens there. It would expand the roles of teachers, principals, and parents as they work to support and educate students. It would also create a new role for the school district as the manager of a portfolio of schools: monitoring performance, adding potentially strong schools, and eliminating weak ones. Finally, it would expand the state's role as an agent of assessment by revamping the testing and assessment system and placing positive incentives behind them for schools and students.

In order to establish a network of schools, five policy changes are needed, whether accomplished through statute, initiative, or charter amendment. Each raises substantive education issues and likely will provoke disagreement among educational interest groups. The fights over these issues are important and worth having; the use of political capital around these issues is likely to be consequential and to lead to a more effective institution.

AUTONOMOUS SCHOOLS AND NETWORKS

For more than a generation, LAUSD has both frustrated and been frustrated by efforts to decentralize. In large measure, LAAMP and LEARN did not persist because they lacked an anchor in political legitimacy. When the reformers tired, the program fell apart. The legal and social structures attached to the conventional hierarchy turned out to be more powerful than the reform organizations, despite the reformers' zeal and philanthropic support.

Meanwhile, the charter school universe began creating its own institutional structures, including a school code, a financing system, and a support infrastructure. By 2001, some 105 charters operated in LAUSD in addition to 162 magnet schools that are freed from some District regulation. Over the years, the form of chartering moved from individual schools, "mom-and-pop charters," to groups of schools operated by Charter Management Organizations (CMOs).

In addition to accommodating the charter schools that now exist, LAUSD needs a way to effectively decentralize the public schools it operates. The statutory tools currently available to charter schools—regulatory codes, financial formulas—can serve as models for legislation or an initiative that would create legitimate autonomy within LAUSD. Charters offer other valuable resources as well, including new management experience and the more compact and flexible labor contracts already negotiated in the charter sector and in the new experimental Belmont Zone of Choice within the District.

The District needs to be legally enabled to follow a similar developmental pattern by creating legally autonomous networks of schools. Legal authority to create autonomous networks, and legitimation of those networks, is an important policy requirement. It would remove the status of the autonomous networks from the favor or disfavor they have with any given superintendent. One of the clear lessons from LAUSD history is that whatever structural arrangement is favored by the current superintendent will not be favored by the next one. Each new chief executive follows the almost-universal managerial instinct to gain control over the unwieldy district by recentralizing or reorganizing its functions. Thus, any attempt to decentralize the district must have a strong anchor in legislation to ensure that it will survive beyond the term of any one superintendent.

The logical geographic form of autonomous networks would be a high school and its feeder schools, something like the clusters that LEARN first envisaged and the School Families that LAAMP enacted. But there are other forms, too. A cluster could be based around identifiable neighborhood lines, or a group of schools could be organized around a theme or idea such as magnet schools or brand-name charter operating organizations like KIPP and Green Dot.

Given legal authorization, the District could entertain petitions to form autonomous clusters from teams of existing school managers who undertook the design of the petition and were committed to its development. Or it could entertain petitions from CMOs, such as Green Dot, which has taken over operation of Locke High School, or the Alliance for College Ready Schools, which spun off from LAAMP and LEARN. Or it could seek petitions from groups of teachers or their union, as is being done in New York. Likewise, the District could expand the Belmont pilot schools model. Or it could follow all of the decentralization paths simultaneously.

This process of evolving into autonomous operating units offers several advantages. First, it allows artful borrowing from the experiences in the charter sector without becoming a charter district as that term is generally understood, as a "locality in which all public schools are charter schools." Second, it would allow schools operating under an autonomous network statute to borrow from the experience of the charter sector without leaving the existing District. Third, autonomous networks would be a means to legally decentralize LAUSD without resorting to a legal breakup of the District, which would most likely simply reproduce the existing organizational problems on a smaller scale. The networks would have the same operating freedoms that existing CMOs possess, and the schools within an autonomous network could legally be charter schools or they could follow the models created by experiments in LAUSD schools. Fourth, the autonomous network idea would allow grassroots connection between schools and community without creating the relatively cumbersome governance arrangements that some other cities, such as Chicago, have attempted.

For teachers and administrators working in District-operated schools, and for the students attending them, autonomous networks would offer the possibility of positive action within LAUSD. The current bifurcation between highly regulated District schools and the much greater freedom of action allowed in the charter sector creates a strong incentive for people who want to make city schools work to exit LAUSD, and it ties the hands of those who stay. It is, in effect, a handicap given to public school reformers, a disadvantage that fairness and equity suggest should be removed.

What would LAUSD become? LAUSD would still be the school district for Los Angeles and the other municipalities where its schools are located, but it would operate more as a hybrid organization than a hierarchy. "Portfolio of schools" has been applied to this idea, but that term has picked up political baggage in its association with outsourcing and for-profit providers. Still, the portfolio notion is an apt one. LAUSD, like a public pension fund or private investor, would put its resources behind the best set of schools that it could. Some of the schools would be traditionally run existing schools while others would be located in the autonomous networks; some would be individual charters, and some would be run by CMOs. LAUSD would retain oversight capability and sufficient accountability to allow denial or renewal of charter status. All the schools would have the same accountability rules for outcomes. Autonomous networks would be reviewed periodically, perhaps every five years, in an examination that was paired with accreditation. But the District would retain no managerial or operating authority over the autonomous networks or the schools within them.

Constructing autonomous network legislation would require addressing a number of tricky policy questions. First, who owns the school buildings and land? LAUSD could retain ownership of the buildings and lease them to the schools and autonomous networks, or a separate building authority could be created to hold and manage educational real estate. Second, under what labor contract would teachers and others work? Given the historic legal test of "community of interest" for forming bargaining units, it would make the most sense for the teachers, at least, to have a separate bargaining unit for each school network. An experiment with this idea is now being conducted in the Belmont High School cluster, where local self-determination has replaced many of the lengthy legalisms in the contract with UTLA. Third, how are disputes between the network and LAUSD to be resolved? What happens if a group of schools wants to become autonomous and the District does not want to grant the petition, or what happens if the autonomous network thinks cancellation of its status is unreasonable? The state superintendent of public instruction or some other umpire should be appointed to resolve these disputes administratively and to keep them out of the courts. Fourth, how are categorical funding and compliance issues to be handled? The charter school sector provides guidance in how these funds can be bundled and their reporting simplified. The key to structuring politics is to subordinate these issues to the overall goal of creating an orderly path to decentralization.

The autonomous network proposal also creates a political situation in which the relationship between the District and charter schools can be rationalized. Supporters of charter schools almost always fail to recognize that the freedom and flexibility those schools enjoy is a function of their exceptionality. As long as there are only a few charter schools, they can open without causing much interruption in the District, and in times of increasing enrollment, their fiscal impact is hardly noticed. Likewise, charter schools can be closed, either for lack of enrollment or for poor performance, and the District can absorb the students. However, when the percentage of charter schools, or any other type of exception-to-the-rule schools, becomes large—more than about 20 percent of the student population, it is said—then increasing flows of students to the charter sector decreases the capacity of the District to reform itself, and charter advocates lose one of their main political arguments, namely that they serve as a spur to reform for the traditional district. Moreover, if there were to be a substantial failure by a charter management organization, the District's capacity to absorb students would be sharply limited.

The policy debate about schooling generally holds that introducing private-sector school management and operations would create a competitive system and that competition would drive the public schools to get better or would allow them to dwindle. Some recent experiments suggest otherwise. In Philadelphia, where state intervention caused a radical restructuring of the schools, the private and public parts appear as more cooperative than competitive, something more like the military-industrial complex that President Eisenhower warned us about.[2] Under superintendent Paul Vallas, the school district made it clear that charter schools were *its* schools, subject to scrutiny and accountability. The district and charter school operators appeared to collaborate over school operations. However, when external evaluations showed that externally managed schools were no more successful than dis-

trict schools that had adopted reforms, CMOs pressured the state government to require Philadelphia to continue contracting out arrangements.[3] If
this is the case, then the hidden hand of the market will not be sufficient to
protect the system from undue influence on the part of educational services
providers. The autonomous network proposed here creates a way that existing district schools can reform in tandem with those run by charter school
operators, groups of adventurous teachers, nonprofit organizations—all
within a systemic legal framework.

Consider how the autonomous network proposal would have the opportunity to restructure the politics of LAUSD in ways that use the new institutional arrangements in an advantageous way. The autonomous networks
aid the development of a constructive pluralistic politics by turning protest
politics into political entrepreneurship. A generation of community activists,
including activist teachers, have found their primary political influence to
be the ability to badger, protest, or demand specific concessions from the
LAUSD board and to jawbone second- and third-level administrators until
they tired and gave in. The autonomous network proposal allows them to
actually build the schools they only dreamed about.

Obviously, the autonomous network proposal re-centers political authority on schools and neighborhoods and makes the system more responsive to
local community organizing. While our proposal does not create elected local
school councils, as Chicago did, it does open the door for potentially influential neighborhood organizations, such as the neighborhood councils that are
creatures of the city council, and the growing number of community-based
organizations, such as the Boyle Heights Learning Collaborative.

The performance of autonomous networks will be easy to monitor. State
and federal accountability requirements provide a public and relatively transparent set of indicators of success or failure, and LAUSD could create a larger
set of indicators if it so wished.

STUDENT-BASED FINANCES

There are two reasons to adopt student-based financing. The first is to make
networks of semi-autonomous schools possible. Only if dollars follow students
to their schools will authority be re-centered on teachers and principals.

The second reason to adopt student-based financing is to change the politics of educational finance. LAUSD has been fiscally impotent for a genera-

Move resource allocation to ind. student to better compete at state level [handwritten annotation]

tion, locked into a state-financed education system in which the local property tax cannot be raised and where the District does not have the authority to levy other kinds of taxes. Now, public education competes for state resources on the basis of competing interest groups of service providers, as, for example, between teachers and prison guards. Moving resource allocations to the individual student level would inject the interests of parents and students directly into that competition. Under the California constitution, public education is not just a political expectation but an entitlement comparable with Social Security and Medicare at the federal level. Connecting politics to an entitlement changes the nature of advocacy and ensures that the amount of the entitlement will receive scrutiny. Instead of budget cuts falling on school administrators (who become bloated bureaucrats for the purposes of budget debates), they fall on children, a much more sympathetic object of support. The question of fiscal adequacy is likely headed to the courts in California. Linking financial distribution to students will undoubtedly bolster the case for adequacy in the courts or in the legislature.

Regarding the linkage between student funding and decentralization, even the short existence of LAAMP and LEARN illustrated the points of tension between school fiscal autonomy and the rest of the system. Categorically funded programs, which make up as much as half the budget of some inner-city schools, come attached to costly and time-consuming compliance mechanisms. This form of remote control greatly limits what schools can do with funds and whether they are decentralized or part of a traditional hierarchy. The most recent research suggests that despite good intentions, the operation of categorical funding programs makes it harder rather than easier for schools to adapt to the needs of their most challenging students.[4]   *Leg'd. req'd* [handwritten annotation]

Legislation is needed to move funds to individual schools in ways that make it possible for teachers and principals to make allocation decisions that are responsive to student needs as they perceive them. The most logical way to do this is to create weighted student formula financing, either uniquely for LAUSD or for all districts in the state. Under a weighted student formula, extra dollars follow students who need a more expensive mix of educational services: special education students and students learning English, for example. Categorical programs do this now, but they generally allocate staff positions to the schools rather than flexible dollars.

The weighted student formula idea is not untried. Its application began in Edmonton, Canada, in the 1970s, and it has been applied in Seattle and

Houston as well as Hawaii, where the entire state rests in a single school system. A variation of the weighted student formula idea is under consideration in New York City, and a Gates Foundation–funded commission to redesign school finance recommends it nationwide.[5] In addition, budgetary devolution has a long history in England, where it was introduced in 1987.[6]

Devolved funding, delivered through a weighted student formula, makes a very big difference in the flexibility of action for schools. UCLA professor William Ouchi, who was LEARN chair in its last years, has long favored weighted student formula financing; he considers it one of the keys to making schools work.[7] The differences in budgetary flexibility between centralized and weighted student formula districts are dramatic. Nearly 92 cents of every operating fund dollar is controlled at the school site in Edmonton versus 7 cents in Los Angeles. Ouchi also presents data that show financially devolved school districts are more educationally effective.[8]

POSITIVE INCENTIVES

The existing standards and assessment system, along with the oversight of program-based categorical funding, have created almost entirely negative incentives for public schools in Los Angeles and elsewhere. If schools are unsuccessful in reaching state or federal achievement targets, they are subject to intervention, close scrutiny, or takeover. If they are successful, nothing happens; they are left alone. There are virtually no direct rewards and few indirect ones, other than the substantial satisfaction of having watched a student "get it." The District is so battered that even successful schools find little recognition of their efforts. Public policy needs to provide positive incentives for those doing the work in schools and classrooms.

Most advocates for incentives in teaching and learning get no further than supporting merit pay for teachers: cash for test scores.[9] In reality, there is a far broader set of incentives, both at the individual and organizational levels, and there are more sophisticated methods of incentivizing teachers other than added pay for high test scores.[10] And teachers should not be first on the incentive list.

In constructing a positive incentive system, it is important to recognize that it is the students, not the teachers, who are the real workers in the educational system. Relatively little attention has been given to how to create incentives for them, from making it socially acceptable to study hard and take

Incentives for students

difficult courses to providing monetary rewards for success. While a number of schools have highly engaging courses of study, such as the Humanitas project, and support systems, such as AVID (Advancement Via Individual Determination), these are largely considered ancillary to the core curriculum and the testing program.

There are large social and economic rewards for obtaining a college degree, but for a student from a working-class background, these are hard to anticipate, and so the reward has little incentive value. And it is a long way off. The rewards for a high school diploma, either in terms of social standing or in monetary rewards, are proportionately less than they were forty years ago. Entry-level jobs for high school graduates do not pay significantly more than those who leave high school during the tenth grade. Although high school graduates make on average $240,000 more than students who do not complete school, the rewards for students accrue over a life time. Thus, in order to be an effective incentive, studying hard in high school and taking a college-ready course of study needs a more proximate payoff. Traditionally, students gain expectations of going to college from their families, but in a community that does not have a tradition of college-going, the prospect of foregone income and substantial expenses make college seem unapproachable.

Probably no greater incentive exists for poor families than a return to free public higher education or a system of early approvals for tuition and expenses scholarships linked to continuing performance in high school. The key to making high school work better for poor and working-class children is to create a pathway to college that is both well lighted and level. Although the case for high tuition at public colleges and universities can be rationalized on the basis that there is a substantial private return to the investment in postsecondary education, part of the payoff for free higher education, at least for the children of the poor, is to make high schools work better. If the job of high school is to prepare students for further education—as is the case with elementary school—rather than preparing students for direct entry into adult work and society, then incentives for students to enter further education become a huge part of what high schools need to offer.

LAUSD and numerous community organizations support creating a pathway to college or high-level technical training. But the existing pathway to college is littered with obstacles that are mostly hidden from parents and students. Despite a 2005 school board mandate, only a small minority of students in LAUSD take a college-ready curriculum, one that includes what are known as the A-through-G requirements, the seven sets of courses required for the University of California and the California State University systems and virtually all private colleges.

Accessing a college-ready curriculum requires that students speak and write English well. Some 54 percent of first grade students in LAUSD enter school designated as English language learners, and the process of qualifying (redesignating) as English fluent is convoluted and requires the alignment of four different indicators, one of them being a test that the student took in the previous school year. Statistically, redesignation counts heavily toward a student being able to take college-ready courses. Of all possible indicators, fifth grade reading scores and whether a student was designated as English fluent best predicted scores on nationally normed tests and passage of the high school exit exam, an examination of Roosevelt High School records shows.[11] In Los Angeles, creating a pathway to college by allowing many more students to access a college-ready curriculum requires a thorough reworking of the elementary English language arts program in order to integrate English language development and the official language arts curriculum. Oddly, they are now run by different offices and are overseen in schools by different program specialists.

Even if students are officially redesignated as English fluent, their placement in secondary school classes is often a function of short diagnostic tests created and administered by middle and high schools. Students who go to community colleges or state university campuses often face similar placement tests, which have high stakes for students but which are not part of the state's formal testing scheme.

The state's testing program offers few incentives for students. It is probably true that the state's assessment scheme pushes schools to emphasize the state standards in instruction and to better monitor student progress toward them, but students experience this as part of a curriculum they are taught that may or may not make school interesting or challenging. However, a student cannot study for the state's testing scheme in the same way that they do for Advanced Placement examinations or an International Baccalaureate examination. Students can study for the California High School Exit Examination, but passing the exam provides the student no particular reward other than the diploma they have already earned by taking and passing classes. Students also need a better system of examinations that they can study for directly, a topic discussed later in this chapter.

As for teachers, it is important to move politics beyond the very narrow focus on test score production. First, teachers generally don't like the idea of being paid according to test results, and UTLA, like most unions, resists it. So, whatever incentive value exists in merit pay comes at a very high political cost. Second, merit pay schemes are devilishly difficult to administer, except those that rely only on supervisor judgment. A proper value-added calculation requires years of data to eliminate the effects of teachers who are assigned high-performing students and others assigned students who have not performed well. Third, almost all departures from the standard salary schedule involve multiple means of gaining salary increments, as is the case in Denver, where an alternative system has been in development since 2000.

The gridlike standard single salary schedule is the nearly universal form of arranging pay for teachers. Rows of the grid represent years of service, and the columns represent additional education beyond the required minimum. Thus, a teacher advances through experience and additional training, not the rating of their principals or supervisors. This form of monetary incentive predates teacher collective bargaining by several decades and is actually a legacy of the old Progressive reforms that produced the first civil service salary schedules on which pay systems for teachers are modeled. The standard single salary schedule endures not because people think it is the best way to pay teachers, but because it is highly rational and easy to administer. It is relatively easy to determine a teacher's qualifications—there are detailed rules for what kinds of professional education count for movement across the columns—and years of service. But this system of paying teachers makes no distinction between a reward and an incentive.

Most of the reward-for-results schemes tried in California became simply happy windfalls for the teachers rather than incentives that changed their practices. An incentive system put in place briefly during the late 1990s created large cash payouts for teachers in some schools. It was never clear that the teachers who received these payouts did anything that other teachers didn't do, and the reward system was discontinued when the state ran short of funds, a frequent cause of incentive plan failure.

However, it is easy to observe teachers responding to incentives. Every year, teachers in Los Angeles earn thousands of salary credit points through continuing education, and several thousand of them have become certified by the National Board for Professional Teaching Standards, responding to the $15,000 salary bonus negotiated by UTLA. Teachers also respond to working at a good school. They flee bad ones as rapidly as they can, but even schools in the most challenging communities are able to keep veteran teachers who feel successful there.

The phrase "pay for knowledge and skill" has entered the lexicon of educational reform as a technique to attach monetary incentives to skills that a school identifies as valuable, rather than the more general attainment of additional college credits.[12] Variations have been tried in several districts, and it is not a huge leap from existing salary practices. In a decentralized, network-style school system, the needed adjustment is to allow skill-based incentives to vary from school to school, thus acting as an incentive to attract teachers to more difficult-to-staff schools. Charter schools now have this freedom, and a system of schools arranged along an autonomous network model need it too.

Providing school-based rewards to join the faculty of a hard-to-staff school provides an incentive for a teacher to participate at that school. But teachers also need incentives to perform. Again, existing practices already differentiate pay according to duties. It is not just the taking on of extracurricular duties that is compensated, but pay is differentiated for work during the school day. There is no good reason that this practice cannot be extended to such areas as working with parents or community organizations.

One can also learn from existing teacher performance incentives for continuing professional education and demonstrated skills. For the last quarter-century, California has operated a teacher evaluation system that involves individual goals and objectives negotiated between a teacher and his or her principal.[13] So called, Stull evaluations can be as rigorous or pro forma as principals make them, but the machinery for substantive review of teachers based on student data and performance already exists.

The primary limitation to the existing system is its principal centeredness. Even if principals have good craft skills in formative evaluation, and many do not, they have difficulty finding time to do a thorough job. In addition, principal-only evaluations hamper the growth of teaching as a profession, as an occupation that creates and enforces standards of good practice for its members. There are alternatives. California has a teacher peer review statute that has been used to good effect in other districts in the state, and UTLA has negotiated such an arrangement for teachers in L.A., though it is regarded as ineffective.[14] Other districts, however, have done much better with the idea.[15]

Peer review is only the beginning of what is possible if public policy is to be directed toward using the relationships between labor and management for education reform. A more promising approach would center on structuring politics in ways that reward interest groups for focusing on commonweal interests or at least longer-term self-interests. Nothing is gained by pretending that self-interest can be ignored or argued away. For example, efforts to wall off the union from interest in or influence over school operations are largely doomed to failure. While one might imagine California as a nonunion state or that the schools might be transformed into a nonunion environment by restrictions on collective bargaining, or that the charter school law could be used to create a nonunion environment, these approaches are doomed either to failure or to very expensive political battles.

Instead, collective bargaining needs to be brought into the twenty-first century by making it work under the assumption that teaching is a profession rather than industrial work. The school board in LAUSD has always negotiated from a position of weakness. Partly this is a function of union support for school board members, who feel beholden to it. But more fundamentally it has been so because the battle lines between the union and the school administration have been drawn in perverse ways. It has been either the administration is going to control things or it is going to give away the store to the union. Administrators disliked LEARN and distrusted their own leaders because Helen Bernstein was heavily involved in LEARN. Union members distrusted Bernstein's involvement for the opposite reasons.

In Los Angeles, the labor contract has generally not been seen as a way to foster education reform. Charles Kerchner and colleagues advocate that union leaders seize the levers of quality and connect them to reform through standards, professional development, and accountability through peer review.[16] In more recent work, they argue that negotiating student outcomes and the means to reach them should be a mandatory subject of bargaining.[17] In order to have a wage agreement, teachers would be required to negotiate student performance goals and to show how the resources they negotiate are aligned to create increased achievement. Like any such requirement, negotiating student outcome measurements could be trivialized, but at a very minimum it would create a political arena in which work rules, teacher compensation, and student achievement would be talked about at the same time.

A STUDENT LEARNING INFRASTRUCTURE

The schools in Los Angeles need better ways of organizing teaching and learning. Reform efforts over the last two decades illustrate polar opposite approaches to managing instruction, and each had conspicuous weaknesses. LEARN and LAAMP sought a professional learning community model, somewhat constructivist in pedagogy and centered on teacher flexibility, development of individual practice, and networks of teachers working together. Beginning in 2000, the District invested heavily in centralized instructional management with a single reading and a single math program for elementary schools, each integrated with citywide testing after each unit of instruction and enforced by a corps of coaches and supervisors. The professional learning community approach was bogged down in labor-intensive processes and was hampered by a vague volunteerism that bred extraordinary engagement for some teachers and superficial enactment by others. Centralized management fostered a compliance mentality, a dampening of innovation and flexibility in schools and classrooms as well as resentment on the part of many teachers.

The investments in computer technology were likewise largely centralized, with similarly uneven results. The District's ability to analyze student progress increased substantially, but the ability to access this system and to use the information it provided was almost entirely mediated by central office staff, subdistrict analysts, or hired consultants. Messages of achievement or failure and their diagnoses came to teachers and students as received wisdom rather than through active efforts to make sense of the teaching and learning process by those engaged in it.

The oscillation between classroom and school-based instructional management and a highly centralized district-based method of gaining coherence in teaching ignores the possibility of increasing the role of students and their families in the management of their own learning. The long-term change in the District has been from a closed system to an open one, a trend that is also found in other professional services. This also continues the long-range shift in public education from a closed system to an open one. And the debate between one-size-fits-all-is-wrong and the value of centralized coherence misses the sea change in technology that has taken place in the last fifteen years.

LEARN, LAAMP, and the District itself invested millions in computer technology and connectivity, but this investment has not changed the teaching and learning process very much. The investments in computer-assisted learning technology during this period were largely homegrown and not easily transferable. Most of the teacher-developed technologies were applications of existing software packages, and most of it was built around presentation or direct instruction rather than interactivity. During the LAAMP era, schools and school families developed web pages that were largely static.

Meanwhile, children and youth throughout the city have dramatically changed how they access and process knowledge, what and how they learn from their environments. The presence of computer connectivity has increased the capacity for learning self-management. In professional relationships outside of education, notably in medicine, increased access to information has changed the relationship between client and professional practitioner.

The "prosumer" relationship between production and consumption foretold by futurist Alvin Toffler has come to pass.[18] Medicine, for example, has come to realize that health maintenance is as much a function of lifestyle control and self-treatment as it is a doctor's treatment. Health maintenance organizations provide their clients handbooks for self-diagnosis and treatment, and websites provide the vigilant consumer with the professionally expected standard of care that patients should receive in the case of serious medical problems, such as stroke or heart attack. Web-based knowledge, including that provided by leading medical schools, can prepare a patient with the foreknowledge to ask intelligent questions of a physician about treatment options or the care he or she is, or is not, receiving.

A student learning infrastructure would have six elements. The first would provide information to students and their parents. At a minimum, parents should have ready access to easily understandable report cards. Currently, the state's annual test score reports provide better guidance about how a student measures up to state standards than do the LAUSD report cards. Parents of English language learners should be able to know their children's progress toward being designated as English fluent, a milestone that makes a college-ready high school curriculum available to those students. Parents should be able to see examples of advanced and proficient work according to state standards along with explanations of why these examples were judged the way they were. Parents should have information about college and other further education options and about the high school coursework that allows a student to transfer to college. Parents should have access to course schedules and the names of their students' teachers and information about how to contact them.

Second, the infrastructure should be a means of communication with parents. If the system is to take seriously the belief that parents are a child's first educators, as reform organizations advocate, then the system of communication about student learning needs to include them. There are already working examples in some school districts of email and web-based communication between teachers and parents, and commercial applications, such as mygradebook.com, are in use. Although not a replacement for face-to-face communication with parents, web-based communications offer the advantages that electronic mail has already demonstrated in other domains. It's asynchronous; teachers and parents can post messages and respond as they are able rather than trying to find a meeting time, which is often difficult for working-class families whose lives often involve multiple jobs. It is immediate and available as needed rather than just once a semester, at parents night or some other occasion at the school.

Third, the learning infrastructure should provide direct assistance to students. Homework help, directed by humans and so-called "intelligent agents" and study guides, should be expanded.

Fourth, the learning infrastructure should begin to open-source the curriculum. While the need for conventional textbooks and support material will continue, the time has long passed for a few publishers to monopolize access to educational material in school. And time has long passed for the city's 35,000 teachers to be merely recipients of curriculum and pedagogy rather than generators of it. The ongoing experiments in open sourcing are dramatically changing knowledge construction throughout the world. Wikipedia, the online encyclopedia that lets its users edit entries and add new ones, is among the ten-most-visited sites on the web.[19] In 2007, Sun Microsystems chairman Scott McNealy started a project, dubbed Curriki, to create a place where educators from any place in the world can post curricula and lesson plans for review by fellow classroom teachers. Curriki and similar ventures would allow educators the ability to tailor content to the needs of their students. Because access is free, it gives teachers and students from all schools access to high-quality material. Unlike many conventional school reforms, these projects have the capacity to spread quickly. More than 15,000 educators have already registered to become Curriki members.[20] The Hewlett Foundation is also supporting open education resources worldwide to produce high-quality digital resources and the tools for creating them.[21]

Fifth, the information infrastructure can offer direct instruction and learning. It can supplement classroom teaching and provide instruction in subjects that are not available in all schools or to students whose schedules do not allow them access to a course. As experience in higher education, corporate training, and the military have shown, web-based instruction seldom replaces conventional face-to-face instruction; it is, however, increasingly valuable as an integrated means to increase the pace, depth, and breadth of learning. The web also changes learning modalities in ways we do not yet completely understand. John Seely Brown, the former chief scientist for Xerox Corporation, called it the "first medium that honors the notion of multiple intelligences."[22] The speed of its development and its presence in our lives makes its integration into the education system imperative.

Sixth, an information infrastructure can allow self-paced examinations and certification of competency in ways that break down the relationship between time spent in classrooms and progress toward graduation from high school. Only when this relationship—one of the most enduring aspects of the Progressive reforms—is broken can we begin to expect substantial productivity gains in public education.

Allowing graduation by examination, which could run parallel with the existing system, effectively decouples demonstrated achievement of academic standards from time spent in a class. It picks up the threads of individualized instructional ideas that were part of the largely experiential and constructivist approach to learning championed by LEARN and LAAMP, although the roots of these ideas are much older. It allows self-pacing, avoids the discrimination attached to slower learners, and provides incentives for students to move as quickly as they can. Allowing time to graduation to be a variable allows the maintenance of a standards-based curriculum for all students.

An external examination system tied to examination also creates a system in which both decentralization and standards-based accountability are possible. Only if there are standards and a transparent accountability system does it make sense to consider decentralizing schools. In standards, we see first that what is called "autonomy" is not unconditional, and autonomous schools are highly dependent on a system that is maintained outside the schools. Infrastructure is important. In policy, there are several options for providing accountability and transparent standards. Most industrial countries use an external examining body that certifies students at the secondary level in different subject areas. The closest that the United States has to this idea is the SAT. The International Baccalaureate is also a good example. Some countries rely on government or quasi-governmental bodies to give these examinations. In the United Kingdom, they are given by private organizations, much like the SAT and the other college entrance exams.

In any technology access issue, questions of equity and equal access arise. Unlike many other issues of equity, however, providing technological access to people of limited financial means appears increasingly easy to solve. The cost of connectivity and hardware is decreasing, and family subsidies through grants or tax credits are among the easier public policy problems to solve. Language access for families who do not read English is also a solvable problem.

VARIETY IN SCHOOLS AND CHOICE AMONG THEM

As a policy intervention, "choice" usually connotes enlarging charter school offerings within a public school district's enrollment area, and in 2007 there were more than 100 charters in operation. In LAUSD, however, choice opportunities are not limited to charters. The District operates 162 magnet schools currently enrolling more than 53,000 students.[23]

The District operates a sophisticated internal choice system involving both preference weights and random choice. It distributes catalogs listing the schools by specialty and location, maintains a website for parents and students seeking admission to the magnet schools, holds parent education sessions, and runs informational programs on its television station.

Indeed, choice has been a part of every reform plan for LAUSD since the 1967 Planning Team report, in which the idea of variety and choice meant an opportunity to "experiment with different types of construction, building plans, room size and equipment . . . new approaches to scheduling and curriculum, new teaching methods and experience."[24] Variation would be used in part to establish model schools, and these were recommended "at all levels of education—elementary, secondary and adult—and in all administrative areas of the city."[25] Magnet schools and a program of intradistrict transfers for students in historically racially isolated schools, called Permits with Transportation, grew rapidly after the 1976 California Supreme Court's desegregation order. LEARN endorsed choice in its 1993 plan, and choice options were mandated under the 2001 federal No Child Left Behind law.

The major problem now is that there are not enough good choices to go around. The District estimates that there will be 70,000 applicants in 2008 for about 12,000 openings. As parents learn when they look at the catalog of options, some schools have application-to-acceptance ratios that resemble Pomona College or Stanford University. Valley Alternative, a 589 student K–12 school in Van Nuys, expects fifty-eight openings; 2,624 students applied in 2007. At the Bravo Medical Magnet on the Eastside, it is expected that only about 30 percent of the applicants will be admitted.[26]

One of the things that these schools do is create *specialness* among students. As was noted more than twenty years ago, "The most obvious way to create more focused educational purpose is to expand upon existing practice: to create more specialty shops."[27] Toward this end, and linked with the autonomous network idea, legislation is needed to create incentives to design novel and focused schools. Both past reforms and current activity, such as the design of the Civitas Academy, suggest that there continues to be a wellspring of innovation among LAUSD teachers who would jump at the opportunity to design and operate their own schools. As the District's massive building program produces more spaces, and as demographics decrease enrollment somewhat, LAUSD will face the fortunate circumstance in which an increase in specialness can take place.

A NEW PROGRESSIVE ERA?

Should we anticipate, or seek, a new progressive era? The word "progressive" has taken on many different meanings. People who now call themselves progressives are "concerned with issues of social and economic justice, democracy, and livability."[28] Many of them are ambivalent about sharing the label with their early-twentieth-century antecedents, because as Robert Gottlieb has observed, in "responding to the excesses of early industrial capitalism, many of these progressives were elite reformers who trusted technological change more than democratic processes and who promoted moral reformation rather than social justice."[29] The earlier Progressives were indeed people of their time and place, full of racial and sexual attitudes that are now out of place. Even John Randolph Haynes, who fought corporate oligarchy and corruption in Los Angeles and represented the Left wing of the Progressive movement, was a eugenicist.[30] They were less critically accepting with business interests than they should have been and rapidly adopted the scientific management business practices of the day.

But the old Progressives had a remarkable civic ideal—never fully met—about a publicly financed education system open to all. Elwood Cubberly, the dean of education at Stanford who wrote the first widely used textbook on school administration in 1916, also wrote a model state statute—some say it was intended for Wisconsin—that provided a statutory guarantee of free universal-access higher education: "Instruction in the university shall be free to all residents of this state, without distinction as to race sex, or sects," something that California has gradually abandoned.[31] From an institutional perspective, what distinguishes the Progressives from those educators who have followed was their ability to get their heads around the entire education system, and in this they stood in stark contrast with most modern reformers.

What would their modern kin be like? Most assuredly they would not all be white Protestants. But, like their predecessors, they would need to wrap their heads around the organizational part of education and the institutional parts, too. They should be able to figure out what the federal government should do and what the states should do, what the roles of nongovernmental organizations and of colleges and universities are. The old Progressives were able to do this, so why is it so difficult to imagine that a new breed of leaders could do the same?

Contemporary progressives accept the most radical notion in education in the last half-century: the assertion that the vast majority of students can learn to a high standard of numeracy and literacy. Thus, it opens the door to a broad swath of Americans, including activists associated with both Republican and Democratic parties. But it precludes elements of both the Right and Left. It excludes those who believe that race and class so mar students of color and of poverty that it is unfair and unjust to expect them to perform well. The "soft bigotry of low expectations" may be a political slogan, but it is grounded in reality. It also excludes those in the "no excuses" camp, who believe that the presence of an effective school or two in high-poverty neighborhoods constitutes proof and that all schools can replicate this success with relative ease and existing resources, if only barriers to success (usually items such as teacher tenure or the collective bargaining contract) were removed. We know better.

Contemporary progressives will need to create a workable balance between elite and populist politics. We believe that what education scholar Anthony Bryk has termed "democratic localism" can flourish within autonomous networks.[32] But the more fundamental realignment of populist and elite conceptions of power comes in reworking our notions of professionalism. The old Progressives fostered a professionalism in which families sent their children to school and put them in the hands of professionals in whom they had faith and confidence. They took comfort in this, and, when they were able, they sought out the best professionals they could, usually by moving to a new school area or district. However, the presence of information technology and an increasingly vigilant consumer movement has changed the power and responsibility relationship between professionals and clients.[33]

Contemporary progressives will also need to thoughtfully redefine the boundary between the private domain of families and the domain of the public or state authority, just as the old Progressives did. Their introduction of mandatory attendance, the more comprehensive curriculum, and the linking of schooling to qualifications to enter the labor force allowed Elwood Cubberly to conclude that "each year the child is coming to belong more to the state, and less and less to the parent."[34] They believed that public schools should be governmental entities, partly out of a belief in commonweal but partly because they believed that good government operations offered the most effective and efficient means of educating students. Contemporary progressives face great public cynicism about the role of government and its capacity to perform. As the idealized form of organization has become less a hierarchy and more a network, and as families routinely have access to nonschool forms of education, public policy will have to answer the question "What is *public*?" The discussion over the matter needs to move beyond the current appropriation of the word by charter school operators on the basis that they get governmental funds or the counterclaim that any form of organization that looks different from a traditional public school district is somehow disloyal.

Restructuring politics is often viewed as either impossible or unnecessary, when, in fact, it is unavoidable. Those who seek a market solution to public education's problems under the guise that markets avoid messiness and failure—conditions associated with politics and interest groups—ignore the fact that structuring markets is a profoundly political act and that market failure was the primary cause of the public education system we now have. A new broad-based progressivism allows educational reform to move from permanent crisis to institutional change.

And that's what we learned from L.A.

Notes

INTRODUCTION

1. Paul M. Possemato, *The Children Can No Longer Wait: An Action Plan to End Low Achievement and Establish Educational Excellence* (Los Angeles, CA: LAUSD, 1989).

PROLOGUE

1. California Department of Education, "1992–93 Enrollment Figures" (accessed October 11, 2007, from www.cde.ca.gov).
2. All LAUSD board meeting quotations and paraphrases taken from board meeting audiotapes, March 15, 1993, Office of the Board Secretariat, LAUSD.
3. The seven board members were Barbara Boudreaux, Warren Furutani, Jeff Horton, Julie Korenstein, Leticia Quezada, Mark Slavkin, and Roberta Weintraub.
4. "Six Phases of a Project," 1993, internal LEARN document, in possession of the authors.
5. Sandra Tsing Loh, "A Drill Can't Fix LAUSD," *Los Angeles Times*, April 28, 2007, A25.
6. See, for example, Nelson W. Polsby, "The Institutionalization of the U.S. House of Representatives," *American Political Science Review* 62, no.1 (March 1968): 144–68; Judith Goldstein and Robert O. Keohane, *Ideas and Foreign Policy: Beliefs, Institutions, and Political Change* (Ithaca: Cornell University Press, 1993); and Terry M. Moe, "Interests, Institutions, and Positive Theory: The Politics of the NLRB," *Studies in American Political Development* 2 (1987): 236–99.
7. Nominally, the District had come into existence only in 1961 with the merger of the Los Angeles Elementary School District and the Los Angeles High School District, but the change was only a formality. The two districts shared the same boundaries and a board that had always governed both elementary and secondary schools. The board also had responsibility for the city's community colleges, although the California legislature devolved that authority to a Los Angeles Community College District in 1969.
8. Judith Raftery, *Land of Fair Promise: Politics and Reform in Los Angeles Schools, 1885–1941* (Stanford, CA: Stanford University Press, 1992), 191.
9. Beth Shuster, "District Needs a Change in Attitudes," *Daily News*, June 6, 1993, vi.
10. David Menefee-Libey et al., "The Historic Separation of Schools from City Politics," *Education and Urban Society* 29, no. 4 (1997): 453–73.
11. David Tyack and Larry Cuban, *Tinkering Toward Utopia* (Cambridge, MA: Harvard University Press, 1995), 84, 85.
12. Raftery, *Land of Fair Promise,* 120.

CHAPTER 1: THE PROGRESSIVES

1. Mike Roos, interview by Charles Kerchner, November 8, 1999.
2. Miles Corwin, "Car Kills Ex-UTLA Chief Helen Bernstein," *Los Angeles Times*, April 4, 1997, B1.
3. Jill Stewart, "The Radical Center Loses a Champion," *New Times Los Angeles*, April 10, 1997.
4. Robert Wycoff, interview by Charles Kerchner and Stephanie Clayton, November 15, 2004.
5. Robert Wycoff, interview by Charles Kerchner, November 11, 1999.
6. Becki Robinson, interview by Charles Kerchner, January 18, 2005.
7. Mary Chambers, interview by Charles Kerchner and Stephanie Clayton, November 15, 2004.
8. Sandy Banks and Stephanie Chavez, "L.A. Schools OK Historic Reforms," *Los Angeles Times*, March 16, 1993, A1.
9. Thornstein Veblen, *The Theory of the Leisure Class: An Economic Study of Institutions* (New York: Macmillan, 1899).
10. William Deverell, "The Varieties of Progressive Experience," in *California Progressivism Revisited,* ed. William Deverell and Tom Sitton (Berkeley, CA: University of California Press, 1994), 1–11; see also George E. Mowry, *The California Progressives* (Berkeley, CA: University of California Press, 1951).
11. David W. Noble, *The Progressive Mind, 1890–1917* (Minneapolis, MN: Burgess, 1981), 76.
12. Raftery, *Land of Fair Promise,* 15.
13. Tom Sitton, *John Randolph Haynes: California Progressive* (Stanford: CA: Stanford University Press, 1992), 14.
14. Sitton, *John Randolph Haynes,* 51, 54–55.
15. Sitton, *John Randolph Haynes,* 27, 28.
16. Deverell, "The Varieties of Progressive Experience," 7.
17. Judith Raftery, "Los Angeles Clubwomen and Progressive Reform," in *California Progressivism Revisited,* 144–74.
18. Raftery, "Los Angeles Clubwomen and Progressive Reform," 148.
19. Raftery, *Land of Fair Promise,* 26.
20. Peter Schrag, *Paradise Lost: California's Experience, America's Future* (Berkeley, CA: University of California Press, 1998).
21. M. C. Bettinger, "Twenty-Five Years in the Schools of Los Angeles," *Historical Society of Southern California* 8–9 (1909–10): 70, as quoted in Raftery, *Land of Fair Progress,* 16.
22. Bettinger, "Twenty-Five Years," 71.
23. Frederick Winslow Taylor, *The Principles of Scientific Management* (New York: Harper, 1911).
24. Noble, *The Progressive Mind,* 39.
25. 2006–2007 enrollment, California Department of Education (accessed October 19, 2007, at http://www.cde.ca.gov).
26. John Fullerton, "Overview of School Finance and the LAUSD Budget," presentation to the Presidents' Joint Commission, August 11, 2005, LAUSD.

27. Mitchell Landsberg, "Mending to Beat the Band," *Los Angeles Times*, January 20, 2007, A1.
28. Lawrence Arthur Cremin, *The Transformation of the School: Progressivism in American Education* (New York: Knopf, 1961), vii.
29. Cremin, *Transformation of the School,* 119.
30. Diane Ravitch, *The Troubled Crusade: American Education, 1945–1980* (New York: Basic Books, 1983). For a range of perspectives on education reform during the Progressive Era, see also Cremin, *Transformation of the School,* and David B. Tyack, *The One Best System: A History of American Education* (Cambridge, MA: Harvard University Press, 1974).
31. Raftery, *Land of Fair Promise,* 5.

CHAPTER 2: WITHDRAWING LEGITIMACY

1. Staff, "Principals Club Department," *Los Angeles School Journal* 3, no. 10 (1919): 7.
2. Vierling Kersey, *Your Children and Their Schools: An Informal Report of the Patrons of the Los Angeles City Schools* (Los Angeles: Los Angeles Board of Education, 1937).
3. Kersey, *Your Children and Their Schools.*
4. David Tyack, Robert Lowe, and Elisabeth Hansot, *Public Schools in Hard Times* (Cambridge, MA: Harvard University Press, 1984), 156.
5. Judith Raftery, *Land of Fair Promise: Politics and Reform in Los Angeles Schools, 1885–1941* (Stanford, CA: Stanford University Press, 1992), 168.
6. Dick Turpin, "L.A. Seniors Rated in Top 27% in Nation," *Los Angeles Times*, September 12 1958, 1.
7. Sam Hamerman et al., *Report of the Los Angeles City Schools Planning Team* (Los Angeles: LAUSD, 1967), 132.
8. Editorial, "A Good School System, but ——," *Los Angeles Times*, March 5, 1963, A4.
9. Deborah Stone, *Policy Paradox: The Art of Political Decision Making* (New York: W. W. Norton, 1998), 137.
10. Raftery, *Land of Fair Promise,* 42, 43.
11. Heinz-Dieter Meyer and Brian Rowan, eds., *The New Institutionalism in Education* (Albany, NY: SUNY Press, 2006), 5.
12. Laurence Iannoccone and Frank W. Lutz, *Politics, Power and Policy: The Governing of Local School Districts* (Columbus, OH: Charles E. Merrill, 1970).
13. Thomas H. Eliot, "Toward an Understanding of Public School Politics," *The American Political Science Review* 53, no. 4 (1959): 1033.
14. Hamerman et al., *Report of the Los Angeles City Schools,* 2.
15. Norma H. Goodhue, "'Growing Pains' of State School System Revealed by Educators," *Los Angeles Times*, January 30, 1949, C1.
16. Editorial, "YES on More Schools," *Los Angeles Times*, May 3, 1963, A4.
17. Editorial, "Thought for Public School Week," *Los Angeles Times*, April 30, 1959, B4.
18. Editorial, "Something Better Than 1%," *Los Angeles Times*, July 19, 1958, B4.
19. Robert E. G. Harris, "Parents Have a Case Against the School," *Los Angeles Times*, February 10, 1950, A4.

20. "Jack Crowther Named New L.A. School Chief," *Los Angeles Times*, December 29, 1961, 1.
21. Susanna McBee, "Educator Sees Union Squeeze on Teachers," *Los Angeles Times*, February 18, 1963, 16.
22. McBee, "Educator Sees Union Squeeze on Teachers."
23. Harry Bernstein, "What Are the Teachers' Long-Range Plans?" *Los Angeles Times*, April 20, 1970, 1-1.
24. Staff, "Vote to Strike," *Los Angeles Times*, April 12, 1970, D5; Editorial, "The Planned Teachers' Strike," *Los Angeles Times*, April 9, 1970, 2-6; John Kendall, "School Officials Plan Action to Block Strike," *Los Angeles Times*, April 9, 1970, 1-3. Whether educational improvement actually trumped paycheck improvement is open to historical debate, according to veteran union leaders.
25. Harry Bernstein, "Teachers' Union Board Recommends Strike on Monday," *Los Angeles Times*, April 8, 1970, 1-1.
26. Editorial, "The Price of School Neglect," *Los Angeles Times*, May 5, 1970, 2-8.
27. Harry Bernstein, "Teachers Strike Cripples City's School System," *Los Angeles Times*, April 14, 1970, 1-1.
28. Harry Bernstein, "Settlement by End of the Week," *Los Angeles Times*, May 5, 1970, 1-1.
29. Harry Bernstein and Jack McCurdy, "Nearly 65% of Teachers Strike, Leaders Claim," *Los Angeles Times*, April 15, 1970, 1-1.
30. Jack McCurdy, "Teachers Returning to Classes Today," *Los Angeles Times*, May 14, 1970, 1-1.
31. Patrick Bushman, "Collective Bargaining in California Public Education: A Historical Perspective" (Ph.D. dissertation, Claremont Graduate School, 1982), 118.
32. Carol McGraw, "L.A. Schools: Integration Fight—No Victor Seen," *Los Angeles Times*, April 6, 1989, 1-1.
33. Raftery, *Land of Fair Promise*, 121–22.
34. Raftery, *Land of Fair Promise*, 189–90.
35. Lawrence B. de Graaf, Kevin Mulroy, and Quintard Taylor, eds., *Seeking El Dorado: African Americans in California* (Seattle, WA: University of Washington Press, 2001), 383, 390.
36. Josh Sides, *L.A. City Limits: African American Los Angeles from the Great Depression to the Present* (Berkeley, CA: University of California Press, 2003), 171.
37. John Caughey, *School Segregation on Our Doorstep: The Los Angeles Distribution in California Public Schools* (Los Angeles: Quail Books, 1966), 18
38. Raftery, *Land of Fair Promise*, 189.
39. Donald Glenn Cooper, "The Controversy Over Desegregation in the Los Angeles Unified School District, 1962–1981" (Ph.D. dissertation, University of Southern California, 1991), 40–41, 266; U.S. Commission on Civil Rights, *A Generation Deprived: Los Angeles School Desegregation* (Washington, DC: U.S. Congress, 1977).
40. Caughey, *School Segregation*, 22.
41. Caughey, *School Segregation*, 10.

42. Caughey, *School Segregation*, 45.
43. Raftery, *Land of Fair Promise*, 171.
44. Douglas Flamming, *Bound for Freedom: Black Los Angeles in Jim Crow America* (Berkeley, CA: University of California Press, 2005), 289. Proposition 14 itself was later thrown out by the California Supreme Court and trumped by the 1964 Civil Rights Act. See Raymond E. Wolfinger and Fred I. Greenstein, "The Repeal of Fair Housing in California: An Analysis of Referendum Voting," *American Political Science Review* 62, no. 3 (1968): 753–69.
45. Raphael Sonenshein, *Politics in Black and White: Race and Power in Los Angeles* (Princeton, NJ: Princeton University Press, 1993), 68–69. Throughout the early 1960s in Los Angeles, conflicts escalated between police officers and groups of young black men. Sides, *L.A. City Limits*, 173–74.
46. Gerald Horne, *Fire This Time: The Watts Uprisings and the 1960s* (Charlottesville, VA: University Press of Virginia, 1995), 377.
47. Irving G. Hendrick, *California Education: A Brief History* (San Francisco: Boyd & Fraser, 1980), 73–74.
48. Jack McCurdy, "Court Orders L.A. School Integration," *Los Angeles Times*, February 12, 1970, 1-1.
49. Orfield would later describe the match-up of the LAUSD versus ACLU as absurdly lopsided in terms of monetary resources. Gary Orfield, "Lessons of the Los Angeles Desegregation Case," *Education and Urban Society* 16, no. 3 (May 1984): 342; William Endicott, "Gitelson Blames Racists for Defeat," *Los Angeles Times*, November 5, 1970, 1-1.
50. HEW continued to grant desegregation monies, and the state continued to distribute these monies to LAUSD. U.S. Commission on Civil Rights, *A Generation Deprived*, 8; and John Caughey, "Decentralization or Integration in Los Angeles?" *Integrated Education: Race and Schools* 52 (July–August 1971): 43–44.
51. Cooper, "The Controversy," 62, 66, 76, 266.
52. Gayle Hopkins, "School Integration in the Los Angeles Unified School District and the Involvement of the Black Community" (Ph.D. dissertation, Claremont Graduate University, 1978); Frank Del Olmo, "Latinos Hit School Integration Plan," *Los Angeles Times*, February 10, 1977, 2-1; U.S. Commission on Civil Rights, *A Generation Deprived*, 107; Orfield, "Lessons," 344–45; Cooper, "The Controversy," 183; and William Trombley, "Metro School Busing Plan Sparks Storm of Outrage," *Los Angeles Times*, January 21, 1979, 1-1.
53. Jack McCurdy, "State High Court Orders L.A. to Integrate Schools," *Los Angeles Times*, June 29, 1976, 1-3; U.S. Commission on Civil Rights, *A Generation Deprived*, 9–10.
54. Orfield, "Lessons," 348; Cooper, "The Controversy," 154.
55. Dick Turpin, "L.A. Pupils Get Low Scores in State Tests," *Los Angeles Times*, January 20, 1966, 3.
56. Jack McCurdy, "L.A. Students Among Poorest Readers in U.S., Tests Show," *Los Angeles Times*, November 3, 1967, 1.
57. Editorial, "A Good School System, but ——," *Los Angeles Times*, March 5, 1963, A4.

58. National Commission on Excellence in Education, *A Nation at Risk: The Imperative for Educational Reform, A Report to the Secretary of Education* (Washington, DC: U.S. Department of Education, 1983), 9.

59. David C. Berliner and Bruce J. Biddle, *The Manufactured Crisis: Myths, Fraud, and the Attack on America's Public Schools* (Reading, MA: Addison-Wesley, 1995).

60. Miles Myers, *Changing our Minds: Negotiating English and Literacy* (Urbana, IL: National Council of Teachers of English, 1996), 1.

61. Eliot, "Toward an Understanding," 1032.

62. Editorial, "The False Face of Federal Aid," *Los Angeles Times*, February 8, 1959, B4.

63. Editorial, "A Homework Assignment on Schools," *Los Angeles Times*, January 29, 1959, B4.

64. Eliot, "Toward an Understanding," 1047.

65. Bonds were approved in 1946, 1952, 1955, 1958, 1960, 1963, and 1966. Hamerman et al., "*Report of the Los Angeles City Schools*, 58.

66. Hamerman et al., "*Report of the Los Angeles City Schools,* 77.

67. Dick Turpin, "State's Booming Population Builds Pressure on Schools," *Los Angeles Times*, September 10, 1962, 1A.

68. Hamerman et al., *Report of the Los Angeles City Schools*, 58–59.

69. "Jack Crowther Named New L.A. School Chief," *Los Angeles Times*, December 29, 1961, 1.

70. Barbara Ehrenreich, *Fear of Falling: The Inner Life of the Middle Class* (New York: Harper Perennial, 1990), 43–44.

71. Ellen Condliffe Lagemann, "A Commitment to Equity: What Matters About the Elementary and Secondary Act of 1965," *Education Week* 24, no. 31 (2005): 60.

72. James S. Coleman et al., "Equality of Educational Opportunity" (Washington, DC: U.S. Government Printing Office, 1966).

73. Hamerman et al., *Report of the Los Angeles City Schools*, 86.

74. He was reelected in 1966 and defeated in 1970 by the much more liberal Wilson Riles, who would serve twelve years. Hendrick, *California Education,* 69.

75. Kurt Schuparra, *Triumph of the Right: The Rise of the California Conservative Movement, 1945–1966* (Armok, NY: M. E. Sharpe, 1998), 81.

76. Michael Kirst et al., *Conditions of Education in California 1994–95* (Berkeley, CA: PACE, 1995), 13.

77. LEARN, "Dear Concerned Citizen" mailing including a letter from Mike Roos; note from Edward James Olmos; "Summary of LEARN's Main Recommendations"; "Petition to the Los Angeles Board of Education"; self-addressed envelope; all undated items ca. October 1992, internal LEARN documents, in possession of the authors.

78. LEARN, "Petition to the Los Angeles Board of Education," ca. October 1992.

79. Helen Bernstein and Richard Riordan, "Don't Atomize the School District," *Los Angeles Times*, October 17, 1990, B7.

80. Sandy Banks, "Poll Gives L.A. Schools Low Marks," *Los Angeles Times*, August 28, 1991, B1.

81. Jean Merl, "Rally Pushes for School Reforms," *Los Angeles Times*, October 22, 1990, B1.

82. "Face to Face with John Mack, Mike Roos—'LEARNing' the Educational System," *Los Angeles Sentinel,* January 16, 1992, B17.
83. Madison Gray, "The L.A. Riots: Fifteen Years After Rodney King," *Time,* April 5, 2007 (accessed on December 10, 2007, from www.time.com/time/specials/2007/la_riot).
84. Mike Roos, interview by Charles Kerchner and Stephanie Clayton, November 15, 2004.
85. Sandy Banks, "Door Opens on Plan to Revamp L.A. Schools," *Los Angeles Times,* January 17, 1992, B1.
86. California Department of Education, California Basic Educational Data Sysem, Enrollment by Grade and School, 2005 (accessed July 12, 2005, from www.cde.ca.gov).
87. Kenneth Starr, *Coast of Dreams: California on the Edge, 1990–2003* (New York: Knopf, 2004), Part V.
88. Jessica Goodheart, "Alliance for Survival," *The Village View,* February 7–13, 1992.
89. Sandra H. Berry, *Los Angeles Today and Tomorrow: Results of the Los Angeles 2000 Community Survey,* Survey R-3075-LA2000 (Santa Monica, CA: RAND, 1988).
90. Berry, *Los Angeles Today and Tomorrow.*
91. Anton quoted in Beth Shuster, "Alliance Plotting a Revolution in L.A. Education," *Daily News,* June 7, 1992, N1.

CHAPTER 3: EXIT AND *ENTRADA*

1. Albert O. Hirschman, *Exit, Voice, and Loyalty: Responses to Decline in Firms, Organizations, and States* (Cambridge, MA: Harvard University Press, 1970), 1.
2. Hirschman, *Exit, Voice, and Loyalty,* 15–16.
3. Hirschman, *Exit, Voice, and Loyalty,* 17, 107.
4. Hirschman, *Exit, Voice, and Loyalty,* 17.
5. Hirschman, *Exit, Voice, and Loyalty,* 83.
6. Edward W. Soja, "Los Angeles, 1965–1992," in *The City: Los Angeles and Urban Theory at the End of the Twentieth Century,* ed. Allen J. Scott and Edward W. Soja (Berkeley, CA: University of California Press, 1996), 428.
7. Irving G. Hendrick, *California Education: A Brief History* (San Francisco: Boyd & Fraser, 1980), 33.
8. Dowell Myers, "Major Changes in the Los Angeles Metropolitan Area between 1960 and 2000," School of Planning, Policy, and Development, University of Southern California (accessed June 4, 2004, at www-rcf.usc.edu/~dowell/new/LA%20trends.htm). It is important to note that both the U.S. census classification and common terminology changed beginning with the 1970 census when Hispanics became an ethnic classification that, ever since, has been essentially racialized and statistically compared with whites, Asians, and African Americans. In popular usage, the term "Anglo" came to apply to any non-Hispanic of European extraction, including ethnic and language groups that were decidedly neither Anglo nor Saxon.
9. Ralph Frammolino, "Breaking Up's Been Hard to Do," *Los Angeles Times,* May 16, 1993, A1. The last community annexed to LAUSD was Topanga in 1962.
10. "Fingertip Facts, 2007–2008" (Los Angeles: LAUSD, 2007).

11. Rodolfo Acuña, *Anything but Mexican: Chicanos in Contemporary Los Angeles* (New York: Verso, 1996), 140.
12. David M. Grant, "A Demographic Portrait of Los Angeles County, 1970 to 1990," in *Prismatic Metropolis: Inequality in Los Angeles*, ed. Lawrence D. Bobo et al. (New York: Russell Sage Foundation, 2000), 51–52
13. John Pitkin, "Three Demographic Waves and the Transformation of the Los Angeles Region, 1970–2000," Population Dynamics Research Group, School of Policy, Planning, and Development," 2004, unpublished paper, University of Southern California.
14. Josh Sides, *L.A. City Limits: African American Los Angeles from the Great Depression to the Present* (Berkeley, CA: University of California Press, 2003), 159–60.
15. J. David Greenstone and Paul E. Peterson, *Race and Authority in Urban Politics: Community Participation and the War on Poverty* (Chicago: University of Chicago, 1973), 29–30.
16. George Sanchez, *Becoming Mexican American: Ethnicity, Culture and Identity in Chicano Los Angeles, 1900–1945* (New York: Oxford University Press, 1993).
17. Lawrence B. de Graaf, Kevin Mulroy, and Quintard Taylor, eds., *Seeking El Dorado: African Americans in California* (Los Angeles: Autry Museum of Western Heritage, with University of Washington Press, 2001).
18. Lonnie G. Bunch, "A Past Not Necessarily Prologue: The Afro-American in Los Angeles," in *20th Century Los Angeles: Power, Promotion, and Social Conflict*, ed. Norman M. Klein and Martin J. Schiesl (Claremont, CA: Regina Books, 1990), 103–4.
19. Lonnie G. Bunch, "'The Greatest State for the Negro': Jefferson L. Edmonds, Black Propagandist of the California Dream," in *Seeking El Dorado*, 129.
20. Bunch, "A Past Not Necessarily Prologue," 120.
21. Hirschman, *Exit, Voice, and Loyalty*, 120; Camille Zubrinsky Charles, "Residential Segregation in Los Angeles," in *Prismatic Metropolis*, 167–219.
22. Vicki L. Ruiz, "We Always Tell Our Children They Are Americans: *Mendez v. Westminster* and the California Road to *Brown v. Board of Education*," *The College Board Review* 200 (Fall 2003): 20–27; Sides, *L.A. City Limits*.
23. Raphael Sonenshein, *Politics in Black and White: Race and Power in Los Angeles* (Princeton, NJ: Princeton University Press, 1993), 31.
24. Lawrence B. de Graaf, "African American Suburbanization in California, 1960 through 1990," in *Seeking El Dorado*, 415.
25. de Graaf, "African American Suburbanization," 419.
26. Victor M Valle and Rodolfo D. Torres, *Latino Metropolis* (Minneapolis, MN: University of Minnesota Press, 2000).
27. Sanchez, *Becoming Mexican American*, 257.
28. Ruiz, *We Always Tell Our Children*, 21, 24.
29. Bobo et al., eds., *Prismatic Metropolis*.
30. Rodolfo Acuña, *Occupied America: A History of Chicanos*, 6th ed. (New York: Harper-Collins, 2006), 3; Pitkin, "Three Demographic Waves," 14; Soja, "Los Angeles, 1965–1992," 442.
31. Pitkin, "Three Demographic Waves," 12, 13.
32. de Graaf, "African American Suburbanization," 421.

33. Acuña, *Anything but Mexican*, 3–5.

34. Pitkin, "Three Demographic Waves," 10.

35. Carlos Munoz Jr., *Youth, Identity, Power: The Chicano Movement* (New York: Verso, 1989).

36. "Classes Boycotted by Student Groups at 2 High Schools," *Los Angeles Times*, March 6, 1968, 3.

37. Jack McCurdy, "Student Disorders Erupt at 4 High Schools; Policeman Hurt," *Los Angeles Times*, March 7, 1968, 3.

38. Quoted in Jack McCurdy, "Demands Made by East Side High School Students Listed," *Los Angeles Times*, March 17, 1968, 1.

39. Muñoz, *Youth, Identity, Power*.

40. Pitkin, "Three Demographic Waves," 3.

41. Educational Demographics Unit, "Selected District Level Data" (Sacramento: California Department of Education, 2008).

42. Allen J. Scott and Edward W. Soja, "Introduction to Los Angeles," in *The City: Los Angeles and Urban Theory at the End of the Twentieth Century*, ed. Allen J. Scott and Edward W. Soja (Berkeley, CA: University of California Press, 1996).

CHAPTER 4: HOLLOWING OUT

1. George Skelton, "A Historic Crossroads on School Reform," *Los Angeles Times*, November 8, 1993, A3.

2. Virgil Roberts, interview by Charles Kerchner, August 25, 2005.

3. Sam Hamerman et al., *Report of the Los Angeles City Schools Planning Team* (Los Angeles: LAUSD, 1967), 58.

4. Hamerman et al., *Report of the Los Angeles City Schools*, 59.

5. Hamerman et al., *Report of the Los Angeles City Schools*, 58–59.

6. Myrna Oliver, "Jack P. Crowther; Led L.A. Schools from 1962 to '70, Fought Cutbacks," *Los Angeles Times*, May 22, 1993, A21.

7. *Serrano v. Priest* [487 Pacific 2d 1241] (1971). The *Serrano* case, filed in Los Angeles Superior Court in 1968, was decided first in 1971 by a California State Supreme Court ruling that invalidated the state's system of locally controlled school finance that had resulted in dramatic differences in the amount of money spent per pupil in the state's schools. The supreme court mandated that the state legislature remedy this inequality, but the legislature proved inadequate to the task, as did two successive governors, Ronald Reagan and Jerry Brown, and State Superintendent of Instruction Wilson Riles. The central controversy was whether to equalize "up"—that is, to increase spending on schools toward the point where poor districts spent as much as richer districts had—or "down" by cutting school spending to the point where rich districts spent as little as poor districts had. The legislature created a convoluted new school financing system that more or less split the difference in 1973, but the court repudiated this as inadequate in a second *Serrano* ruling in 1976. The court demanded that the legislature devise a full remedy by 1980, after which the court would take a more active role. No decisive follow-up case ever emerged. For a more detailed history, see

Michael Kirst, "Evolution of California State School Finance with Implications from Other States" (Stanford, CA: Stanford University Institute for Research on Education Policy and Practice, 2006).

8. The proposition passed by a narrow margin, with 50. 8 percent voting in favor and 49. 2 percent voting against. "State Vote on Propositions," *Sacramento Bee*, November 10, 1988, A6.

9. Herbert A. Sample, "Proposition 98 Would Insulate Schools from Budget Cuts," *Sacramento Bee*, October 8, 1988, A11.

10. Herbert A. Sample, "Prop 98 Brochure Unveiled: Honig Uses His Own Campaign Treasury," *Sacramento Bee*, October 21, 1988, A3.

11. Kirst, "Evolution."

12. Roy Romer, "Los Angeles Schools: Learning Curve from the Superintendent's Chair, Things are Looking Up, with System Wide Gains," *Los Angeles Times*, September 7, 2003, M1.

13. Legislative Analyst's Office, "Education 2002–03 Analysis," 2002 (accessed July 17, 2007, from http://192.234.213.2/analysis_2002/education/ed_an102.pdf); Stephen J. Carroll et al., *California's K–12 Public Schools: How Are They Doing?* (Santa Monica, CA: RAND, 2005), 39–40.

14. "School Finance Highlights 2007–08," (Mountain View, CA: EdSource, December 2007).

15. Stephen Frank and Jonathan Travers, "Strategic Review of FY06 District & School-Level Resources" (Boston, MA: Education Resource Strategies, 2007). LAUSD also invested heavily in professional development, allocating 6.1 percent of its operating budget to that purpose, nearly $10,600 per teacher, including the funds allocated to coaches and that to pay teachers for attending weekly staff development meetings during what is called "banked time."

16. Merle Price, interview by Jeanne Fryer, November 10, 2005.

17. "First to Worst," *The Merrow Report*, first broadcast February 1, 2004.

18. Ellen Condliffe Lagemann, "A Commitment to Equity: What Matters About the Elementary and Secondary Act of 1965," *Education Week* 24, no. 31 (2005): 60.

19. Hamerman et al, *Report of the Los Angeles City Schools*, 2.

20. Hamerman et al, *Report of the Los Angeles City Schools*, 99.

21. Hamerman et al, *Report of the Los Angeles City Schools*, 108–9.

22. Hamerman et al, *Report of the Los Angeles City Schools*, 131, 174.

23. Richard Rothstein, *Where's the Money Going? Changes in the Level and Composition of Education Spending, 1991–1996* (Washington, DC: Economic Policy Institute, 1996), 14, 18.

24. Frank and Travers, "Strategic Review," 10.

25. William Lowe Boyd and Charles Taylor Kerchner, eds., *The Politics of Excellence and Choice in Education: Yearbook of the Politics of Education Association* (Philadelphia: Falmer, 1988).

26. Bill Honig, "The Educational Excellence Movement: Now Comes the Hard Part," *Phi Delta Kappan* 66 (June 1985): 678; Michael Fallon, "California Assembly Passes Sweeping Education-Reform Measure," *Education Week* 2, July 27, [1983]; Paul Barry, "A

Man Between Two Worlds: Bill Honig," *The College Board Review* 132 (Summer 1984): 9–13, 31–33; and Dan Walters, "Bill Honig: Education's Cheerleader Is Long on Ideals but Short on Administrative Achievement," *California Journal* 16, no. 4 (April 1985): 145–47.

27. Boyd and Kerchner, *The Politics of Excellence and Choice in Education.*

28. Marshall Smith and Jennifer O'Day, "Systemic School Reform," in *The Politics of Curriculum and Testing*, ed. Susan Fuhrman and Betty Malen (Philadelphia: Falmer, 1991), 233–67.

29. Bill Honig, *Last Chance for Our Children: How You Can Help Save Our Schools* (Reading, MA: Addison-Wesley, 1987).

30. Bill Honig, interview by Charles Kerchner, October 18, 2004.

31. Judith Raftery, *Land of Fair Promise: Politics and Reform in Los Angeles Schools, 1885–1941* (Stanford, CA: Stanford University Press, 1992).

32. Michael Kirst et al., *Conditions of Education in California 1994–95* (Berkeley, CA: PACE, 1995), 13. For example, with Assembly Bill 2565, the California legislature in 1961 passed a sweeping reorganization of the state's curriculum, specifying subject and course requirements including a mandate that all of the state's elementary school children be provided with foreign language instruction. In response to howls from elementary principals and teachers across the state, the legislature quickly backed off on this latter requirement, but they continued to increase state instructional mandates. In 1965, the Miller-Unruh Reading Act mandated expanded reading instruction. Under strong political and legal pressure, the state required bilingual instruction for non–English speaking children. The state revised and expanded the "minimum academic standards for graduation" in 1969, and California's superintendent of public instruction, Wilson Riles, successfully advocated an Early Childhood Education Act in 1972. This movement continued throughout the 1970s, for example in 1977 with AB 3408, sponsored by Santa Barbara assemblyman (later senator) Gary Hart, which expanded the requirements for high school graduation to include, by 1980, minimal proficiency in reading, writing, and mathematics. See Irving G. Hendrick, *California Education: A Brief History* (San Francisco: Boyd & Fraser, 1980), 69–81.

33. Elaine Woo, "L.A. School District, Teachers' Union Negotiate Contract Issues," *Los Angeles Times*, September 10, 1988, 2-3. The prior contract was extended until a new contract was signed or until either party cancelled it.

34. "New Strategy by Teachers Union," *Los Angeles Times*, September 29, 1988, 2-2.

35. Elaine Woo, "L.A. School District Threatens to Dock Pay of Teachers If They Boycott Activities," *Los Angeles Times*, October 11, 1988, 2-3, and "Tests Postponed: Teachers Refuse to Handle Exams," *Los Angeles Times*, October 18, 1988, 2-1.

36. Elaine Woo, "Teachers Union Rejects 3-Year, 16.9% Pay Hike," *Los Angeles Times*, October 6, 1988, 2-1.

37. The SBM program, modeled on SBM reforms initiated in Dade County by Britton and his assistant, Joseph Fernandez, instituted Shared Decision-Making councils to be elected at each campus and charged with developing a specific plan for raising student achievement. The councils would also have authority to set policies for student discipline, staff development, event scheduling, school equipment, and the school's

discretionary budget. A districtwide elected "central council" would review their plans and, for those they approved, secure necessary waivers from district and state mandates and oversee their performance. Keena Lipsitz, "Site Based Management in the Los Angeles Unified School District," 1994, unpublished paper, Pomona College. LAUSD's version of SBM initially drew national attention and praise for offering a creative solution to intractable labor-management hostility in the public school system. More importantly, it promised a substantial expansion of teachers' professional roles beyond classroom instruction and into the actual management of schools as well as a clear focus on student learning schoolwide.

38. Elaine Woo, "Teachers Union Faces Charges Over Boycott of Certain Chores," *Los Angeles Times*, October 26, 1988, 2-4.

39. Sam Enriquez and Larry Gordon, "L.A. Teachers Strike as Talks With District Fail," *Los Angeles Times*, May 15, 1989, 1-1; and Larry Gordon, "Half of Students in L.A. District Stay Home as 21,000 Teachers Walk Out," *Los Angeles Times*, May 15, 1989, A1.

40. Sam Enriquez and Larry Gordon, "Talks Resume in Teachers' Strike; End May Be In Sight," *Los Angeles Times*, May 25, 1989, 1-1, and "Teachers, Board OK Pact; Classes Resume Today," *Los Angeles Times*, May 26, 1989, 1-1.

41. Sandy Banks, "Teachers OK Pact With 3% Pay Cut," *Los Angeles Times*, December 20, 1991, B1.

42. Prior to the 1961 consolidation of the Los Angeles school district, the taxes for the elementary, secondary, and junior colleges had been separate. However, the superintendent and the school board for all three districts were the same. The board members were elected at-large and there were seven offices. These offices were numbered, with all of the even numbered offices up for election in the same year and all of the odd numbered offices up for election two years later. Primaries were held in the first week of April in odd-numbered years along with other municipal offices. A candidate had to receive over 50 percent of the vote in order to win a seat. If no candidate won the required amount, the two top candidates would face a run-off in the last week of May. School board members held four-year terms beginning on July 1 after they were elected and ending on June 30. See Raftery, *Land of Fair Promise*; David Menefee-Libey et al., "The Historic Separation of Schools from City Politics," *Education and Urban Society* 29, no. 4 (1997): 453–73.

43. Hamerman et al, *Report of the Los Angeles City Schools*, 58–59; Timothy Almy and Harlan Hahn, "Ethnic Politics and Racial Issues: Voting in Los Angeles," *Western Political Quarterly* 24, no. 4 (1971): 719–30; and Hendrick, *California Education*, 72.

44. Supporting UNESCO during this period meant that one favored UNESCO's work in support of peace and disarmament, a world communication and information order, human rights, and racial equality. See Hamid Mowlana, "The U.S. Decision to Withdraw from UNESCO," *Journal of Communication* 34, no. 4 (1984): 136–41.

45. Eric Malnic, "Pair Re-elected to School Board," *Los Angeles Times*, April 7, 1965, 3; editorial, "Board of Education Endorsement," *Los Angeles Times*, May 13, 1965, A4; "3 Key Endorsements Given to Rev. Jones," *Los Angeles Times*, May 21, 1965, 3; and Richard Bergholz, "Edelman, Jones, Lamport Elected," *Los Angeles Times*, May 26, 1965, 1.

46. Richard Bergholz, "City Votes Today on 4 Candidates and Bond Issues," *Los Angeles Times,* May 31, 1967, 3, and "Wilkinson and Nava Elected; Library, Police Bonds Defeated," *Los Angeles Times*, June 1, 1967, 1.

47. Jack McCurdy, "Castro Restored to Teaching Job," *Los Angeles Times*, October 4, 1968, 1.

48. William Johnston, "Campaigns and Elections," in *The Doc Newman Story* (Privately published, 2005), 8.

49. Johnston, *The Doc Newman Story*, 4.

50. Johnston, *The Doc Newman Story*, 41.

51. Johnston, *The Doc Newman Story*, 44.

52. In the meantime, the voters had approved a ballot proposition that allowed voters who lived outside the Los Angeles city limits but inside the school district boundaries to vote on city charter amendments that affected them. These voters, it was thought, would favor district rather than citywide representation. See "District School Elections Urged," *Los Angeles Times*, June 9, 1978, B28.

53. Jack McCurdy, "Proposed Education Board Electoral Districts Outlined," *Los Angeles Times*, October 17, 1978, C1; "2 on School Board Attack Districting Proposal," *Los Angeles Times,* October 18, 1978, B24; and "Prop M. Districting to Fix Political Makeup of Board," *Los Angeles Times,* November 6, 1978, A3.

54. Sam Enriquez, "Incumbent's Race for School Board Includes Plenty of Brickbats to Dodge," *Los Angeles Times [Valley Edition]*, January 8, 1989, 2-4.

55. Rich Connell, "L.A. Schools Election," *Los Angeles Times*, March 21, 1989, 2-1; and Sam Enriquez, "Teachers Give a Lesson in Power at the Polls," *Los Angeles Times*, June 8, 1989, 2-1.

56. Rich Connell, "Gershman Tops Foe," *Los Angeles Times*, April 1, 1989, 2-3, and "L.A. Schools Election: It's a Three-Way Tug of War," *Los Angeles Times*, March 21, 1989, 2-1; Sam Enriquez, "District Is Flunking, Say School Board Challengers," *Los Angeles Times*, April 2, 1989, 2-4; and Sam Enriquez, "Razor-Thin Split Forces Runoff in School Board Vote," *Los Angeles Times*, April 21, 1989, 2-1.

57. Sam Enriquez, "Teachers Union," *Los Angeles Times,* April 17, 1993, B3; and Stephanie Chavez and Jean Merl, "Korenstein and Slavkin Reelected to School Board," *Los Angeles Times*, April 21, 1993, A19.

58. Amy Pyle, "26 File Papers to Seek 4 L.A. School Board Seats," *Los Angeles Times*, January 18, 1995, B3, and "2 Conservatives Target Horton on AIDS, Gay Issues," *Los Angeles Times*, April 7, 1995, B1.

59. Doug Smith, "Candidates Give Differing Views of L.A. Unified," *Los Angeles Times*, March 18, 1999, B1; Louis Sahagun, "Schools Candidates Trade Barbs at Last Forum," *Los Angeles Times*, April 8, 1999, B5; Rick Orlov, "Mayor-Backed Candidates," *Daily News*, April 2, 1999, N4; Louis Sahagun and Doug Smith, "Issues May Be Scarce," *Los Angeles Times*, April 11, 1999, B1; and "New Era at School Board," *Los Angeles Times*, April 15, 1999, B8.

60. Louis Sahagun and Doug Smith, "Riordan Takes Pride in School Slate's Showing," *Los Angeles Times*, April 15 1999.

61. Los Angeles City Ethics Commission, "2007 LAUSD Election" (accessed July 17, 2007, from http://ethics.lacity.org/efs/public_election.cfm).
62. Mike Roos, interview by Charles Kerchner and David Menefee-Libey, July 14, 2005.
63. Virgil Roberts, interview by Charles Kerchner, August 19, 2005.

CHAPTER 5: NEW IDEAS

1. For a more detailed examination of these reform plans and tracking the ideas as they developed, see David Menefee-Libey, Charles Taylor Kerchner, and Laura S. Mulfinger, "The Persistence of Ideas in Los Angeles School Reform," in *The Transformation of Great American School Districts: How Big Cities are Reshaping Public Education*, ed. William Lowe Boyd, Charles Tayor Kerchner, and Mark Blyth (Cambridge, MA: Harvard Education Press, 2008).
2. Gerald Grant and Christine Murray, "The Second Academic Revolution," in *The Politics of Education and the New Institutionalism: Reinventing the American School*, ed. Robert L. Crowson, William Lowe Boyd, and Hanne B. Mawhinney (New York: Falmer, 1996), 93–100.
3. Paul M. Possemato, *The Children Can No Longer Wait: An Action Plan to End Low Achievement and Establish Educational Excellence* (Los Angeles: LAUSD, 1989), 17.
4. Sam Hamerman et al., *Report of the Los Angeles City Schools Planning Team* (Los Angeles: LAUSD, 1967).
5. Paul M. Possemato, *Priorities for Education: A Design for Excellence* (Los Angeles: LAUSD, 1986).
6. Possemato, *The Children Can No Longer Wait*.
7. Elaine Woo and Larry Gordon, "Board OKs Plan to Reverse Low School Achievement," *Los Angeles Times [Home Edition]*, March 28, 1989, 1.
8. *For All Our Children: Better Educational Results in the Los Angeles Public Schools*, (Los Angeles: LEARN, 1993).
9. Peggy Funkhouser, interview by Charles Kerchner, January 30, 2004.
10. Mark M. Blyth, *Great Transformations: Economic Ideas and Institutional Change in the Twentieth Century* (Cambridge, UK: Cambridge University Press, 2002), 18. See also Moe, "Interests, Institutions, and Positive Theory"; and Judith Goldstein, *Ideas, Interests, and American Trade Policy* (Ithaca, NY: Cornell University Press, 1993). Blyth's approach to examining institutional change in education can be found in William Lowe Boyd, Charles Taylor Kerchner, and Mark Blyth, eds., *The Transformation of Great American School Districts: How Big Cities are Reshaping Public Education* (Cambridge, MA: Harvard Education Press, 2008).
11. Paul Thomas Hill, Christine Campbell, and James Harvey, *It Takes a City: Getting Serious about Urban School Reform* (Washington, DC: Brookings Institution Press, 2000).
12. These included the Industrial Areas Foundation–affiliated organizations: UNO (United Neighborhood Organizing Committee based in East Los Angeles), SCOC (South Central Organizing Committee, based in South Central L.A. and Compton), EVO (East Valleys Organization, based in the San Gabriel and Pomona valleys), and VOICE ([San Fernando] Valley Organized in Community Efforts).

13. The leadership included Richard Riordan (L.A. mayor), William Anton (LAUSD superintendent), Helen Bernstein (UTLA president), Robert Wycoff (ARCO president), Phillip Williams (Times Mirror vice president, publisher of the *Los Angeles Times*), Roy Anderson (retired Lockheed CEO), John Mack (Urban League), Virgil Roberts (LAEP chair), Rosalinda Lugo (UNO), John Singleton (Security Pacific Bank vice president), Joe Alibrandi (Whittaker Corp. CAO and cochair of Kids 1st), William Ouchi (UCLA management professor and later deputy mayor). Some of the names changed as the campaign unfolded, but not the breadth of representation.

14. Mary Chambers, interview by Charles Kerchner, March 3, 2004; and Virgil Roberts, interview by Charles Kerchner, September 10, 1999.

15. Members of the LEARN Executive Working Group and their affiliations at the time are as follows (the names of the original Working Group members are in bold): **Joseph Alibrandi**, member California Business Roundtable, CAO Whittaker Corporation; **Roy Anderson**, chair 2000 Partnership, chair Lockheed Corp.; **William Anton**, superintendent LAUSD; Walter Backstrom, managing director Los Angeles City and County School Employees, Local 99, SEIU; **Helen Bernstein**, president UTLA; John F. Bookout III, managing partner McKinsey and Co., Inc.; Eli Brent, president AALA; Sally Burkett, parent Overland Avenue School; Mary Chambers, vice president LEARN; John Cooke, president Disney Channel; Richard Farman, Southern California Gas Company; David Fleming, attorney Latham and Watkins; Peggy Funkhouser, president LAEP; Warren Furutani, president Los Angeles Board of Education; Dan Garcia, vice president Warner Brothers; Antonia Hernandez, executive director Mexican American Legal Defense and Education Fund; Irene Hirano, executive director Japanese American National Museum; **Rosalinda Lugo**, Southern California IAF Network; **John Mack**, president Los Angeles Urban League, Black Leadership Coalition on Education; Theodore Mitchell, dean UCLA Graduate School of Education; **William Ouchi**, UCLA Anderson School of Management; Leticia Quezada, president Los Angeles Board of Education; Gilbert Ray, attorney O'Melveny and Myers, member Christopher Commission; **Richard Riordan**, founder Kids 1st, founder Riordan and McKinzie; **Virgil Roberts**, chairman LAEP, chairman Dick Griffey Productions/Solar Records; Mike Roos, president and chief executive officer LEARN; William Rusnack, LAEP, Los Angeles Urban League, ARCO; John Singleton, chairman Workforce LA, chairman Security Pacific Corporation; Mark Slavkin, president Los Angeles Board of Education; Sidney Thompson, superintendent LAUSD; Franklin Ulf, chairman and CEO U.S. Trust Company of California; Richard Weston, American Jewish Committee, Major Clients Agency; **Phillip Williams**, chairman California Chamber of Commerce Education Committee, vice president Times Mirror Company, president Workforce LA; **Robert Wycoff**, chairman LEARN, chairman California Business Roundtable, president ARCO. Tammi J. Chun, "Facilitating Organizational Change Through Community-Based Coalitions: The Los Angeles Educational Alliance for Restructuring Now's Efforts in the Los Angeles Unified School District," 1994, unpublished paper, Pomona College.

16. Robert Wycoff, interview by Charles Kerchner, November 11, 1999; and Denise Hamilton, "Roos Faces Big Task on School Reform," *Los Angeles Times*, February 27, 1991, B1.

17. "Draft of LEARN Timeline," 1993, internal LEARN document, in possession of authors.

18. The poll was also supported by LAEP and the 2000 Partnership.

19. Sandy Banks, "Poll Gives L.A. Schools Low Marks," *Los Angeles Times*, August 28, 1991, B1.

20. Chun, "Facilitating Organizational Change," 36–41; LEARN, "How It All Began," *Learning Curve*, November 11, 1991.

21. Chambers interview, 2004; and Chun, "Facilitating Organizational Change," 43.

22. Chun, "Facilitating Organizational Change," 43–44; Chambers interview, 2004; LEARN, "Draft of LEARN Timeline."

23. Sandy Banks, "Teachers OK Pact with 3% Pay Cut," *Los Angeles Times*, December 20, 1991, B1.

24. Sandy Banks, "Door Opens on Plan to Revamp L.A. Schools," *Los Angeles Times*, January 17, 1992, B1; Cheryl W. Thompson, "Panel to Push School Reforms," *Daily News*, January 17, 1992, N4; Charles Cooper, "Education Reform Launched," *Highland Park News-Journal and Herald*, January 22, 1992; Catherine M. Carey, "Los Angeles Community Mobilizes to Restructure LAUSD Through LEARN," *United Teacher*, January 31, 1992; John D. Wagner, "Black Leaders Back Plan," *The Wave*, January 24, 1992.

25. Robert A. Rosenblatt and Stuart Silverstein, "U.S. Jobless Rate Hits 8-Year High," *Los Angeles Times*, June 6, 1992, A1; Kenneth J. Garcia, "Dire Warnings of Budget Cuts Turn Out to Be Real This Time," *Los Angeles Times*, June 14, 1992, B3.

26. Sandy Banks, "Plan Would Tie School Pay to Pupil Performance," *Los Angeles Times*, February 26, 1992, B1; Ann Bradley, "Fueled by Sense of Crisis, Coalition Forges Plan to Rebuild L.A. Schools." *Education Week* 11, no. 36 (May 27, 1992): 1.

27. Bradley, "Fueled by Sense of Crisis," 1. "Education Reform is Essential to Revitalize Los Angeles, Says LEARN," May 28, 1992; and *LEARN: Action Update:* "Final Month of Task Force Meetings," May 29, 1992, both internal LEARN documents, in possession of the authors.

28. Bradley, "Fueled by Sense of Crisis," 1.

29. Frank Clifford, "Corporate Suites Become Arena for Activist Politics," *Los Angeles Times*, April 6, 1992, A1.

30. David Ferrell, "Rich and Poor, Black and White Voice Anger," *Los Angeles Times*, April 30, 1992, A1; editorial, "Stop the Violence, Start the Renewal," *Los Angeles Times*, May 1, 1992, B6; Melvin L. Oliver, "It's the Fire Every Time, and We Do Nothing," *Los Angeles Times*, May 1, 1992, B7; James Flanigan, "Can L.A. Answer Cry for Economic Equality?" *Los Angeles Times*, May 3, 1992, D1; Lynell George, *No Crystal Stair: African-Americans in the City of Angels* (London: Verso, 1992); James H. Johnson Jr., Walter C. Farrell, and Chandra Guinn, "Immigration Reform and the Browning of America: Tensions, Conflicts and Community in Metropolitan Los Angeles," *International Migration Review* 31, no. 4 (Winter 1997): 1055–95.

31. *LEARN: Action Updates:* "LEARN Task Force Sessions Underway," May 15, 1992; "LEARN Offers Support to Rebuild LA Effort," May 22, 1992; "SEIU and AALA to Join Working Group," June 5, 1992, internal LEARN documents, in possession of the authors.

CHAPTER 6: LEARN

1. Mike Roos, interview by Charles Kerchner and David Menefee-Libey, July 14, 2005.

2. Sidney Thompson, interview by Charles Kerchner, November 2, 2004.

3. Howard Fine, "Departing Crusader (Interview with Public Affairs Consultant Mike Roos)," *Los Angeles Business Journal*, September 6, 1999 (accessed January 14, 2008, from www.thefreelibrary.com/Departing+Crusader—a055905398).

4. Career highlights: math teacher, Pacoima Junior High School, 1956–65; assistant principal, Maclay Junior High, 1965–69; principal, Markham Junior High, 1969–71; principal, Crenshaw High, 1971–76; deputy area administrator, 1976–78; administrative consultant in Office of Associate Superintendent for Business and Personnel, 1978–81; area assistant superintendent, 1981–82; associate superintendent, school operations, 1982–86; deputy superintendent, school operations, 1986–92. Charisse Jones, "Thompson Appointed to Helm of L.A. Schools," *Los Angeles Times*, October 6, 1993, B1.

5. Sidney Thompson, interview by Charles Kerchner, November 2, 2004.

6. Stephanie Chavez, "Schools Battle Is Rehearsal for Latinos," *Los Angeles Times*, October 5, 1992, B1, and "Acting Chief to Get Top Schools Job, Sources Say," *Los Angeles Times*, May 1, 1993, B1. Several sources confirmed an understanding that if Thompson were named superintendent, he was to be followed by a Latino, Zacarias, if he was available, which he was in 1997 when Thompson resigned.

7. Stephanie Chavez, "Thompson Gets 2-Year Contract to Lead Schools," *Los Angeles Times*, May 21, 1993, B1.

8. Judy Burton, interview by Benjamin Diehl, July 29, 1994.

9. Steve Proffitt, "Head of L.A.'s Teachers' Union Struggles With a Constricting Budget," *Los Angeles Times*, September 6, 1992, M3; Editorial, "How to Avoid a Strike," *Los Angeles Times*, September 16, 1992, B6.

10. Beth Shuster, "Bernstein Predicts Strike Authorization," *Daily News*, October 19, 1992, N1; Stephanie Chavez, "L.A. Teachers Give Union OK to Call Strike," *Los Angeles Times*, October 23, 1992, A1; Stephanie Chavez and Jean Merl, "Judge Halts Deep Pay Cuts for L.A. Teachers," *Los Angeles Times*, November 6, 1992, A1; Beth Shuster, "L.A.s' Teachers OK Strike by Big Margin," *Daily News*, October 23, 1992, N1; "Judge Blocks Teachers' Pay Cuts," *Daily News*, November 6, 1992, N1; "LAUSD Won't Seek Pay-cut Alternatives," *Daily News*, November 18, 1992, N1; Phillip Gollner and Beth Shuster, "LAUSD to Seek Meeting of State Board," *Daily News*, November 20, 1992, N10; Stephanie Chavez, "State Board Meets Today on Schools Crisis," *Los Angeles Times*, November 24, 1992, B1; Sandy Harrison and Beth Shuster, "State School Board Waives Salary Rule," *Daily News*, November 25, 1992, N1.

11. Shuster, "LAUSD Won't Seek Pay-cut"; Harrison and Shuster, "State School Board Waives Salary Rule"; Stephanie Chavez, "Meeting Fails to Bring Teachers, District Closer," *Los Angeles Times*, December 4, 1992, B1.

12. Beth Shuster and Kevin Stone, "Strike Decision Up to Teachers," *Daily News*, December 1, 1992, N1; Stephanie Chavez, "Board Approves Other Contracts, Enrages UTLA," *Los Angeles Times*, December 8, 1992, B1, and "L.A. Teachers Authorize Strike Feb. 22," *Los*

Angeles Times, December 11, 1992, A1; Jack Cheevers and Henry Chu, "Report Questions School District's Deficit Figure," *Los Angeles Times*, December 31, 1992, B1; Mike Comeaux and Beth Shuster, "LAUSD Says Budget 'Hole' of $73 Million Doesn't Exist," *Daily News*, January 6, 1993, N1.

13. Mike Roos, interview by Charles Kerchner and Stephanie Clayton, November 15, 2004; Roos interview, 2005.

14. Sandy Harrison, "Brown Meets with District Leaders in Bid to Avert Strike," *Daily News*, January 13, 1993, N4; Stephanie Chavez and Jerry Gillam, "Brown and Teachers Union Hold Discussion," *Los Angeles Times*, January 15, 1993, B1.

15. Stephanie Chavez, "Talks on Schools Dispute Resume," *Los Angeles Times*, February 2, 1993, B8; Sandy Harrison, "Animosity Slows Mediation, Brown Says," *Daily News*, February 3, 1993, N1; Mark Katches, "Brown Calls Contract Talks Close, Cautious," *Daily News*, February 16, 1993, N1; Stephanie Chavez, "Teachers Divided on New Contract Offer," *Los Angeles Times*, February 22, 1993, B1.

16. Thompson interview, 2004.

17. Chavez, "Teachers Divided"; Kevin Stone, "Bernstein Doubts Strike Will Occur," *Daily News*, February 22, 1993, N1.

18. Sandy Harrison and Beth Shuster, "Union Head Fears Teacher Protest Vote," *Daily News*, February 24, 1993, N1; Beth Shuster, "Specter of Strike Grows Again," *Daily News*, February 26 1993, N1; Beth Shuster, "Paycheck Changes on Hold," *Daily News*, March 2, 1993; Stephanie Chavez, "Brown Asks Clinton to Provide Federal Funds for L.A. Schools," *Los Angeles Times*, March 10, 1993, B1; Beth Shuster, "School Deal Not Finalized," *Daily News*, March 11, 1993, N1.

19. Sandy Harrison and Beth Shuster, "State Poses Threat to District's Plans," *Daily News*, March 17, 1993, N1; Stephanie Chavez and Dan Morain, "Settlement of L.A. Teachers Dispute All but Signed, Brown Says," *Los Angeles Times*, March 19, 1993, B3; Sandy Harrison and Rick Orlov, "Brown-Wilson Clash Over District Deal Intensifies," *Daily News*, March 19, 1993, N1.

20. Beth Shuster, "Brown Insists District Ratify Teachers Accord," *Daily News*, April 1, 1993, N1; Stephanie Chavez, "Plans Laid for School Layoffs, Program Cuts to Meet Shortfall," *Los Angeles Times*, March 23, 1993, B1; Jeanne Mariani and Beth Shuster, "LAUSD's Fiscal Status Downgraded," *Daily News*, March 30, 1993, N1; Sandy Banks and Stephanie Chavez, "County to Check Schools' Finances in Takeover Step," *Los Angeles Times*, March 30, 1993, B1.

21. Beth Shuster, "Thompson Rebuffs Brown: No Funds, No Teachers Pact," *Daily News*, April 2, 1993, N1; Sandy Harrison, "LAUSD Board Courting Strike, Brown Warns," *Daily News*, April 4, 1993, N1.

22. Sandy Harrison and Rick Orlov, "Brown-Wilson Clash Over District Deal Intensifies," *Daily News*, March 19, 1993, N1.

23. Stephanie Chavez, "School Board Moves Toward Ratifying Teachers Pact," *Los Angeles Times*, April 6, 1993, B3; Jeanne Mariani, "School Board Draws Up Fiscal Plan," *Daily News*, April 13, 1993, N4; Sandy Banks, "Pact Blocked; Threat of Teacher Strike Renewed," *Los Angeles Times*, April 20, 1993, A1.

24. Mike Roos, interview by Charles Kerchner and Stephanie Clayton, November 15, 2004; Sandy Banks, "Funds Pursued to Avert Teacher Strike," *Los Angeles Times*, April 21, 1993, B1.

25. Banks, "Funds Pursued"; Beth Shuster, "Teachers Plan Strike Vote Next Week," *Daily News*, April 21, 1993, N4.

26. Sandy Harrison and Jeanne Mariani, "State Finds Funds for Schools," *Daily News*, April 27, 1993, N1; Jeanne Mariani, "L.A. Gets $35 Million for Schools," *Daily News*, April 28, 1993, N1; Stephanie Chavez, "Taxpayer Group Won't Challenge School Pact Again," *Los Angeles Times*, May 1, 1993, B3; Sandy Banks and Stephanie Chavez, "Teachers Union Leaders Oppose Reform Plan," *Los Angeles Times*, May 4, 1993, A1.

27. Betsy Bates, "100 Schools Flood District with LEARN Applications," *Daily News*, April 24, 1993, N1.

28. Beth Shuster and Jeanne Mariani, "District Accepts Roster of 42 LEARN Schools," *Daily News*, May 11, 1993, 1.

29. Shuster and Mariani, "District Accepts Roster."

30. The UTLA Members Against LEARN Committee, "Stop LEARN Now" (1993), p. 31, LEARN Archives, Leavey Center for the Study of Los Angeles, Loyola Marymount University, Los Angeles.

31. Banks and Chavez, "Teachers Union Leaders Oppose."

32. Lois Timnick, "New Day is Dawning for L.A. Schools," *Los Angeles Times*, August 22, 1993, J1.

33. Stephanie Chavez, "Re-Educating the Educators," *Los Angeles Times*, July 26, 1993, B1.

34. Nancy Vogel, "TV Ads Escalate in Campaign Over School Vouchers," *Los Angeles Times*, July 26, 2000, A3.

35. Associated Press, "Bill to Break Up LAUSD Dies in Assembly," *Daily News*, September 12, 1993, N13.

36. Kimberly Kindy, "Governor Signs Legislation to Ease LAUSD Breakup," *Daily News* August 3, 1995, N1.

37. Editorial, "For the Educational Good of All," *Los Angeles Times*, July 31, 1993, B4.

38. Editorial, "Ten Reasons That Things Are Getting a Bit Better," *Los Angeles Times*, August 2, 1993, B6; editorial, "Los Angeles Turning Points: Three Monumental Reforms," *Los Angeles Times*, August 15, 1993, M4.

39. Stephanie Chavez, "37 Schools Selected to Pioneer Reform," *Los Angeles Times*, May 18, 1993, B3. A total of thirty-seven schools were originally approved, but only thirty-four joined.

40. Judy Burton, interview by Charles Kerchner, March 14, 2008.

41. Judy Burton, interview by Benjamin Diehl, July 29, 1994.

42. Burton interview, 1994.

43. Benjamin Diehl, "Field Notes: Cluster Leaders Meeting," 1993, unpublished paper, Pomona College.

44. Diehl, "Field Notes," paragraph 18.

45. Burton interview, 2008.

46. Theodore Caplow, *Managing an Organization* (Orlando, FL: Holt, Rinehart and Winston, 1983).

47. Burton interview, 1994.

48. Judy Burton, interview by Charles Kerchner, February 14, 2000.

49. Burton interview, 1994.

50. Burton interview, 1994.

51. Sid Thompson, "Inter-Office Correspondence to All Principals: LEARN Schools Budget Misconceptions," 1994, internal LAUSD document, in possession of the authors.

52. "White Paper: Budget Decentralization," 1997, internal LAUSD document, in possession of the authors.

53. Charisse Jones, "School Equality Decree OK'd by L.A. Board," *Los Angeles Times* March 17, 1992, A1.

54. Becki Robinson, interview by Charles Kerchner, January 18, 2005.

55. Merle Price, interview by Jeanne Fryer, November 10, 2005.

56. William Ouchi, interview by Charles Kerchner, August 31, 2005.

57. Rick Redding, "Teachers, Principals LEARN to Pull Together as a Team," *News-Pilot*, July 16, 1993, A1.

58. Jeanne Mariani, "Educators Learn Team Leadership," *Daily News*, July 16, 1993, 6.

59. Stephanie Chavez, "Re-Educating the Educators," *Los Angeles Times*, July 26, 1993, B8.

60. Terri Hardy, "Thompson Upbeat on New Year: Administrators Told LAUSD 'Over Hump,'" *Daily News,* August 31, 1995, N1.

61. Howard Lappin, interview by Jeanne Fryer, November 4, 2005.

62. Bruce Matsui, "Impact of UCLA's Advanced Management Program (AMP) Training on LEARN Cohort IV Schools," 1998, unpublished paper, Claremont Graduate University.

63. Office of the Superintendent, "Superintendent's Call to Action for Improving Student Achievement, 1995–2000," 1996, internal LAUSD document, in possession of the authors.

64. "Superintendent's Call to Action," 4.

65. "Superintendent's Call to Action," 1–3. There were additional goals for health and human services, school safety and intergroup relations, and parent involvement, including opening 100 new parent centers by 1996.

CHAPTER 7: LAAMP

1. William Celis "Clinton Hails Annenberg's $500 Million Education Gift," *New York Times*, December 18, 1993, 9.

2. Christopher Ogden, *Legacy: A Biography of Moses and Walter Annenberg* (Boston: Little, Brown, 1999), 539.

3. Edward B. Fiske, "Annenberg to Give $50 Million to United Negro College Fund," *New York Times*, March 3, 1990, 1.

4. Barbara Cervone, letter to Virgil Roberts, March 3, 1997, internal LAAMP document, in possession of the authors; Joel L. Fleishman, *The Foundation: A Great American Secret* (New York: Public Affairs, 2007), 196.

5. In its beginnings, LAAMP had only one *A*; the Annenberg *A* was inserted during the organization's first year of operation after Maria Casillas realized that there was another nonprofit, the Los Angeles Men's Project, which served the homeless, using the same acronym. The name change also signaled LAAMP's connection with the national Annenberg Challenge.

6. Mike Roos, interview by Charles Kerchner and David Menefee-Libey, July 14, 2005.

7. Casillas quoted in Richard Colvin, "Educator Named to Run School Reform Effort," *Los Angeles Times*, February 8, 1995, B3.

8. *Memorandum of Understanding by and among The Los Angeles Unified School District, the Annenberg Foundation and The Los Angeles County Alliance for Student Achievement* (Los Angeles: LAUSD, 1996), 6 (hereafter *MOU*): "In the event LAAMP concludes that LAUSD has not met the conditions for a subsequent year's grant, LAAMP shall notify the District in writing and allow reasonable opportunity, not less than 30 nor more than 90 working days, for District to cure such defect."

9. *MOU*, 4.

10. Roos interview, 2005.

11. Paul T. Hill, Lawrence C. Pierce, and James W. Guthrie, *Reinventing Public Education: How Contracting Can Transform America's Schools* (Chicago: University of Chicago Press, 1997).

12. For a detailed analysis of LAAMP's revenue and expenses, see Charles Taylor Kerchner et al., *The Impact of the Los Angeles Metropolitan Project on Public Education Reform* (Claremont, CA: Claremont Graduate University, 2000).

13. Mark Slavkin, interview by Charles Kerchner, October 10, 2005.

14. Dan Katzir, interview by Charles Kerchner, March 8, 2005.

15. Laura M. Desmione, "Linking Parent Involvement with Student Achievement: Do Race and Income Matter?" *The Journal of Educational Research* 93, no. 1 (1999): 11–30.

16. See Anne T. Henderson, *Parent Participation-Student Achievement: The Evidence Grows* (Columbia, MD: National Committee for Citizens in Education, 1981).

17. Reginald M. Clark, *Family Life and School Achievement: Why Poor Black Children Succeed or Fail* (Chicago: University of Chicago Press, 1983).

18. James P. Comer, "Educating Poor Minority Children," *Scientific American* 259, no. 5 (1988): 42–48; Gary Putka, "Some Schools Give Parents Crucial Roles in Educating Children," *Wall Street Journal*, December 30, 1991, A1–A2; Chuck Freadhoff, "How Parents Improve Schools: 'Parental Involvement' May Be Vital to Reforms," *Investor's Business Daily*, May 15, 1992.

19. LEARN, *For All Our Children*, 15.

20. *Executive Summary—Implementing LEARN: Perspectives of School and District Stakeholders* (Los Angeles: Evaluation and Training Institute, 1996), iii.

21. LAAMP had three major parent involvement programs or initiatives: Parents as Learning Partners (PLP), the Parent Institute for Quality Education (PIQE), and Families in Schools.

22. Ruth Yoon, interview by DeLacy Ganley, April 13, 1999.

23. Yoon interview, 1999.

24. Yoon interview, 1999; Kerchner et al., *The Impact*, 32

25. Preliminary research data lend some support to this conclusion. There were higher reading and language arts achievement results in PLP schools than in comparative schools, controlling for teacher and student characteristics. Additionally, in the PLP setting, teachers and parents tended to have a higher quality of communication, parents reviewed their children's homework and read aloud to their children more frequently, and students were motivated to read and complete their math homework more frequently. However, comparisons of teacher behaviors, parent experiences with teachers, and student achievement in math do not widely differ between settings that had a PLP program and those that did not. Denise Quigley, *Parents and Teachers Working Together to Support Third-Grade Achievement: Parents as Learning Partners (PLP) Findings,* CSE Technical Report 530 (Los Angeles: CRESST/UCLA, 2000).

26. Eva L. Baker and Joan L. Herman, *The Los Angeles Annenberg Metropolitan Project: Evaluation Findings* (Los Angeles: Graduate School of Education & Information Studies, UCLA, 2003), 39.

27. Families in Schools (FIS) offers a continuum of programs from pre-K to high school that enable parents to serve as their child's first teacher, as advocates for their children's education, and as allies of public schools in ensuring that their children learn to their fullest potential. It was initially headed by Ruth Yoon.

28. The Boyle Heights Learning Collaborative, which started as a project of the Los Angeles County Alliance for Student Achievement, another LEARN and LAAMP spin-off, moved to FIS and Casillas became president of the organization. Yoon later became administrative coordinator of the LAUSD Early Childhood Education Division.

29. Kerchner et al., *The Impact.*

30. Lawrence B. Friedman et al., *The Technology Initiatives of Five School Families in the Los Angeles Annenberg Metropolitan Project: December 1998 through June 2000* (Naperville, IL: Evaluation and Policy Information Center, 2000), 11.

31. Friedman et al., *The Technology Initiatives of Five School Families;* Joseph Shim, "Leaving a Legacy in LAUSD During LEARN and LAAMP Reform Movements: Were Any Reforms Sustained?" 2005, unpublished paper, Claremont Graduate University.

32. Education Counts, found at www.edweek.org, allows comparison of states along a number of technology-related and other indicators.

33. Sterling C. Lloyd, "Technology Counts, Times 10," *Education Week* 26, no. 30 (2007): 31–32.

34. Comparison made using www.edweek.org data (accessed January 9, 2008).

35. Theodore Mitchell recalls that when the LAAMP proposal was being written, Theodore Sizer criticized the plan because it did not identify a specific problem it was trying to solve. "We talked about a major problem in L.A. being transiency rates and from this emerged the notion of a family of schools" that would provide pathways and support for students. Theodore Mitchell, interview by Charles Kerchner, September 16, 1999.

36. Priscilla Wohlstetter and Andrew K. Smith, "A Different Approach to Systemic Reform: Network Structures in Los Angeles," *Phi Delta Kappan* 81, no. 7 (2000): 508.

37. Kerchner et al., *The Impact,* 30.

38. Kerchner et al., *The Impact,* 34.

39. Mike Roos, interview by Charles Kerchner, November 8, 1999.

40. Alonzo would later become a superintendent of Local District 4.
41. Richard Alonzo, interview with Charles Kerchner, April 27, 2005.
42. *North Hollywood: Status Report on the Use of Data* (Los Angeles: LAAMP, 1999).
43. *North Hollywood Status Report.*
44. Merle Price, interview by Jeanne Fryer, November 10, 2005.
45. Price interview, 2005.
46. Judy Burton, interview by Charles Kerchner, December 12, 2003.
47. Burton interview, 2003.
48. For a list of the schools and a summary of their programs see Kerchner et al., *The Impact*, 28–42.
49. Dorothy J. Jackson, "The Effects of Elementary Principals' Perceptions of the History of Reforms in LAUSD on Their Regard for LEARN and Other Reforms" (Ph.D. dissertation, UCLA, 1996), 160.
50. John Stuppy, who worked with LEARN while at UCLA, collected email responses from participants and circulated them to an email list in 1995: "Issues, Suggestions and Problems Feedback," internal LEARN document, in possession of the authors.

CHAPTER 8: IMPLEMENTATION

1. John Stuppy, who worked with LEARN while at UCLA, collected email responses from participants and circulated them to an email list in 1995: "Issues, Suggestions and Problems Feedback," internal LEARN document, in possession of the authors.
2. Those interested in the literature should begin with Jeffrey Pressman and Aaron Wildavsky, *Implementation: How Great Expectations in Washington Are Dashed in Oakland; or, Why It's Amazing That Federal Programs Work at All, This Being a Saga by Two Sympathetic Observers Who Seek to Build Morals on a Foundation of Ruined Hopes* (Berkeley, CA: University of California Press, 1973). This exemplifies first-generation implementation studies that focused on the difficulty of the task. A second generation of studies worked to identify factors that made successful implementation more and less likely, as exemplified by Paul Peterson, Barry Rabe, and Kenneth Wong, *When Federalism Works* (Washington, DC: Brookings Institution, 1986). Attempts at a third generation that could offer a general theory of implementation, have included Malcolm L. Goggin, Ann O'M. Bowman, James P. Lester, and Laurence J. O'Toole Jr., *Implementation Theory and Practice: Toward a Third Generation* (Glenview, IL: Scott, Foresman, 1990), and, more recently, Meredith I. Honig, ed., *New Directions in Education Policy Implementation: Confronting Complexity* (Albany, NY: SUNY Press, 2006).
3. Virgil Roberts, interview by Charles Kerchner, August 19, 2005.
4. Virgil Roberts, interview by Charles Kerchner, September 10, 1999.
5. Everett M. Rogers and F. Floyd Schoemaker, *Communications of Innovations: A Cross-Cultural Approach* (New York: Free Press, 1971), 135. The large literature on innovations has at least two points of tangency with LAUSD as a case of institutional change. The product innovation cycle introduced in Rogers and Schoemaker is one of them. The second is the organization behavior or organizational sociology contribution to institutional theory and research. This is well reviewed by Brian Rowan and Cecil G.

Miskell, "Institutional Theory and The Study of Educational Organizations," in *Handbook of Research on Educational Administration*, ed. J. Murphy and K. S. Louis (San Francisco: Jossey-Bass, 1999).

6. The "tipping point" popularized by Malcolm Gladwell, first in a magazine article "The Tipping Point," *New Yorker*, June 6 1996, and later in a popular book, *The Tipping Point: How Little Things Can Make A Big Difference* (Boston: Little, Brown, 2000), has its origins in epidemiology as the moment at which a virus begins spreading with more people getting sick than getting well. As such, it is an important amendment to the usual ideas about educational change because it adds the notion of natural or spontaneous spread. In education, see for example, Jonathan Crane, "The Epidemic Theory of Ghettos and Neighborhood Effects on Dropping Out and Teenage Childbearing," *American Journal of Sociology* 96, no. 5 (1991): 1226–59.

7. Stuppy, "Issues," 8.

8. As in most of LEARN, the planning process was highly participatory with representatives of the school administration, LEARN, and UCLA involved. See "Discussion Session on Developing a School Site Action Plan," 1993, p. 5, internal LEARN document, in possession of the authors.

9. Camellia Avenue Elementary School, "LEARN Site Action Plan," 1995, 2.

10. Robert Frost Middle School, "LEARN Site Action Plan," 1995, 2.

11. Camellia, "LEARN Site Action Plan," 4.

12. Frost, "LEARN Site Action Plan," 10–13.

13. Frost, "LEARN Site Action Plan," 8.

14. Pressman and Wildavsky, *Implementation*.

15. LAEP, "The Los Angeles Educational Partnership: Learning Community Program," 1995, 1.

16. Linda Friedrich et al., *The Learning Community Program Evaluation, Year 3: 1996–1997, Final Report to Los Angeles Educational Partnership* (Stanford, CA: Center for Research on the Contexts of Teaching, 1997), 4, citing Judith Warren Little, "Norms of Collegiality and Experimentation," *American Educational Research Journal* 19, no. 3 (1982): 325–40; Susan J. Rosenholtz, *Teachers' Workplace: The Social Organization of Schools* (White Plains, NY: Longman, 1989); and Milbrey W. McLaughlin and Joan E. Talbert, *Contexts That Matter for Teaching and Learning: Strategic Opportunities for Meeting The Nation's Educational Goal* (Stanford, CA: Center for Research on the Context of Secondary School Teaching, 1993).

17. See Little, "Norms of Collegiality"; Milbrey W. McLaughlin, "What Matters Most in Teachers' Workplace Context?" in *Teachers Work: Individuals, Colleagues and Contexts*, ed. Judith Warren Little and Milbrey W. McLaughlin (New York: Teachers College Press, 1993), 79–103; McLaughlin and Talbert, "Contexts That Matter"; Fred M. Newmann and Gary G. Wehlage, *Successful School Restructuring* (Madison, WI: Center of Organization and Restructuring of Schools, 1995); Karen Seashore Louis, Helen M. Marks, and Sharon Kruse, "Teachers' Professional Community in Restructuring Schools," *American Educational Research Journal* 33, no. 4 (1996): 757–98; and Friedrich et al., "The Learning Community," 4.

18. Its original funding came from the Ford Foundation and the Public Education Fund. LAEP then established itself as a local education fund.
19. Peggy Funkhouser, "Remarks at Washington Mutual Breakfast for Urban Education Partnership," 2005, p. 1, in possession of the authors. Also see Peggy Funkhouser, *History of the Los Angeles Educational Partnership* (Los Angeles: LAEP, 2000).
20. Funkhouser, "Remarks," 1.
21. These were supported by more than $1 million in initial grants and pledges raised to support the new organization and launch these programs. The local business community and private foundations joined in collaborative private efforts to invest in finding solutions for the problems in public schools. The early funders were ARCO, Pacific Bell, GTE, TRW, First Interstate Bank, and Carnation joined by major multiyear grants from the Ford, Stuart, Rockefeller, and Carnegie foundations (Funkhouser, *History*, 4).
22. Day Higuchi, interview by Charles Kerchner, February 10, 2000.
23. In 2005, the Urban Education Partnership, the successor organization to LAEP, announced that the graduation rate of Humanitas students was 77 percent compared to 46 percent for same school peers. See Urban Education Partnership, "Urban Education Partnership Study Finds LAUSD Students in Humanitas Program Closing the Achievement Gap," press release, September 9, 2005 (accessed March 16, 2006, from www.laep.org/pdf/news-releases/Humanitas.pdf).
24. The mission of LAEP was changed to that of a national contract service provider, and the organization was renamed the Urban Education Partnership. Funkhouser retired in 2000, but came out from retirement in 2005 to head UEP, which had fallen on hard times.
25. Michael Fullan, *Change Forces: Probing the Depths of Educational Reform* (New York: Falmer, 1993), 22–24.
26. Friedrich et al., "The Learning Community," 4.
27. Friedrich et al., "The Learning Community," 5.
28. Friedrich et al., "The Learning Community," 5–6, citing "Theory of Action Letter," December 1995.
29. Friedrich et al., "The Learning Community," 9.
30. Friedrich et al., "The Learning Community," 20.
31. Friedrich et al., "The Learning Community," 18.
32. The first summer institute was held at California State Polytechnic University, Pomona.
33. Dee Nishimoto, interview by Marco Villegas and Anthony Ortiz, June 3, 2004.
34. Suzie Oh, interview by Marco Villegas and Anthony Ortiz, April 12, 2004.
35. Stuppy, "Issues," 1; Dan Chernow, interview by Marco Villegas and Anthony Ortiz, June 24, 2004.
36. Stuppy, "Issues," 2.
37. Stuppy, "Issues," 3.
38. Stuppy, "Issues," 4.
39. Ronni Ephraim, interview with Charles Kerchner, March 10, 2008.
40. Nishimoto interview, 2004.

41. Judy Johnson and Diane Glinos, interview by Charles Kerchner, November 2, 2004.

42. Friedrich et al., "The Learning Community," 43

43. Friedrich et al., "The Learning Community," 43.

44. Roberts interview, 1999.

45. Dorothy J. Jackson, "The Effects of Elementary Principals' Perceptions of the History of Reforms in LAUSD on Their Regard for LEARN and Other Reforms" (Ph.D. dissertation, UCLA, 1996).

46. Stuppy, "Issues," 1.

47. Maria Casillas, interview by Charles Kerchner, January 25, 2000.

48. Friedrich et al., "The Learning Community," 54.

49. Jackson, "The Effects," 163. The finding that time was a major issue surprised Jackson; there were no questions in her study directed toward time usage or availability.

50. Henry Mintzberg, *The Nature of Managerial Work* (New York: Harper & Row, 1973); William J. Martin and Donald J. Willower, "The Managerial Behavior of High School Principals," *Educational Administration Quarterly* 17, no. 1 (1981): 69–90.

51. Jackson, "The Effects," 157–58.

52. Jackson, "The Effects," 158.

53. Friedrich et al., "The Learning Community," 9.

54. Friedrich et al., "The Learning Community," 20.

55. Friedrich et al., "The Learning Community," 10.

56. Friedrich et al., "The Learning Community," 10.

57. Friedrich et al., "The Learning Community," 19.

58. Friedrich et al., "The Learning Community," 32.

59. Bob Baker and Sandy Banks, "Lessons in School Reform," *Los Angeles Times*, February 1, 1993, A1.

60. The state had previous experience with the California Assessment Program that had introduced writing samples into the state's testing scheme, a departure from multiple-choice tests. It was eliminated from the budget by Governor George Deukmejian in 1990. See Ruth Mitchell, "Deukmejian Gets Dunce Cap for Spiking Innovative School Assessment Program," *Los Angeles Times*, August 19, 1990, M5.

61. Mitchell, "Deukmejian Gets Dunce Cap."

62. For a summary of the political process, see PACE, *Conditions of Education in California 1994–95* (Berkeley, CA: Policy Analysis for California Education, 1995).

63. Jodi Wilgoren and Richard O'Reilly, "Scoring of School Tests Found To Be Inaccurate," *Los Angeles Times*, April 10, 1994, A1.

64. Stuppy, "Issues," 8.

65. Judy Burton, interview by Charles Kerchner, February 14, 2000.

66. Ronni Ephraim, interview by Charles Kerchner, March 10, 2008.

67. Charles Taylor Kerchner et al., *The Impact of the Los Angeles Metropolitan Project on Public Education Reform* (Claremont, CA: Claremont Graduate University, 2000), 45.

68. Ephraim interview, 2008.

69. Kerchner et al., *The Impact.*, 47.

70. The STAR (Standardized Testing and Accountability System) continues, although its underlying tests have changed, making trend analysis difficult. See Stephen J. Carroll

et al., *California's K–12 Public Schools: How Are They Doing?* (Santa Monica, CA: RAND, 2005).

71. Carla Rivera, "More Effort to Pass Exam Urged," *Los Angeles Times*, July 22, 2006, B3; 2006–07 Accountability Progress Report, California Department of Education (accessed on November 19, 2007, at http://ayp.cde.ca.gov/reports/).

72. Jack McDonough, *Strategic Alignment Framework* (Los Angeles: UCLA School of Management, 1993). 8–9.

73. *For All Our Children: Better Educational Results in the Los Angeles Public Schools* (Los Angeles: LEARN, 1993), 8.

74. *For All Our Children*, 8.

75. Judy Burton, interview by Charles Kerchner, March 14, 2008.

76. Burton interview, 2008.

77. Jackson, "The Effects," 82.

78. Anthony Handy interview in Marco Villegas and Anthony Ortiz, "Principal Professional Development: Los Angeles Unified School District," 2004, p. 10, unpublished paper, Claremont Graduate University.

79. Jackson, "The Effects." Jackson interviewed sixteen principals from schools on L.A.'s Westside, eight of whom were involved in LEARN.

80. Jackson, "The Effects," 9.

81. This section draws on field research conducted by Marco Villegas and Anthony Ortiz. See Villegas and Ortiz, "Principal Professional Development."

82. Villegas and Ortiz, "Principal Professional Development," 24.

83. Stuppy, "Issues," 5.

84. Stuppy, "Issues," 5.

85. Stuppy, "Issues," 6.

86. LAEP, "Los Angeles Educational Partnership Learning Community Program: Meeting of the Evaluators," 1998, 9.

87. Jackson, "The Effects," 180.

88. At that time, LAUSD used Harcourt Brace's Stanford 9. The District had just switched from the California Test of Basic Skills making long-term comparisons impossible.

89. Doug Smith, "Score Gains Seen Under Reform Programs," *Los Angeles Times*, November 4, 1998, B2.

90. Smith, "Score Gains," 3.

91. The evaluation organization was known as the Los Angeles Consortium for Evaluation. It was headed by Eva Baker at UCLA and Priscilla Wohlstetter at USC. A subcontract to document the operations of the LAAMP board and staff was carried out by Charles Kerchner at Claremont Graduate University.

92. Joan L. Herman and Eva L. Baker, *Los Angeles Annenberg Metropolitan Project Evaluation Findings* (Los Angeles: Los Angeles Consortium for Evaluation, 2003), vi. The report continued, "Using advanced statistical techniques that take into account the effects of student and school backgrounds and socioeconomic status characteristics, we find no significant differences between LAAMP and non-LAAMP schools for reading, language arts, or mathematics performance. That is, taking into account student

school characteristics, we found that participation in LAAMP had no significant effect on student performance" (26).

93. Herman and Baker, *LAAMP Evaluation Findings,* 21.

94. Jeffrey A. White and Steven Cantrell, *Evaluation of Major LAUSD Reform Programs: API Growth from 1999 to 2002* (Los Angeles, CA: Program Evaluation and Research Branch of Los Angeles Unified School District, 2003), 12.

95. Evaluation and Training Institute, "The Purpose of the LEARN School Report Card: Summary Findings," 1998, pp. 1, 4, LEARN internal document, in possession of the authors.

96. Merle Price, interview by Jeanne Fryer, November 10, 2005.

97. Not everyone writes as positively about M-Form organizations. John Brackman, for one, considers them "a vestige of the early twentieth century." See John Backman, *The M-Form Organization Dysfunction* (2005; accessed October 4, 2007, from www.rediff.com/money/2005/jun/09bspec.htm).

98. William G. Ouchi, *Theory Z: How American Business Can Meet the Japanese Challenge* (Reading, MA: Addison-Wesley, 1981); William G. Ouchi, *The M-Form Society* (Menlo Park, CA: Addison-Wesley, 1984).

99. William G. Ouchi, *Making Schools Work: A Revolutionary Plan To Get Your Children the Education They Need* (New York: Simon & Schuster, 2003). 14, 17, 245.

100. Ouchi, *Making Schools Work,* 16.

101. William Ouchi, interview by Charles Kerchner, August 31, 2007.

102. Howard Lappin, interview by Jeanne Fryer, November 4, 2005.

103. Ouchi interview, 2007.

104. Ouchi interview, 2007.

105. Ouchi interview, 2007.

106. Amy Bruce et al., "Los Angeles Educational Partnership Learning Community Program: Meeting of the Evaluators," 1998, p. 15, internal LAAMP document, in possession of the authors.

107. Judy Johnson, "Memorandum to Mike Roos," 1995, 2, 5.

108. Ouchi interview, 2007.

109. Ouchi interview, 2007.

CHAPTER 9: PERMANENT CRISIS

1. "Los Angeles Times Interview: School Board Candidates," *Los Angeles Times,* March 14, 1999, M3.

2. Louis Sahagun, "Few Angelenos Give School Board Good Grades," *Los Angeles Times,* April 4, 1999, A1.

3. Louis Sahagun and Doug Smith, "Los Angeles Elections: Buoyed by Hayes' Win, School Reformers Plan Major Changes," *Los Angeles Times,* June 10, 1999, A1.

4. Sid Thompson, interview by Charles Kerchner, March 11, 2008.

5. Mike Roos, interview by Charles Kerchner and David Menefee-Libey, July 14, 2005.

6. Louis Sahagun, "L.A. School Board Gives Zacarias High Marks," *Los Angeles Times,* July 15, 1998, B1.

7. Bill Boyarsky, "In the Big School Play, the Board's the Heavy," *Los Angeles Times*, April 24, 1997, B1.

8. In 2008, it remains unfinished, although construction restarted in response to community pressure to do something about the overcrowding conditions at the old Belmont High School.

9. See, for example, Doug Smith, "Experts Tell of Explosion Risk at Belmont," *Los Angeles Times*, June 16, 1999, 8; Patt Morrison, "Belmont, Where School Spirit is High-Octane," *Los Angeles Times*, October 29, 1999, 1.

10. Her retirement was short lived. She later worked as a representative of the Bill and Melinda Gates Foundation, and when the successor organization to LAEP fell on hard times, she went back to head it.

11. The *Times* would have an unhappy existence as a property of the Chicago Tribune Company, and in 2007 controlling interest was obtained by real estate entrepreneur Sam Zell.

12. Virgil Roberts, interview by Charles Kerchner, August 19, 2005.

13. "A School System Is a Terrible Thing to Waste," *L.A. Weekly*, October 27, 1999 (accessed May 17, 2007, from http://www.laweekly.com/news/news/a-school-system-is-a-terrible-thing-to-waste/6221/?page=7).

14. Louis Sahagun, "Riordan Funds for L.A. School Board Races Come with Strings Attached," *Los Angeles Times*, March 25, 1999, B1; Rick Orlov, "Riordan Slate Near $2 Million," *Los Angeles Daily News*, April 2, 1999, N4.

15. "Committee on Effective School Governance" (accessed February 9, 2005, from www.laamp.org/administrators/cesg_members.html).

16. CESG, "Financial Report, July 13, 1999," internal LAAMP document, in possession of the authors.

17. CESG, "Los Angeles Unified School District Governance—Our Future at Risk," 1999, internal LAAMP document, in possession of the author.

18. CESG, "LAUSD—Our Future at Risk," 5.

19. CESG, "LAUSD—Our Future at Risk," 7.

20. CESG, "LAUSD—Our Future at Risk," 5.

21. Louis Sahagun and Doug Smith, "Issues May Be Scarce, but Passion and Politics Aren't," *Los Angeles Times*, April 11, 1999, B1.

22. Doug Smith, "Riordan-Backed School Board Candidates Up the Ante with Ads," *Los Angeles Times*, April 1, 1999, B1.

23. Louis Sahagun, "School Board Hopefuls' Forum Erupts in Shouts," *Los Angeles Times*, April 10, 1999, B5.

24. Howard Blume, "And Another Thing," *L.A. Weekly*, November 3, 1999, 1.

25. Richard Lee Colvin and Louis Sahagun, "Riordan in Discussions about Next Schools Chief," *Los Angeles Times*, August 14, 1999, A1.

26. Louis Sahagun, "Cortines Sets to Work on Plans for District," *Los Angeles Times*, November 6, 1999, 1.

27. Louis Sahagun and Kristina Sauerwein, "L.A. Unified Appoints 11 Leaders for Subdistricts," *Los Angeles Times*, June 16, 2000, B1.

28. Editorial, "A Bad Fit for LAUSD: The School Board's Selection of Romer Gave Short Shrift to the Basic and Most Crucial Issue: Who Is the Best Person to Lead the LAUSD," *Los Angeles Times*, June 7 2000, B10.

29. Jon Fullerton, "Overview of School Finance and the LAUSD Budget: Presentation to the Presidents' Joint Commission" (Los Angeles: Board of Education, 2005), internal LAUSD document, in possession of the authors; see also http://www.masspike.com/bigdig/background/index.html (accessed July 17, 2007).

30. David B. Tyack, *The One Best System: A History of American Urban Education* (Cambridge, MA: Harvard University Press, 1974).

31. Greg Gero, "Lost in Translation: The Cases of Learning Walks and Lesson Study in the Los Angeles Unified School District," 2006, p. 9, unpublished paper, Claremont Graduate University.

32. Jean Merl, "Charter Schools Promote Reform; Group Target's L.A.'s Mayoral Candidates in a $1.5 Million Campaign to Secure Endorsements of its Efforts to Reshape Education System," *Los Angeles Times*, February 17, 2004, B3.

33. Howard Blume, "Decrepit District Is Tough to Demolish," *Los Angeles Times*, January 2, 2005, M2.

34. Joel Rubin and Jessica Garrison, "City Control of Schools Advocated; Mayor Should Appoint Board of Education as One Step in a Broad Transformation of the District, Villaraigosa Tells Panel of Legislators," *Los Angeles Times*, June 18, 2005, B1.

35. Roy Romer, *State of the Schools Address* (Los Angeles: LAUSD, 2006) (accessed July 18, 2007, from http://notebook.lausd.net/pls/ptl/docs/PAGE/CA_LAUSD/FLDR_LAUSD_NEWS/FLDR_ANNOUNCEMENTS/STATE%20OF%20SCHOOLS%20SPEECH45450.PDF).

36. Evergreen Solutions, LLC, "Diagnostic Phase I Review in the Los Angeles Unified School District, Final Report," April 6, 2007, in possession of the authors.

37. Jim Newton, "Familiar Ring to Mayor's Agenda; Villaraigosa's Focus on Expanding the LAPD and Controlling Schools Echoes Riordan's Goals," *Los Angeles Times*, April 24, 2006, B1.

38. Howard Blume, "Mayor Drops School Fight; Villaraigosa Abandons the Court Battle Over L.A. Unified Control but Says He Realized the Key Goal: to Spark Dialogue," *Los Angeles Times*, May 19, 2007, A1.

39. Naush Boghossian, "Mayor Jettisons School Takeover-Court Case Moot with New Board," *Daily News*, May 19, 2007, N1.

40. Antonio Villaraigosa, *The Schoolhouse: A Framework to Give Every Child in LAUSD an Excellent Education* (Los Angeles: Office of the Mayor, 2007).

41. Graham T. Allison, *Essence of Decision: Explaining the Cuban Missile Crisis* (Boston: Little, Brown, 1971).

42. Kathleen Thelen, "Historical Institutionalism in Comparative Politics," *Annual Review of Political Science* 2, no. 1 (1999): 369–404.

43. Frank H. Knight, *Risk, Uncertainty and Profit* (New York: Houghton Mifflin, 1921).

44. Mark M. Blyth, *Great Transformations: Economic Ideas and Institutional Change in the Twentieth Century* (Cambridge, UK: Cambridge University Press, 2002), 11.

CHAPTER 10: CHARTER SCHOOLS

1. Assembly Bill 544, passed in 1998, increased the statewide cap to 250 in 1998–99, with an additional 100 allowed each year after that. It also eliminated a ten school-per-district limit. For a brief legislative history, see Brian Edwards and Mary Perry, *Charter Schools in California: An Experiment Coming of Age* (Palo Alto, CA: EdSource, 2004).

2. "Chamber Sends Senator Roberti Letter in Support of LEARN, Charter Schools," *Southern California Business*, August 1993, cited in Chun, "Facilitating Organizational Change."

3. Proposition 174, titled the Parental Choice in Education Act, provided vouchers in the amount of $2,600 for each child to be used in private schools. The proposition was overwhelmingly defeated in November 1993. "California's Schools: No Vouchers, Yet," *The Economist*, November 6, 1993, 25.

4. Hart quoted in Carl Ingram, "Governor Signs Legislation to Allow Charter Schools; Education: New Law Permits Independently Run Pubic Institutions Where Only the Basics are Taught," *Sacramento Bee*, September 22, 1992, A3.

5. *California Education Code*, Section 47601.

6. Maria Perez et al., *Charter Schools in California: A Review of their Autonomy and Resource Allocation Practices* (Stanford, CA: American Institutes for Research, 2006).

7. Joseph Murphy and Catherine Dunn Shiffman, *Understanding and Assessing the Charter School Movement* (New York: Teachers College Press, 2002).

8. California Department of Education (accessed September 4, 2007, from http://cde.ca.gov).

9. California Charter Schools Association (CCSA), "LAUSD Charter Demographic and Performance Data, 2006," CCSA internal document, in possession of the authors.

10. Joel Rubin, "Give Him an A for Ambition," *Los Angeles Times*, February 20, 2007, A1.

11. Eric Crane and Brian Edwards, *California's Charter Schools: Measuring Their Performance* (Mountain View, CA: EdSource, 2007).

12. Crane and Edwards, *California's Charter Schools*, 3; and CCSA, "LAUSD Charter Demographic and Performance Data."

13. LAUSD, "Policy for Charter Schools in the Los Angeles Unified School District," June 25, 2002.

14. Mike Roos, interview by Charles Kerchner and David Menefee-Libey, July 14, 2005

15. Mark Slavkin, interview by Benjamin Diehl, 1994.

16. Merle Price, interview by Jeanne Fryer, November 10, 2005.

17. Price interview, 2005.

18. LAUSD, "Policy for Charter Schools."

19. Price interview, 2005.

20. Price interview, 2005.

21. LAUSD, "Policy for Charter School," 2.

22. LAUSD, "Policy for Charter School," 2.

23. LAUSD, "Policy for Charter School," 2.

24. Caroline Hendrie, "Romer Raises Stakes in L.A. Charter Fight," *Education Week*, May 21, 2003, 1

25. Howard Blume, "Legacy May Impede New Charter Official," *Los Angeles Times,* December 26, 2007, B1.

26. Caprice Young, interview by Charles Kerchner and Laura Mulfinger, August 28, 2007.

27. Howard Lappin, interview by Jeanne Fryer, November 4, 2005.

28. Aspire Public Schools, "Business Plan, 2004," 7 (accessed on August 15, 2007, from www.nea.org/edstats/images/05rankings-update.pdf).

29. Don Shalvey, interview by Charles Kerchner, August 22, 2007

30. Aspire Public Schools, "Results" (accessed on August 15, 2007, from www.aspirepublicschools.org/?q=results).

31. Shalvey interview, 2007.

32. Aspire Public Schools (accessed on August 15, 2007, from www.aspirepublicschools.org).

33. Shalvey interview, 2007.

34. Green Dot Public Schools (accessed August 16, 2007, from www.greendotpublicschools.org).

35. Barr, in Rubin, "Give Him an A."

36. Regalado quoted in Sam Dillon, "Union-Friendly Maverick Leads New Charge for Charter Schools," *New York Times,* July 24, 2007, A1.

37. Sam Dillon, "Union-Friendly Maverick Leads New Charge for Charter Schools," *New York Times,* July 24, 2007, A1.

38. Ed-Data (accessed January 3, 2008, from www.ed-data.k12.ca.us/).

39. Virgil Roberts, interview by Charles Kerchner, August 19, 2005.

40. The New Schools Venture Fund was started in 1998 by social entrepreneur Kim Smith and venture capitalists John Doerr and Brook Byers in order to transform public education by supporting education entrepreneurs, helping them to grow their organizations to scale and connect their work to broader systems change. See http://newschools.org (accessed August 16, 2007).

41. William Ouchi, interview by Charles Kerchner, August 31, 2007.

42. Foshay went from being one of the "31 lowest achieving schools in LAUSD" in 1989 to a K–12 school that the *Los Angeles Times* called a "Model of Education Reform." In 1996, it was honored as a "California Distinguished School"; in 1998, *L.A. Magazine* named it one of the "Ten Best Schools in Los Angeles," and in 2000, *Newsweek* named it the "95th Best High School in the U.S.A." In 1995, *Reader's Digest* called Lappin a "Hero in American Education," and in 1997 he was named "California Principal of the Year." Governor Pete Wilson also referred to him as a "California Hero" in his 1998 State of the State speech. Howard Lappin was the director of the Urban Learning Centers at LAEP and the principal of Foshay Learning Center in the LAUSD. He became principal of Foshay Junior High School in 1989 (in 1994, it changed its name to Foshay Learning Center). Since then it has become a K–12 school. Lappin retired from Foshay in 2001. Alliance Public Schools (accessed January 6, 2008, from http://www.laalliance.org/staff.html).

43. Alliance Public Schools (accessed January 6, 2008, from http://www.laalliance.org/staff.html).

44. Lappin interview, 2004.

45. Lappin interview, 2004.
46. Caprice Young, "Empowering Teachers and Parents with Charter Schools Can Bring New Opportunities To Urban Communities," *USC UrbanEd* (Fall/Winter 2005): 27.
47. Howard Blume, "2 More L.A. Schools Take Control," *Los Angeles Times*, January 30, 2008, B2.
48. California Charter Schools Association (accessed August 27, 2007, from www.my-school.org).
49. CCSA, www.my-school.org (accessed August 27, 2004).
50. CCSA, www.my-school.org (accessed August 27, 2004).
51. The High Tech High Graduate School of Education, located in San Diego, opened in September 2007. See http://gse.hightechhigh.org (accessed January 9, 2008).
52. Mike Roos praised Siart's management skills; nonetheless, the position went to then LAUSD deputy superintendent Ruben Zacarias. "Ex-Banker Bids for LAUSD Job," *Daily News*, April 18, 1997, N4.
53. ExED (accessed January 9, 2008, from www.exed.net).
54. Pacific Charter School Development, www.pacificcharter.org (accessed January 17, 2008).
55. PCSD, www.pacificcharter.org (accessed January 17, 2008).
56. Howard Blume, "L.A. Charter Schools Get a Financial Boost; Philanthropist Eli Broad Is Donating $23.3 Million to Jump-Start 17 New Campuses Run by Two Major Groups," *Los Angeles Times*, January 17, 2008.
57. Thouraya Raiss. "Charter Schools Advocate Reed Hastings to Speak April 12," *Stanford Online Report,* April 5, 2000 (accessed September 25, 2007, from http://news-service.stanford.edu/news/2000/april5/hastings-45.html).
58. Shalvey interview, 2007.
59. Founded in 2005 and based in Colorado, the Charter School Growth has provided awards totaling nearly $30 million to twelve high-quality charter operators who will add 44,000 new seats in schools by 2012. National in scope, thus far it has funded charter operators in Arizona, California, Colorado, the District of Columbia, Illinois, New Jersey, New York, North Carolina, Oregon, and Texas. Charter School Growth Fund (accessed September 25, 2007, from http://www.chartergrowthfund.org).
60. Martin Carnoy et al., *The Charter School Dust-Up: Examining the Evidence on Enrollment and Achievement* (New York: Teachers College Press, 2005).
61. Crane and Edwards, "California's Charter Schools."
62. Crane and Edwards, "California's Charter Schools."
63. California Department of Education, "2007 AYP LEA Overview" (accessed November 19, 2007, from www.cde.ca.gov).
64. Young interview, 2007.
65. Young interview, 2007; Shalvey interview, 2007.
66. Joel Rubin and Howard Blume, "Green Dot Charter Organization to Take Over Locke High School," *Los Angeles Times,* September 12, 2007, B3.
67. Joel Rubin, "Green Dot Plans School in N.Y. City," *Los Angeles Times,* June 28, 2007, B6.
68. Roberts interview, 2005.

69. Shalvey interview, 2007.
70. Paul T. Hill, Lawrence C. Pierce, and James W. Guthrie, *Reinventing Public Education: How Contracting Can Transform America's Schools* (Chicago: University of Chicago Press, 1997).
71. California Department of Education, "Update of Enacted Charter School Legislation, May 5, 2004" (accessed November 19, 2007, from www.cde.ca.gov/sp/cs/lr/cslegsummmay05.asp).
72. *California Education Code,* Section 47604.33
73. Young, in Howard Blume, "Legacy May Impede New Charter Official," *Los Angeles Times*, December 26, 2007, B1.

CHAPTER 11: BEYOND CRISIS

1. This has been the case in Chicago, where the Commercial Club of Chicago has been the vehicle for business involvement and had influence over the schools for more than a century. See Dorothy Shipps, *School Reform, Corporate Style: Chicago, 1880–2000* (Lawrence, KS: University Press of Kansas, 2006).
2. David Tyack, "Public School Reform: Policy Talk and Institutional Practice," *American Journal of Education* 100, no. 1 (1991): 10–11.
3. James Madison, "The Federalist No. 10: The Same Subject Continued: Union as a Safeguard against Democratic Faction and Insurrection." The Federalist Papers (1787–88) (accessed June 10, 2008, from http://thomas.loc.gov/home/histdox/fed_10.html).
4. Alliance for a Better Community (accessed March 18, 2008, from http://afabc.org/history.html).
5. New Schools Better Neighborhoods (accessed December 14, 2007, from www.nsbn.org).
6. This observation applies to school districts nationally. See Mark Blyth, "Studying Educational Systems with the Tools of Institutional Theory," in Boyd et al., *The Transformation*.
7. Stephen J. Carroll et al., *California's K–12 Public Schools: How Are They Doing?* (Santa Monica, CA: RAND, 2005). Sylvia A. Allegretto, Sean P. Corcoran, and Lawrence Mishel, *The Teaching Penalty: Teacher Pay Losing Ground* (Washington, DC: Economic Policy Institute, 2008).
8. Jane J. Mansbridge, ed., *Beyond Self-Interest* (Chicago: University of Chicago Press, 1990).
9. Peter Schrag, *Paradise Lost: California's Experience, America's Future* (Berkeley, CA: University of California Press, 1998), 167.
10. Schrag, *Paradise Lost,* 166.
11. Schrag, *Paradise Lost,* 195.
12. "Marion Joseph," *Learning Matters*, January 30, 2004. (accessed December 14, 2007, from www.pbs.org/merrow/tv/ftw/joseph.html).
13. Sid Thompson, interview by Charles Kerchner, November 2, 2004.
14. Howard Blume, "L.A. Unified Warned That It Falls Short of State Standards; With 98 Other Districts It Faces Penalties Under NCLB," *Los Angeles Times*, November 29, 2007, B3.

15. Tyack, "Public School Reform," 10.
16. Schwarzenegger's Second Inaugural address, January 5, 2007 (accessed January 16, 2008, from http://gov.ca.gov/index.php?/press-release/5049/).
17. Baumgartner and Jones introduce the idea of "punctuated equilibrium." See Frank R. Baumgartner and Bryan D. Jones, *Policy Dynamics* (Chicago: University of Chicago Press, 2002); and Frank R. Baumgartner and Bryan D. Jones, *Agendas and Instability in American Politics* (Chicago: University of Chicago Press, 1993).
18. Charles E. Lindblom, "The Science of Muddling Through," *Public Administration Review* 19, no. 2 (1959): 79–88.
19. Anthony Downs, "Up and Down with Ecology—The 'Issue-Attention Cycle,'" *Public Interest* 28 (Summer 1972): 38–50.
20. Malcolm L. Goggin et al., *Implementation Theory and Practice: Toward a Third Generation* (Glenview, IL: Scott, Foresman/Little, Brown, 1990); B. Guy Peters, *American Public Policy: Promise and Performance*, 5th ed. (New York: Chatham House, 1999).
21. Marshall Smith and Jennifer O'Day, "Systemic School Reform," in *The Politics of Curriculum and Testing*, ed. Susan Fuhrman and Betty Malen (Philadelphia, PA: Falmer, 1991), 233–67. See also David Menefee-Libey, "Systemic Reform in a Federated System: Los Angeles at the Turn of the Millennium," *Education Policy Analysis Archives*, 12, no. 60 (October 2004), available at http://epaa.asu.edu/epaa/v12n60.
22. In 1993, just 23 percent of U.S. households owned a computer; by 2003, 62 percent owned a computer and 55 percent had access to the Internet. U.S. Bureau of the Census, "Computer Use and Ownership Data: 1993, Table A" (accessed February 28, 2008, from www.census.gov/population/socdemo/computer/report93/compusea.txt); and U.S. Bureau of the Census, "Computer Use and Ownership Data: 2003, Figure 1" (accessed February 28, 2008, from www.census.gov/prod/2005pubs/p23-208.pdf).
23. On this point, see Lorraine M. McDonnell, "Creating the Political Conditions for Major Changes in School Finance Policy," School Finance Redesign Project, Evans School of Public Affairs, University of Washington, 2007.
24. Blyth's research on economic change also shows how a new set of ideas was able to disembed liberalism in the 1970s. Assembling a set of ideas about monetarism, rational choice, public choice theory, and supply side economics, business interests were able to make the case that inflation was a greater threat to the nation than was unemployment and that the only proper government intervention was to let the market clear. Government intervention was to be aimed at inflation. Business interests revitalized and invested heavily in ideas. The American Enterprise Institute, which had been quietly operating since the 1940s, saw its budget increase more than tenfold in the 1970s. Business-oriented philanthropists founded scores of think tanks to spread and give academic credence to their ideas. Donations from Joseph Coors, Richard Mellon Scaife, and William Simon underwrote the Heritage Foundation's founding in 1973. The Hoover Institute on War, Revolution and Peace found similar benefaction and moved from its original emphasis to champion market approaches to social problems. Simon, in particular, was important in guiding the Olin Foundation's investment in a conservative ideology and the founding of smaller think tanks around the country. See Mark M. Blyth, *Great Transformations: Economic Ideas and Institutional Change in the Twentieth Century* (Cambridge, UK: Cambridge University Press, 2002), 126–57.

25. Joel L. Fleishman, *The Foundation: A Great American Secret* (New York: Public Affairs, 2007), 271.

26. Thomas S. Kuhn, *The Structure of Scientific Revolutions* (Chicago: University of Chicago Press, 1970).

27. Elwood P. Cubberly, *Public School Administration: A Statement of the Fundamental Principles Underlying the Organization and Administration of Public Education* (Boston: Houghton Mifflin, 1916).

CHAPTER 12: FIVE POLICY LEVERS

1. Paul T. Hill, *Charter School Districts,* Progressive Policy Institute, 2001 (accessed December 14, 2007, from http://www.ppionline.org/ppi_ci.cfm?contentid=3365&knl gAreaID=110&subsecid=134). See also *State Policy Options for Creating Charter Districts* (Denver, CO: Education Commission of the States, 2003) and other ECS publications on same subject.

2. Eva Gold et al., *Blurring the Boundaries: Private Sector Involvement in Philadelphia Public Schools* (Philadelphia, PA: Research for Action, 2005).

3. Jolley Bruce Christman, Eva Gold, and Benjamin Herold, *Privatization "Philly Style": What Can Be Learned from Philadelphia's Diverse Provider Model of School Management* (Philadelphia, PA: Research for Action, 2006).

4. Christopher Cross and Marguerite Roza, *How the Federal Government Shapes and Distorts the Financing of K–12 Schools* (Seattle, WA: School Finance Redesign Project, 2007).

5. School Finance Redesign Project, *Funding Student Success: How to Align Education Resources with Student Learning Goals* (Seattle, WA: University of Washington Center for Reinventing Public Education, 2008). For papers and recommendations from the project, see www.schoolfinanceredesign.org (accessed July 19, 2007).

6. Interestingly, school-level control of funds, which were introduced under Conservative prime minister John Major, were retained during the long tenure of Tony Blair's Labor government.

7. William G. Ouchi, *Making Schools Work: A Revolutionary Plan to Get Your Children the Education They Need* (New York: Simon & Schuster, 2003), 81.

8. William Ouchi, Bruce Cooper, and Lydia Segal, "The Impact of Organization on the Performance of Nine School Systems: Lessons for California," *California Policy Options: UCLA School of Public Policy and Social Research* (Winter 2003): 125–40.

9. Editorial, "Year of Education, Still; Budget Cuts or Not, a Few Inexpensive Measures Could Vastly Improve California's Schools," *Los Angeles Times*, January 12, 2008, A20.

10. For example, Douglas Mitchell and colleagues differentiate rewards and incentives and examine incentives at the individual, group, and organizational levels. See Douglas E. Mitchell, Flora Ida Ortiz, and Tedi K. Mitchell, *Work Orientation and Job Performance: The Cultural Basis of Teaching Rewards and Incentives* (Albany: SUNY Press, 1987).

11. Charles Taylor Kerchner and Laura Steen Mulfinger, *Creating a Culture of Literacy in Boyle Heights: A Report to the Community on the Creation of the Boyle Heights Learning Collaborative* (Claremont, CA: Claremont Graduate University, 2007).

12. Allan Odden and Carolyn Kelley, *Paying Teachers for What They Know and Do: New and Smarter Compensation Strategies to Improve Schools* (Thousand Oaks, CA: Corwin, 1997).

13. The Stull Act (named after its principal sponsor, Assemblyman John Stull) requires all school districts in California to adopt a uniform set of guidelines for use in evaluating the professional competence of their certificated personnel. The act went into effect on September 1, 1972.

14. LAUSD and UTLA, *2006–2009 Agreement* (2006; accessed December 19, 2007, from www.utla.net/contracts/index.php). See Article 10-A for peer review agreement.

15. Charles Taylor Kerchner and Julia Koppich, "Organizing Around Quality: The Union Struggle to Organize Mind Workers," in *Teacher Unions and Educational Policy: Retrenchment and Reform*, ed. Ron Henderson, Wayne Urban, and Paul Wolman (Boston: Elsevier/JAI, 2004), 187–222. Charles Taylor Kerchner, "The Modern Guild: The Prospects for Organizing around Quality in Public Education," in *Transforming Unions*, ed. Jon Brock and David Lipsky, Industrial Relations Research Association Series (Urbana, IL: University of Illinois Press, 2003).

16. Charles Kerchner, Julia Koppich, and Joseph Weeres, *United Mind Workers* (San Francisco: Jossey-Bass, 1997). Charles Taylor Kerchner, Julia E. Koppich, and Joseph G. Weeres, *Taking Charge of Quality: How Teachers and Unions Can Revitalize Schools: An Introduction and Companion to* United Mind Workers (San Francisco: Jossey-Bass, 1998).

17. Charles Taylor Kerchner and Julia Koppich, "Negotiating What Matters Most: Collective Bargaining and Student Achievement," *American Journal of Education* 113 (2007): 349–65.

18. Alvin Toffler, *Powershift: Knowledge, Wealth and Violence at the Edge of the 21st Century* (New York: Bantam Books, 1990).

19. Corey Murray, *Curriki Offers New World of Course Content*, eSchool News, 2007 (accessed November 17, 2007, from www.eschoolnews.com/news/top-news/index.cfm?i=45616 &CFID=75486&CFTOKEN=95886468).

20. Curriki was developed particularly with the needs of rural schools and those in developing nations (accessed January 16, 2008, from www.curriki.org).

21. See Marshall S. Smith and Catherine M. Casserly, "Creating a Foundation for Open Knowledge: Technology Assessment of Web-Based Learning" (accessed January 14, 2008, from www.hewlett.org/Programs/Education/OER/Publications/Creating+a+ Foundation+for+Open+Knowledge.htm).

22. John Seely Brown, "Growing Up Digital: How the Web Changes Work, Education, and the Ways People Learn," *Change* 32 (March/April 2000): 11–20.

23. "Parents/Guardians to Receive 2008-2009 Magnet/Permits with Transportation/Public School Choice Brochures by Mail," press release, November 14, 2007, LAUSD Office of Communications.

24. Sam Hamerman et al., *Report of the Los Angeles City Schools Planning Team* (Los Angeles: LAUSD, 1967), 251.

25. Hamerman et al., *Report of the Los Angeles City Schools*, 126.

26. "2008–2009 Choices," 5, 18, LAUSD Office of Student Integration Services (accessed November 28, 2007, from http://echoices.lausd.net/BrochureEnglish.pdf).

27. Arthur Powell, Eleanor Farrar, and David Cohen, *The Shopping Mall High School: Winners and Losers in the Educational Marketplace* (Boston: Houghton Mifflin, 1985), 316.

28. Robert Gottlieb et al., *The Next Los Angeles: The Struggle for a Livable City* (Berkeley: University of California Press, 2005), 5. See for a summary the word's use applied to Los Angeles.

29. Gottlieb, *The Next L.A.*, 22.

30. Tom Sitton, *John Randolph Haynes: California Progressive* (Stanford: CA: Stanford University Press, 1992).

31. Elwood P. Cubberly, *State and County Educational Reorganization: The Revised Constitution and School Code of the State of Osceola* (New York: Macmillan, 1922), 103.

32. Anthony S. Bryk and Sharon G. Rollow, "The Chicago Experiment: Enhanced Democratic Participation as a Lever for School Improvement," Issue Report no. 3 (Fall 1992), Center on Organization and Restructuring of Schools, Madison, WI.

33. For a discussion of professions and their place in society, see Donald A. Schon, *The Reflective Practitioner: How Professionals Think in Action* (New York: Basic Books, 1983), 287–354.

34. Quoted in David Tyack and Elisabeth Hansot, *Managers of Virtue: Public School Leadership in America, 1820–1980* (New York: Basic Books, 1982), 103. A similar change took place in the business sector. The evolution of company law represented an initial departure from narrow private property rules and a move toward general public corporations. Originally, the corporation was a legal device that extended public powers to individuals outside of government. Creation of a general law of corporation moved the boundaries between public and private. Public protections and authority to form enclaves of private capital were made generally available, vastly expanding the private realm. At the same time, regulation of the newly powerful private sector and unprecedented intrusion of the state into economic life followed. See Ronald L. Jepperson and John W. Meyer, "The Public Order and the Construction of Formal Organization," in *The New Institutionalism in Organizational Analysis*, ed. Walter W. Powell and Paul J. DiMaggio (Chicago: University of Chicago Press, 1991), 212.

About the Authors

Charles Taylor Kerchner is a research professor at Claremont Graduate University (CGU). His recent work on institutional change builds on a foundation of academic work in educational organizations, policy, and teachers unions. As a companion to this book, he is coeditor (with William Lowe Boyd and Mark Blyth) of *The Transformation of Great American School Districts,* also published by Harvard Education Press. He received his PhD from Northwestern University and, prior to joining the CGU faculty in 1976, he was assistant director of the Illinois Board of Higher Education and a reporter and editor at the *St. Petersburg Times* in Florida.

David J. Menefee-Libey is a professor of politics at Pomona College, where he serves as coordinator of the Program in Public Policy Analysis. He is lead author of "The Persistence of Ideas in Los Angeles Public School Reform," a chapter in *The Transformation of Great American School Districts.* Menefee-Libey received his PhD in political science from the University of Chicago. Before joining the Pomona faculty in 1989, he was a Research Fellow at the Brookings Institution and did research on education policy in the Washington, D.C., office of the RAND Corporation.

Laura Steen Mulfinger is a doctoral candidate at Claremont Graduate University, where she has focused her research in the areas of K–12 public education policy, urban school reform, and student achievement. From 2002 to 2006 she served as coresearch director of the external evaluation team for the Boyle Heights Learning Collaborative. Her dissertation is a study of the Society of Students, a social capital and social/emotional learning program that began in as part of the Boyle Heights collaborative. Before beginning her doctoral studies at CGU, Mulfinger worked in the fields of institutional advancement and philanthropy, primarily in the areas of education, health care, and social services.

Stephanie E. Clayton is a doctoral student in history at the University of Southern California. She received her MA in American history from Claremont Graduate University in 2004. Her primary research interests are the history of scientific racism and the creation of mental institutions in California and the West from the late nineteenth century to the World War II era.

Index

Page references followed by an italic *f* or *t* indicate information contained in figures and tables, respectively